Parenthood and Immigration in Psychoanalysis

This book presents a comprehensive overview of psychoanalytic work with immigrant mothers, fathers, and their children, combining clinical examples and contemporary research to explore ways in which psychoanalysts can work and shape appropriate therapeutic settings.

Written by an international range of contributors, from Europe, the US, and the Middle East, the chapters examine how psychoanalysts, especially when they too are immigrants, can best support those in a transcultural situation against the backdrop of increasing migration from conflict, persecution, war, or poverty. They share a clinical and societal commitment. While showing how the existing literature on immigration focuses rightly on traumatic elements, the chapters in this text also demonstrate how creativity must be considered while shaping a psychoanalytic perspective. The text brings together case material and research to illuminate how the therapeutic and theoretical processes of psychoanalysis, at times combining anthropology and sociology, can lead to the construction of new therapeutic settings mostly for non-Western families in contexts of higher psychopathological risks: neo-natal period, international adoption, and social isolation.

Written in a practical, accessible style, *Parenthood and Immigration in Psychoanalysis* is essential reading for practicing psychoanalysts, paediatricians, psychotherapists, and counsellors, as well as researchers and clinicians in a range of fields, including perinatal, sociology, cultural studies, and social work.

Marie Rose Moro, MD, PhD, is a professor at Paris University, France. She is a child/adolescent psychiatrist and psychoanalyst (Paris Psychoanalytic Society SPP), researcher, and writer. She is a specialist in transcultural psychiatry and is the founder of the transcultural journal, *L'autre* and an international transcultural association (AIEP).

Geneviève Welsh, MD, is a psychiatrist, psychoanalyst (Paris Psychoanalytic Society SPP) and a group analyst. She has created a consultation and group therapy settings for immigrants (ASM13, France) and works in private practice.

Parenthood and Immigration in Psychoanalysis

Shaping the Therapeutic Setting

Edited by
Marie Rose Moro and Geneviève Welsh

Routledge
Taylor & Francis Group

LONDON AND NEW YORK

Cover image: Geneviève Welsh

First published 2022
by Routledge
4 Park Square, Milton Park, Abingdon, Oxon OX14 4RN

and by Routledge
605 Third Avenue, New York, NY 10158

Routledge is an imprint of the Taylor & Francis Group, an informa business

British Library Cataloguing-in-Publication Data
A catalogue record for this book is available from the British Library

Library of Congress Cataloging-in-Publication Data
Title: Parenthood and immigration in psychoanalysis : shaping the
  therapeutic setting / edited by Marie Rose Moro and Geneviève Welsh.
Description: Abingdon, Oxon ; New York, NY : Routledge, 2022. | Includes
  bibliographical references and index. | Summary: "This book presents a
  comprehensive overview of psychoanalytic work with immigrant mothers,
  fathers and their children, combining clinical examples and contemporary
  research to explore ways in which psychoanalysts can work and shape
  appropriate therapeutic settings. Written in a practical, accessible
  style, Parenthood and Immigration in Psychoanalysis is essential reading
  for practicing psychoanalysts, paediatricians, psychotherapists and
  counsellors, as well as researchers and clinicians in a range of fields,
  including perinatal, sociology, cultural studies and social work"--
  Provided by publisher.
Identifiers: LCCN 2021044232 (print) | LCCN 2021044233 (ebook) | ISBN
  9781032005614 (hbk) | ISBN 9781032005508 (pbk) | ISBN 9781003174684
  (ebk)
Subjects: LCSH: Parenthood. | Immigrant families. | Children of immigrants.
  | Psychoanalysis. | Clinical psychology.
Classification: LCC HQ755.8 .P3782 2022 (print) | LCC HQ755.8 (ebook) |
  DDC 306.874--dc23
LC record available at https://lccn.loc.gov/2021044232
LC ebook record available at https://lccn.loc.gov/2021044233

ISBN: 978-1-032-00561-4 (hbk)
ISBN: 978-1-032-00550-8 (pbk)
ISBN: 978-1-003-17468-4 (ebk)

DOI: 10.4324/9781003174684

Typeset in Times New Roman MT Std
by KnowledgeWorks Global Ltd.

Para mi padre,
"Caminante, no hay camino, se hace el camino al andar" -
"Walker, there is no path, the path is made by walking" -
Tribute to Isidoro Moro Gomez (1933–2016)
From Salamanca to Charleville-Mézières
For Dad,
« It is a long way from Tipperary »
Tribute to William Patrick Welsh (1920–2019)
From Glasgow to Algiers and Paris

Contents

Acknowledgements

Gratitude to Lisa Revai, Lola Martin-Moro, Gabrielle Maas, Suzy-Jane Tanner for their translations, proofreading: their patience was unwavering. Maya Chami for the front cover.

To Fatima Titouh, Mahmoud Boudarene, Michèle Fiéloux, Jacques Lombard, Anne Yvonne Guillou.

To our husbands, Michel Jouve and Dominique Martin

To Zhu Xiao- Mei and Jean Sebastien Bach: thank you for the Goldberg variations.

To Tereza Berganza for her sublime "Anda, jaleo" (Federico Garcia Lorca).

Marie Rose Moro & Geneviève Welsh

Contributors

Salman Akhtar, MD, is Professor of Psychiatry at Jefferson Medical College and a Training and Supervising Analyst at the Psychoanalytic Centre of Philadelphia. He has served on the editorial boards of the International Journal of Psychoanalysis, the Journal of the American Psychoanalytic Association, and the Psychoanalytic Quarterly. His more than 300 publications include 82 books, of which 18 are solo-authored. S Akhtar has delivered many prestigious addresses and lectures worldwide. He is the recipient of many awards among which the highly prestigious Sigourney Award (2012) for distinguished contributions to psychoanalysis. S Akhtar is an internationally sought speaker and teacher, and his books have been translated in many languages. A true Renaissance man, S Akhtar has served as the Film Review Editor for the International Journal of Psychoanalysis and is currently serving as the Book Review Editor for the International Journal of Applied Psychoanalytic Studies. He has published 9 collections of poetry and serves as a Scholar-in-Residence at the Inter-Act Theatre Company in Philadelphia.

Milena Claudius, PhD, is a psychologist in private practice and teaches in the Counseling Department at Webster University in Geneva, Switzerland. Her scholarship focuses on mental health across cultures, psychological trauma, as well as risk and resilience in acculturation. She holds a doctoral degree in Counseling Psychology from Boston College.

Mayssa' El Husseini, PhD, is a clinical psychologist and family therapist at the Maison de Solenn - Cochin Hospital in Paris - Assistant Professor at University of Picardie Jules Verne; researcher at the Centre for the History of Science, Society and Conflicts (CHSSC EA 4289); affiliated researcher at INSERM (CESP), Paris University (France). Psychoanalyst, she is currently a candidate at Psychoanalytical Society of Paris (SPP). As a consultant for international NGO's, she has worked with migrants and displaced populations in Lebanon, Haiti, Turkey, Greece, and France, in contexts of war, natural disasters and pandemics. Her research and publications focus on trauma, the impact of trauma and critical contexts on countertransference and international adoption. Her publications can be found on research gate: https://www.researchgate.net/profile/Mayssa-El-Husseini

Lia Fort-Jacques is a child and adolescent psychiatrist at the Lannemezan Hospital (France). After studying at the Ecole Supérieure des Beaux-Arts in Bordeaux, she obtained a degree in philosophy, studied medicine at the University of Bordeaux. She did her internship in psychiatry at the University of Poitiers, during which she gained experience in the field of perinatal psychic care as well as in transcultural medicine at the University Hospital of Bordeaux. Her doctoral thesis (2019) entitled "Fathers in exile on the perinatal scene" focuses on the place of migrant fathers in perinatal care, in the family sphere, and in the reception they receive in institutions. Co-author of an article to be published on this issue in the journal L'autre, cliniques, cultures et sociétés (www.revuelautre.com).

Aurélie Harf, MD-PhD, is a child and adolescent psychiatrist and a family therapist at the Maison de Solenn, Cochin Hospital in Paris: www.maisondesolenn.fr. She is in charge of a day care unit for adolescents. She is the founder of the International Adoption consultation unit in this department. She is the director of research at INSERM (CESP) Paris University. Her main research topics are international adoption, parenting, school refusal, how to assess therapies... She is expert on family therapy and multifamily therapy. She has written a lot of international articles and collective books. Her last one is Benoit L, Harf A, Moro MR. La phobie scolaire. Retrouver le plaisir d'apprendre. Paris: Vigot Maloine; 2020.

Estelle Gioan is a clinical psychologist at the Transcultural Consultation of the Bordeaux University Hospital since 2004 (France). She treats women who are victims of violence. She has worked for several years with people in very precarious situations and in a family welcome centre. She is a member of the Ethnotopies association as a perinatal referent. She has been conducting workshops for pregnant women, parents, mothers and their babies and young children. Since 2007, she conducts the Maternity and Families in Exile Meetings, for professionals and volunteers who work with migrant families. She participates in the French-speaking transcultural platform "Mental health, perinatality and migration". She is co-author of the collective work Bébés d'ici, mères d'exil, edited by Claire Mestre, Erès, 2016.

Gabriela Guzman†, MD was a child and adolescent psychiatrist (University of Chile). She had a master's degree in psychopathology and psychoanalysis (Paris University, France), a Postgraduate university degree in attachment (Universidad del Desarrollo, Chile), a Postgraduate university degree in infant mental health (Paris University, France) and a Postgraduate university degree in transcultural psychiatry (Paris 13 University, France). Her main interests were psychopathology in adolescence, adolescent suicide and self-harm behaviours, eating disorders in adolescence, transcultural clinical practice and consultation-liaison psychiatry. She has contributed to several books on transcultural topics.

Julia Kristeva, PhD is a writer, psychoanalyst, and professor emeritus at the University of Paris. She is a training member of the Psychoanalytical Society of Paris (SPP) and Doctor Honoris Causa of several universities where she teaches regularly in the United States, Canada, and Europe. Commander of the French Legion of Honour, Commander of the French Order of Merit and the first laureate of the Holberg Prize in December 2004, Kristeva was awarded the Hannah Arendt Prize in 2006 and the Vaclav Havel Prize in 2008. Julia Kristeva created in 2008 the Prize Simone de Beauvoir for the freedom of the women. She is the author of some thirty books. Her work has been published in English and most of her books are available in major languages throughout the world. Bibliography in www.kristeva.fr

Claire Mestre, MD, PhD is a psychiatrist-psychotherapist, doctor in anthropology, and writer, director of the transcultural consultation of the Bordeaux University Hospital (France). She conducts transcultural psychotherapy for adults and families with babies. For more than 20 years, she has been promoting access to care for foreigners, including the promotion of interpreting in medical and social settings, prevention for babies in exile, psychological care for exiled victims of intentional violence and unaccompanied minors. She is president of Ethnotopies association involved with collectives, foundations, and agencies. Research field: transcultural psychiatry in France, Chad, and Madagascar. She teaches anthropology at the University of Bordeaux and is co-organizer of the University Diploma "Transcultural Medicine and Care". Co-editor of the journal L'autre, cliniques, cultures et sociétés (www.revuelautre.com). Among her publications: Maladies et violences ordinaires dans un hôpital malgache. L'Harmattan; 2013. She has edited Bébés d'ici, mères d'exil, Erès; 2016.

Marie Rose Moro, MD, PhD, is a psychoanalyst member of the Psychoanalytical Society of Paris (SPP) and member of IPA. She is Full Professor at Paris University. She is a child/adolescent and adult psychiatrist. She is trained in philosophy and anthropology in Sorbonne University and writer. Director of the Department of Adolescent Psychiatry, La Maison de Solenn in Cochin Hospital in Paris (France, www.maisondesolenn.fr).

In the field of transcultural psychiatry, she has worked with immigrants' families and their children for more than thirty years and has developed specific settings for them in public hospitals. She is in charge of a research department in adolescent and transcultural psychiatry. She has been a humanitarian advisor in war-affected countries for about 30 years with Doctors Without Borders. She has delivered many prestigious addresses and lectures worldwide and her article and books have been translated in many languages. She is officer of the French Legion of Honour in 2021, officer of the French Order of Merit in 2014. Bibliography in: www.marierosemoro.fr

Rahmeth Radjack, MD, PhD, is a child/adolescent and adult psychiatrist currently working in the Department of Adolescent Psychiatry, La Maison de Solenn in Cochin Hospital in Paris (France, www.maisondesolenn.fr). She is in charge of child psychiatry consultations at the Port Royal maternity hospital (Paris). She is a specialist in transcultural psychiatry. She also trained in philosophy in Tours. She is in charge of a weekly transcultural consultation at the Maison de Solenn. She has coordinated a participative action-research program on the adaptation of the transcultural setting to unaccompanied minors, and a research on issues related to radicalism. She regularly gives transcultural training to professionals working in the field of perinatal care and child protection. She has 71 publications in peer reviewed journals and has contributed to 11 books.

Sara Skandrani, PhD is a clinical psychologist and family therapist at the Maison de Solenn - Cochin Hospital in Paris (France). Psychotherapist in the International Adoption consultation unit (France, www.maisondesolenn.fr). She is also Assistant Professor at Paris Ouest Nanterre University and researcher in the field of adolescent psychiatry, international adoption, and transcultural psychotherapy. She has written many international articles about transcultural topics in peer reviewed journals and has contributed to many books. Bibliography at https://loop.frontiersin.org/people/679838/publications

Olivier Taïeb, MD, PhD is an adolescent and adult psychiatrist who works in Avicenne Hospital, Sorbonne Paris Nord University, in Bobigny, in the north of Paris. He is also a psychodrama and group psychoanalytic therapist. He directs a day care centre for adolescents with a psychodynamic approach. His research focusses on qualitative, narrative, and transcultural issues in psychiatry. He is interested in memories and childhood narratives. Previously, he was in charge of an addiction unit. He has written many international articles, has contributed to several books and has published a solo-authored book in French Les histoires des toxicomanes. Récits et identités dans les addictions, PUF, 2011.

Saskia von Overbeck Ottino, MD, is a psychoanalyst, training member and vice president of the Société Suisse de Psychanalyse SSPsa (IPA). She is a child, adolescent, and adult psychiatrist, head of the migrant mental health and ethnopsychoanalysis unit (MEME), at the Geneva University Hospital. She is the chair of the forum "Psychoanalysis, Migration and cultural Identities" at the EPF and the president of the Association Santé Mentale: Suisse-Rwanda (ASMSR). She has been working for more than 30 years with refugee families, founding cross-cultural psychiatric units and organizing training courses. In Rwanda, she leads a development project in child psychiatry. Her main field of interest is the resonances between conscious and unconscious issues in the ethnopsychoanalytical clinic.

Pratyusha Tummala-Narra, Ph.D. is a Professor of Counselling, Developmental and Educational Psychology and Director of Doctoral Training in Counselling Psychology at Boston College (USA). She is also in Independent Practice. Her research and scholarship focus on immigration, trauma, race, and cultural competence and psychoanalytic psychotherapy. Tummala-Narra is an Associate Editor of the Asian American Journal of Psychology, Associate Editor of Psychoanalytic Dialogues, and Senior Psychotherapy Editor of the Journal of Humanistic Psychology. She is a Fellow of the American Psychological Association, and with APA Division 39 and Division 45. She is the author of Psychoanalytic Theory and Cultural Competence in Psychotherapy, published by APA (American Psychological Association) Books in 2016. Her edited book, Trauma and Racial Minority Immigrants: Turmoil, Uncertainty, and Resistance, was published by APA Books in January 2021

Geneviève Welsh, MD, is a psychiatrist and psychoanalyst (Psychoanalytical Society of Paris, SPP). She works both in private and public practice (ASM13, Paris). She has chaired a psychiatric department in charge of South East Asian refugees, mainly Cambodians, created group settings for exiled patients and parents. She has served as a member of the IPA group on "Terror and Terrorism" (2002-2005) and has contributed to many IPA congresses, to workshops and panel of EPF. She has been a member of the EPF Forum on "Psychoanalysis, Migration and cultural Identities" since 2015. Her publications focus on: psychosis, refugees and immigrants, genocides and collective traumas, resistance in extreme situations, terror and terrorism, transcultural situations, and group psychoanalysis. She has contributed to several books and has translated in French many articles and one book: (2015) The Groups Book (2010) by Caroline Garland (Taylor & Francis Ltd).

Preface

Julia Kristeva

The metamorphoses of parenthood

In a globalized world with its flows of migrants, parenthood is changing. We focus here on these metamorphoses as the backdrop to the different chapters in this book. Migrants are becoming parents in a world where the family has changed: broken families, recomposed families, single parents, and now gay parents. It is, however, on the basis of the notion of hetero-parenthood, conceptualized according to the model of biological links, that we endeavour to apprehend and accompany the trends and changes in parenthood – in terms of varying forms of parenthood. And indeed, migrants contribute to these metamorphoses. What do we know about parenthood? Or more precisely, do we know what it is that plays out when individuals present themselves as parents, when they plan to be parents, and when they become parents? What are the desires, the memories, the life histories that are within us, escape us and are handed on in this experience that seems so natural? Can we not go back in human time, as we are invited to by ethnology, anthropology, and psychoanalysis? Beyond the "symptom", these disciplines offer ways to explore the event and reappraise the history of parenthood (the experience of being a father or a mother for the man and the woman) – a history made up of affects and values that continuously hover between instability and emergence. This memory forms strata in present-day customs, so that the two protagonists (the ancient and the modern), in particular in the Western world, brandish or proclaim certain indisputable, essential components of the "principle of parenthood", characterizing human beings since the prehistoric era. We can term it the "emergent principle of parenthood", since it is open to the environment, but cannot escape from the previous states of society: the past is inscribed in it, and emergence depends on what has gone before to be able to draw away from it.

After the legislator, the conference of biologists, gynaecologists, sociologists, psychoanalysts, and other specialists of the family will have the delicate task of identifying the different facets of this continually emergent parenthood, of harmonising them, so as to move on from "equality for all" to the "multiple universe" (or "multiverse") of singularities of families today, also present in each of us. Without separating the paternal from the maternal, we need to lend an ear to the paternal *per se*, from the outset, in the shared experience of parenthood: "three-ness" applies for the paternal sphere whenever there is a father and a mother.

I will briefly sum up two lines of approach to the logics and the depths of parenthood, indissociable from becoming human: the shift from the primitive hoard to the family requires the instatement of homoeroticism within social intercourse, and within paternity, as can be seen in the social changes at present underway. Further to this, paternity does not obviate the genital organization of the libido (despite what certain theorists suggest). Heterosexuality (in the sense of the psychic dimension of genitality and sexual difference, including psychic bisexuality, and in the sense of their inscription in the social contract) is a late, ill-assured acquisition. It is still a major issue for each of us: in the setting of parenthood of course, and more widely in social relationships.

A theoretical fable: Claude Lévi-Strauss, when exploring the elementary structures of parenthood and the multitude of variants, discovered a fundamental logic of patrilinear and matrilinear societies: men exchange women. Sigmund Freud for his part, well known and widely criticized for his conceptualizations (the unconscious, the Oedipus, etc.) favoured theoretical fictions and exaggerated ("psychoanalysis only tells the truth when it exaggerates" – Adorno) to reach his readers more readily: he talked of the inconceivable enormity of what he learnt from dreams, myths, and literature. Thus, on the subject of family and marriage, he drafted the narrative of the primitive hoard. In the Indo-European world, in line with Claude Lévi-Strauss's "elementary structures of parenthood", the term "marriage" relates to the alliance between men.

The conquering and promiscuous man establishes an alliance with another man when choosing his wife (the sister or daughter): *maritare* in Latin means to match or to join; but *marya* (in Farsi) takes on the meaning of the desiring, fierce, young man, and the daunting warrior. The condition of the mother, *matrimonium*, signifying that the woman is captured or taken by the man and is destined to procreate (that is to say to be the mother of the man's son) appears only at a late stage in Roman law, and finally merges with *maritare*, despite have nothing in common with the term. The meaning of marriage changes thereafter: it is no longer reduced to its role of a social alliance between men, it becomes the instrument of procreation, under the control of the man-father, while the mother is merely the worker, the servant or even the slave.

In contrast, the Chinese ideogram 姓 *xing*, which means "the family name" is made up of the pictogram女 *nü* – woman – on the left of the phonic complex生 *sheng* – grow, be born, life. In contrast to the Western world with the patronym, the Chinese family name is that of the woman-mother,

literally "born from the woman". Thus, the Chinese family name was originally the name of the clan in the matrilinear era, a feminine name, dating
back to the matrilinear family. Thus, the eight great names in Confucian
matriarchal Chinese Antiquity all contained the pictogram 女 *nü* – woman
(which did not prevent Confucian males from binding the feet of women,
with the resulting extremely painful consequences). Thus, matrilinear societies appear as having more respect for the procreative matrimonial function.

Heterosexuality cannot be called upon either as the surest and sole way to
give life or to guarantee generational transmission. It is linked to the intensity of eroticism, and this leads to extreme vulnerability. It took Freud's
genius to put words on what each of us senses: procreation that obsesses
humans is not a natural act, and even less a sovereign act. By this very act
(which should not be forgotten when the paternal is deduced from the other
act, that of the murder of the father), the difference of the sexes is proclaimed
in a cascade of fantasies that construct the psyche. What are they?

There is vulnerability in the fury of the primitive scene, the epitome of an
original and universal fantasy: fusion and confusion of man and woman,
the exuberant loss of energies and identities, affinity between life and death
– heterosexuality is not solely a discontinuity (I am another, alone before
the other) normalized by continuity (fusion to give life). The principle of
fatherhood and of parenthood itself is thus neither an abstraction nor an
assemblage of substitutes or functions, it takes shape in the heterosexual
dyad of the two parents.

Because according to Lacan "there is no gender relationship", the sexual
couple perpetuates itself by way of a third party: "contingent love" (Sartre
and Beauvoir), sublimation (lifework, vocation, undertaking, calling, sport,
hobby, community, church...), and at the summit the Creator, the third person, "He" with a capital letter, impersonal, eternal, and outside dialogue,
who sums up, supports and perpetuates the parental "three-ness" and
its meaning. Alongside, the heterosexual couple (whether or not they are
believers) hopes for a third party to whom they have given life, and for lack
of eternity see themselves in the horizontality of passing time. It is the child
who restores the generational chain: he is the sign (existence) of the reality within symbolic transcendence, which has become trans-generational
transmission. Parenthood is not solely the production of citizens with their
super-ego. In the unbearable fantasy of the primitive scene, parenthood
erects subjectification as the pivot, the eclipse, and the re-launching of time.

What is a father? What is a mother? Let us return to the paternal, and the
paternal alone, if we can put it that way. In the light of homoeroticism and
at the zenith of conquering, unsustainable heterosexuality, it is not paternity that disaggregates. It is parenthood, and the heterosexual dimension
within us that is the "problematic component" (as suggested by Georges
Bataille): heterosexuality is *the* problem, the foundation of three-ness, and
in this sense the ultimate personal and universal issue.

When equality removes the differences between man and woman, and when what is missing no longer exists, the impossible and death also disappear: in vitro fertilization, the renting of a uterus, and research by gynaecologists and endocrinologists are attempts to do away with them. Our ability to give meaning to the achievements of science and technology and to freedom from restrictive codes is threatened by unfettered drives seeking immediate and absolute satisfaction. Thus, between genitality that cannot be entertained and the transmission of social codes (morals, education, professional training) only the rights of the child – a recent addition to human rights - appear as being able to contain the tensions and finalise the principle of parenthood. But a child's rights derive from the experience and the philosophy of the parents, provided that the parents actually take an interest in the issue. I do not suggest replacing the paradigm of the murder of the father, nor the Christ-centred paradigm of the dead father, which would leave us only a name, or merely a principle. I suggest a new manner of envisaging this issue via the paradigm of the primitive scene and, thus, to envisage the effects of parenthood in the construction of contemporary psychosexualities, in a context that is increasingly open.

This means that starting from psychic bisexuality, the metamorphoses of the original parenthood are numerous. Being a father and a migrant is a complex situation, since to the process we have just described is added migration and life in a setting other than that into which you were born, an experience that destabilizes all your references. This book explores what happens for all those migrants, men, women, mothers, fathers, who wish to form a family, here or elsewhere, in a world that is itself searching for the meaning and the role of the family.

It is important to accompany each family project – adoption, filiation – in personalized manner taking each case into account. Nothing new? It is more necessary than ever. Between the biblical family and the Chinese family, each of which claims ascendance over the coming millennium, there is no other choice for Europe and the Americas. Without giving in to the temptation of a policy of psychoanalysis (which would go against its deontology) psychoanalysis is perhaps the only response to this emergency: not the disappearance, but the dissemination of the individual in its incommensurable singularity; for this, psychoanalysts are not just there to witness, they also remind and, thus, enable the emergence of the individual. If we are convinced of this, we can make ourselves understood.

Introduction

Geneviève Welsh

Welcome to this book: we are on the threshold of the door you have just opened to read it, and perhaps wonder about the picture on the cover? Let me tell you its story; it is connected to the title.

According to Dr Fatima Titouh, a psychoanalyst and a friend of mine, in Kabylia, a Berber-speaking region in northeast Algeria, there is a long history of people leaving their villages to go far away or abroad, sometimes without hope of return. To speak to the absent, women would go at sunset to a house on top of a windswept, barren hill and stand by a special window, "ttaq bbwadu" uttering words to be carried by the wind to the absent ones. It is important to note that the window has to be in a house on top of a high-perched mountain, near the place where the wind blows, and near the stars. Thus, they share a conversation with the absent. They would also draw and paint on the walls: bodies, signs, dots, arrows drawn from the ancestral repertoire. These symbols can be found on pottery and tapestry: they are passed on as a duty of transmission, like tales and songs.

With this photo, which I shot in such a house, I wanted to pay tribute to these silent figures. When I saw these drawings and heard the story of the window of the wind, I was moved, thinking of songs of exile from my own cultural background: their words might be those of the ones left behind or the emigrants' voices. Of course, nowadays in the era of phone calls and internet, communication is different, and in Kabylia, many relatives hold a cell phone bought for them, but in more remote or poorer parts of the world, who knows what the wind blows to the absent loved ones?

We wanted to pay a tribute to them since the book will be dealing with immigrants who become parents in a different country to that where they were born and to their parents who will not witness their access to parenthood.

The origins of the book

In July 2015, a panel on Parenthood and Migration was held in Boston IPA (International Psychoanalytic Association) Conference on "Changing worlds, the shape and use of psychoanalytic tools today". Among the

DOI: 10.4324/9781003174684-1

panellists were many contributors of this book: Salman Akhtar, Usha Tummala Narra (USA), Marie Rose Moro, Geneviève Welsh (France), and Gabriela Guzman (Chile). Right after the meeting, it was Salman Akhtar's idea to gather our papers into a book and to extend the issues that had just been tackled during the panel. No doubt now the impetus given 6 years ago was sustained and gained momentum. It is noteworthy that most of the contributors are psychoanalysts who have shaped settings and developed theories in the field of immigration and transcultural situations in Europe and the USA. In addition, most of the contributors are also immigrants themselves and none of them is a native English speaker.

This book is an attempt to put together their therapeutic experiences, their professional and personal cultures: their differences and similarities construct a space where psychoanalysis will shed light on vulnerabilities and creativity in parenthood and immigration.

Parenthood: The Western contemporary context

As Julia Kristeva rightly pointed out in the preface, parenthood is undergoing metamorphoses related to the many methods for attaining kinship through advances in reproductive medicine. Making parents is a topic for many contemporary studies in Western societies. Indeed, models of parenthood are questioned and reinterpreted all over the world. This backdrop is perhaps a favourable circumstance for the immigrant that western professionals are questioning the many different aspects of parenthood and decentring from a model based on nuclear families and heterosexuality.

In French, the word "parentalité" is recent; it was introduced in the eighties in the French dictionary "Le Petit Robert". It stemmed from Paul Claude Racamier et al. (1961), a French psychoanalyst who wrote on parenthood as a dynamic interaction implied by the psychic work that has to be done both by mothers and fathers, based on Therese Benedek's pioneering work on parenthood (Benedek, 1959).

The concept of parenthood has several meanings and has undergone constant changes in the academic field. Basically, two trends can be stressed for the purpose of this book:

- It was viewed as a developmental phase by psychoanalysts such as Benedek (1959), as a process of construction of parental positioning through their fantasies and the reactivation of archaic investments where pregenital elements dominate, a kind of crisis leading to a new identity.
- It has also an anthropological dimension: for instance, in Esther Goody's work (Goody, 1982) five functions of parenthood are defined: procreation, nurturing, education, identity assignment, and access to adulthood.

Parenthood is not natural, innate, it is an ability to gain, and a social construct that is changing even more since it has been possible to separate sexuality and procreation. It is a dynamic process that keeps developing on the individual level (every child is affiliated to his parents) and collective level (through social regulations). Parenthood is at the crossroads of sociology, anthropology, history, and psychoanalysis. As we shall see in the following chapters, clinical work will confirm what Godelier (2005) has stated: "One needs more than a man and a woman to make a child". Nowhere a man and a woman are sufficient to make a child he insisted, meaning that other agents are intervening to complete the foetus in all the societies he had studied, and even in Europe (Barraband et al., 2005).

Psychoanalysis and immigration

To date, we did not find any other book regarding specifically parenthood and immigration in psychoanalysis. The importance of immigration in the history of psychoanalysis at its beginnings has been overlooked in the psychoanalytic literature apart from the germane book by Rebecca and Leon Grinberg (1986, Spanish first edition). The contemporary refugee influx in Europe and the USA have inspired contributions to question the position of immigrant analysts with their patients and the position of analysts towards immigrants: a book "Immigration in Psychoanalysis, Locating Ourselves" (Beltsiou, 2016) has invited foreign-born psychoanalysts to discuss aspects of their practice with immigrant patients and an article on contemporary psychoanalytic views on the experience of immigration (Ainslie et al., 2013) has emphasized the necessity to take into account not only the psychic reality but also the social context.

Yet the experience of analysts in exile has "only recently been explored in depth by psychoanalysts and historians" (Beltsiou, 2016) presumably because it takes time to link the trauma immigrant psychoanalyst had faced to their clinical practice. Indeed, as Dori Laub poignantly stated (Beltsiou, 2016), when asked to write an essay on his experience as an immigrant, it makes a difference to have a normative immigrant experience and to feel being a "perpetual refugee from an overwhelming life-threatening situation constantly pursuing (me)".

Psychical reality is made of several spaces

The main point in the field of psychoanalysis and immigration is that psychical reality is not limited to a single space without accounting for the links that the subject maintains with others and the social environment. Therefore, we then need to refer to *several spaces* of psychical reality: intrapsychic, intersubjective, and transsubjective. We are all subject of the unconscious and subject of groups. The psychoanalyst's stance in dealing with immigrants

can be described through the lens of two psychoanalytic tools: group analysis and *countertransference*. What has been called *"cultural countertransference"* is of paramount importance. Cultural countertransference was a
significant theoretical contribution made by Georges Devereux (1908–1985).
His work is still influential in the trend of ethnopsychoanalysis, based on the
concept of complementarity, countertransference, and decentring, which is
the common background of many contributors of this book.

According to Laplanche and Pontalis (1967) transference is "a repetition
of infantile prototypes that are lived out with a deep feeling of reality". In
a way, the analyst's reactions to his patient can be seen as a kind of transference he can analyze through his analytical training. Devereux (1967)
discovered that culture is an important and useful component in the transference-countertransference field, rather than a dimension threatening the
neutral expected stance of the psychoanalyst or an obstacle that has to be
brushed away in order to attain the purity and the depth of unconscious offshoots. It is all the more important when patient and analyst are of different
cultural backgrounds. In Devereux's terms, what matters in transcultural
situations is the countertransference, namely the cultural dimension of the
analyst's reactions that have to do with his groups of belonging and not only
with his unconscious personal reactions. This dimension can be very useful if
the analyst is able to observe his reactions by stepping aside, decentring from
his perceived conscious and unconscious reactions, and see how he can attribute them to his primary and secondary groups of belongings (Rouchy, 1995),
Namely, the cultural countertransference is compounded by the reactions
related to the analyst's personal history but also to the history of the society
he belongs to, to politics, to balance of power, to the strength of prejudices
(Moro, 2011, my translation). This stance has been developed by Delanoe
and Moro (2016) who describe the "cultural transference" as a component of
the transference-countertransference process, along the lines of five logical
patterns structuring the relationship between the therapist and the patient,
leading to speak of a "socio-cultural transference rather than cultural transference": power balance, humanitarian moral stance, post- colonial relations,
racialized social relations, cultural domination in a global world.

As we shall see in the chapters of the book, there is an oscillation in
accounting for the weight of the external reality compounded of culture,
social constraints, prejudices, racism, and the weight of unconscious issues
on the side of the analyst and the patient.

Group analysis field and anthropology

We need to add to the countertransference psychoanalytic issue, two other
components: group analysis and anthropology. These components are
explicitly used in their clinical work mostly by the European contributors
of this book.

Indeed, the missing link between the intrapsychic field of identification, to the social field of identity is related to what group analysts refer to as "groups of belonging" whether primary ("natural", family groups) or secondary (socially instituted). Thus, based on the acknowledgment of the groups we belong to, we can think of the conditions for metabolizing what is the psychic reality and the external reality, the differentiation between me and non-me, the space within the group and the space outside the group. This distinction also enables to account for the way these groups are transmitted across generations and for the effects on the transmission of personal and social traumas. All these ingredients are of paramount importance to take into account with immigrants in general especially when they attempt to found their family.

Many contributors have been trained in anthropology and have developed a competence based on the idea that anthropology can nourish and stimulate psychoanalytic thinking As Corin (2012) stated "Anthropology and psychoanalysis meet on a shared imperative to listen to the other in their own terms rather than from pre-existing knowledge… The destabilizing power associated with otherness is particularly important to preserve in a contemporary world where making another's otherness opaque parallels a difficulty to make room for otherness within oneself". Yet if we warmly agree on this shared meeting point, we have to take into account that the methods differ on certain points, namely the time anthropologists spend making fieldwork, and the scarcity of anthropologists who have both a psychological and an anthropological competence enabling them to link ethnographic data to clinical material, as will be illustrated in the chapter on spirit possession and motherhood.

Shaping the therapeutic setting

Distinct models have been shaped in different countries according to the history of migration, health politics and ideologies. In my view, there are at least three possibilities to shape therapeutic settings for immigrant patients: one is to consider that only immigrant therapists sharing the same cultural and ethnic background are in the best position, a second possibility is to integrate the immigrants in the general mental health service, and the third one, shared by most of the contributors of this book, is to create new settings in the general public hospitals or in private practice, according to their specific needs.

Along the lines of the first, there is the psychiatric care at San Francisco General Hospital where ethno-racial units were designed in the eighties: Asian, Afro American, and Latino patients were referred respectively to Asian, Afro American, and Latino staffs. According to Grossi (2018), this approach to the care put across as progressive, revives in fact "fixed categories of race largely inherited from essentialist thought" and serves to "increase the number of health professionals recruited from ethno-racial minorities".

As for the second possibility, the general ideology is to propose an equal access to mental health care to all subjects. But quite often then, psychiatrists feel helpless when encountering patients from non-European origins and lose their clinical capacities or tend to give a standard medical approach based on symptoms and prescriptions. The follow up is then meagre all the more because immigrants are often homeless and are not fully integrated in the regular active list of patients. The third possibility is to find an approach based on transcultural theory and the specific needs of immigrants. We shall now briefly develop the history of a pioneering setting of an ethnopsychiatric consultation in Paris (France).

A brief history of the creation of a transcultural consultation setting in France for immigrant families: Avicenne and Cochin

Interestingly, the creation of this consultation resulted from a kind of serendipity: it was not designed by a political agenda. The three steps that marked its creation are connected to haphazard circumstances. First, its birthplace, the "Franco-Muslim" hospital is paradoxically directly related to colonization. The "Franco-Muslim" hospital was founded in the north-eastern suburb of Paris in 1935 and was meant for the Muslim indigenes of the French North African colonies. It was supposed to treat colonial subjects according to their culture and traditions, but also to protect the centre of Paris from infectious diseases supposedly affecting the colonized patients. This indicates "a conflict-laden field of ongoing debates about the practices of understanding and representing immigrants as the modern Other" (Sturm et al., 2008).

Later, the hospital was integrated into the public network of Paris Hospitals and was then opened to the general public: in this suburb, the patients were either underprivileged or immigrants. It became a university teaching hospital in 1971. The change of its name occurred in 1978 for "Avicenne", transcription of the name of Ibn Sina (980–1037), a famous Persian physician and philosopher, and a transcultural author of his time, who translated Hippocrates and Galien's texts in Arabic (Moro & Gomez, 2004).

Serge Lebovici, (1915–2000), a pioneer in the field of child psychoanalysis and the head of the Child and Adolescent Department of Avicenne decided to create a consultation for immigrants in the eighties; he called Tobie Nathan, a psychologist who had been a follower of George Devereux. Nathan invented and set up an ethnopsychiatric consultation with interpreters, cultural brokers, and many therapists of different cultural backgrounds. The evolution of his setting led to rough debates especially when he distanced it from a psychoanalysis-based setting and turned it into a setting meant to remind the patients of the traditional ways of healing according to cultural representations.

In 1987, Marie Rose Moro started a study with Lebovici on the specific vulnerability of children born to immigrant parents. This second generation was different from the first generation of immigrants because they did not know their parents' native country. They were living in a transcultural situation and double group belonging that transmitted inside the home and that experienced outside the home. In 1989, Moro created a consultation for children of immigrant descent and their families, enabling the passage from one world to another, from one tongue to another, based on the central concept of "métissage" (hybridization). This setting provides immigrant parents and their children with a group of therapists of different cultural backgrounds and mother tongues, trained in anthropology, psychology, and psychoanalysis.

In 2008, the same setting was started in Cochin, a university hospital in the centre of Paris. The same kind of setting was adapted to the context of international adoption, mixed couples, and unaccompanied minors. Training, research, and ethnopsychoanalytic journal, "l'Autre", were set up. Today the International Ethnopsychoanalytic Association has federated multiple transcultural settings that have been developed in France and Europe.

The multi-layered experience of parenthood in immigration, viewed in different psychoanalytic therapeutic settings in Europe and in the USA

Motherhood and fatherhood

Moro describes the context of her therapeutic setting in which she analyzes and discusses the situation of an African mother and her difficulties forming an interaction with her baby on phantasmatic, imaginary, and cultural levels and shows how to organize a psychotherapeutic approach designed to be meaningful for both the psychoanalyst and the patient. In European society, in which her clinical practice is located and has been shaped by different waves of postcolonial migration and migrants' transnational practices, she argues that immigration should consequently be a focus of psychoanalytical concerns.

In the next chapter, the concept of "paternal involvement" (Mestre) refers to paternal positions and roles with regard to children's care and education. The concept emerges in the context where the area of baby care is pervaded by the arguments of feminism, the influence of institutions, and scientific knowledge disseminated by the media. In the setting of exile, paternal involvement in the perinatal scene can be particularly relevant when the mother is prevented because of ill health. The fathers are then called upon and have to face two difficulties: their situation of exile and the newness of their position regarding the baby. They are only variously supported by the different care institutions. In the setting of the transcultural care, consultations and workshops on adapting to a newly born baby implemented at Bordeaux hospital (France), Mestre observes fathers' attitudes and their psychic evolution, calling on concepts such as the "paternal space" where fathers occupy the "third place". The references here are to anthropology and psychoanalysis. Clinical situations have shown that this paternal positioning is acquired in opposition to their own traditions, and in social situations that disqualify them. Nevertheless, fathers do commit themselves, at the cost of psychological tension, because they support their spouses and are anxious to pass their culture and their values on to their babies. Institutions need to back up this involvement so as to foster this fathering process.

The perinatal period: A higher vulnerability risk among refugee parents

Considering the cultural dimension is useful to improve healthcare during the perinatal period. Indeed, first-time migrant pregnant women are prone to psychological vulnerability due to isolation and the challenge of dealing with other forms of baby care.

In Paris, Radjack's team has built multidisciplinary interventions strategies, taking into account the cultural and social contexts of mothers and the specificities of the pathologies encountered in these transcultural situations. She has developed three different ways to practice transcultural interventions during the short stay of mothers in the maternity ward:

Cultural mediation (with an interpreter) in the hospital room in the presence of the mother and the baby.

A transcultural and cosmopolitan therapeutic group (with therapists from different cultural backgrounds).

A support and discussion group (sharing of experiences between migrant mothers, focusing on different ways of mothering across cultures, and blending multiple mothering techniques).

These three types of transcultural practices are adapted and used according to the temporality and singularity of each of the mother-infant dyads. The aim of this chapter is also to provide useful transcultural skills for any healthcare worker who accompanies a family during the perinatal period. It highlights the cultural aspects to which attention should be paid in the representation of pregnancy, the needs of a child, obstetrical complications or post-natal problems.

In Switzerland too, for parents seeking asylum from countries ravaged by war like Afghanistan, Eritrea, or Syria, the peripartum period is one of significant risk for them and their infants. Moreover, near than half of refugee women experience maternal depression and their children experience elevated rates of attachment disorders and developmental disturbances. To address the needs of this vulnerable population Saskia von Overbeck Ottino at the Geneva University Hospital proposes a systematic screening and consultation which is integrated in the routine pregnancy follow-up and in collaboration with the child mental health unit. Violence experienced before, during, and after migration can imperil the parental couple's and family's functioning, thus weakening the baby-to-be need for an extra- and intra-psychic protective shield. In a new environment, the mother but also the father often feel isolated, separated from familiar milestones, and confused. The language barrier, culture-bound fears or the lack of information may hinder parents in finding appropriate help. Psychoanalysis, contrary to what is often thought, is well equipped to approach the resonances between the different referentials in play, collective-cultural, and singular, or the entanglements between the conscious and unconscious processes as well as the counter-transferential questions at stake. Clinical examples illustrate the clinical work with mothers.

Immigrant mothers and their internal life

Pratyusha Tummala-Narra and Milena Claudius show that although the maternal figure has been viewed as playing a key role in the well-being of human beings, the internal life of mothers has not been adequately recognized or addressed in developmental theories. In fact, for over a century, psychoanalytic and non-psychoanalytic theories have perpetuated a decontextualized view of mothers and the mothering process. In this chapter, they review literature concerning the context of immigration, focus on the subjectivity of immigrant mothers as shaped by the interaction between the individual and social context, and argue that a psychoanalytic lens that integrates contextual understandings is critical to addressing the intrapsychic and interpersonal lives of mothers who either immigrate to the U.S. and of women who become mothers post-migration in the U.S. They then explore the internal life of mothers and the complicated ways in which immigrant mothers negotiate the mothering process and their identities in the face of cultural change and upheaval. They also provide a brief case vignette to illustrate the complexity of mothering in an immigrant context.

In a private practice setting, Welsh France illustrates a clinical example in which the complexity of cultural transference and countertransference develop. Djenaba, an African woman, married to a Caucasian French man gave birth to a baby girl. She was referred to the analyst because she could not take care of her baby. A diagnosis of depression had been made but when a trustful relationship was established, she told the analyst that she was afraid of offending the spirit who was her invisible lover, possessing her since adolescence. The analyst had to check her cultural countertransferential reactions regarding "possession" and to overcome a kind of uncanny feeling through a collaborative work with anthropologists. When Djenaba emerged from her melancholia, she had to face conflicts with her husband who could not cope either with her trances or with her African way of being a mother.

Children of immigrant descent, internationally adopted children are facing specific challenges

Akhtar (USA) lists and describes comprehensively the many specific challenges faced by children of immigrants. To be sure, such dilemmas exist side by side with the ubiquitous intrapsychic and interpersonal problems of childhood and adolescence. The hardships caused by being a child of immigrants and the ordinary phase-specific developmental difficulties rarely stand apart. More often than not, the two symbolize each other, defend against each other, or get condensed and accentuate the emotional intensity of whatever is going on at a given moment. It then becomes hard to tear them apart. Nonetheless, the specific burdens upon children of immigrants do warrant individual consideration. These include (i) straddling between cultures, (ii) experiencing shame at having parents who are "different" from the parents of friends and peers, (iii) feeling taxed by the high expectations of their parents, (iv) having tight restrictions on their autonomy, (v) being forced into the role of their parents' teachers and "translators", (vi) managing the guilt induced into them by immigrant parents, (vii) parental prohibition on socialization, especially dating, drinking, and mingling with the opposite sex, (viii) facing discrimination and prejudice, and (ix) having to defend their being "American". Examples from clinical settings as well as social experiences will be provided to highlight the above-mentioned issues.

A research study conducted in Paris (El Husseini) shows substantial differences between the literature from English-speaking countries and that from France and Europe in general. Approximately 30 000 children are adopted across national borders each year. A review of the literature on the cultural belonging of these internationally adopted children and a clinical vignette will introduce to the specific difficulties met in international adoption.

The objective of the study is to start from the discourse of French adoptive parents to explore their representations of their child's cultural belonging and their positions (their thoughts and representations) concerning connections with the child's country of birth and its culture. The study includes 51 French parents who adopted one or more children internationally. Each parent participated in a semi-structured interview, focused on the adoption procedure and their current associations with the child's birth country. The interviews were analyzed according to a qualitative phenomenological method, Interpretative Phenomenological Analysis. The principal themes that emerged from the analysis of the interviews made it possible to classify the parents into three different groups.

The first group maintained no association with the child's country of birth and refused any multiplicity of cultural identities. The second group actively maintained regular associations with the child's country of birth and culture and affirmed that their family was multicultural. Finally, the third group adapted their associations with the child's birth country and its culture according to the child's questions and interests. Exploring parental representations of the adopted child enable professionals involved in adoption to provide better support to these families and to do preventive work at the level of family interactions.

Adolescents born to immigrant parents in South America also face specific challenges. Guzman (Chile) shows how immigration from neighbouring countries (Peru, Argentina, Bolivia, Ecuador, Colombia) has increased considerably over the past ten years. This immigration is mostly related to the search for better employment opportunities to achieve better living standards. In clinical settings, she has encountered adolescents born in Chile from immigrant parents. Their parents frequently have high expectations regarding their education and their future occupations. How do these adolescents cope with this pressure? How do they grow up in a country other than that of their parents? How can a consulting adolescent psychiatrist in a public hospital with limited time assigned to each patient assess these issues from an ethno-psychoanalytic point of view? To illustrate these aspects, she discusses the case of an adolescent with Peruvian parents who attempted suicide after being sexually abused by another adolescent.

Portrait of an immigrant couple in literature: Ashima and Ashoka, by Jhumpa Lahiri, in the Namesake (2003)

This book is a day-to-day chronicle of an Indian couple who settled in Boston and became parents of a son they named Gogol. It could be used as a textbook on parenthood and immigration for anyone who would like to become familiar with the many details of the complexity of the process.

Jhumpa Lahiri illustrates thoughtfully the components of the difficulties faced by immigrant parents when they speak so eloquently of the issues we will tackle in this book. First, the fear of motherhood in exile: *"motherhood (…) that it was happening so far from home, unmonitored and unobserved by those she loved, had made it more miraculous still. But she is terrified to raise a child in a country where she is related to no one, where she knows so little, where life seems so tentative and spare" (page 4).* And she goes on with the feeling of exile which does not amount only to the feeling of loss. It is also moving to see the importance she gives of trying to cook food that reminds of the homeland during pregnancy. The naming of her husband and of her son follow rules that are not familiar in the USA. The paternal stance is evoked by her husband while Ashima is in labour. And, last but not least, the feeling of isolation: taking this feeling of isolation into account is one of the most important roots of our work with immigrant parents.

References

Ainslie, R., Tummala-Narra, P., Harlem, A., Barbanel, L., & Ruth, R. (2013). Psychoanalytic views on the experience of immigration. *Psychoanalytic Psychology*, 30(4), 663–679. doi:10.1037/a0034588

Barraband, M., Gassmann, X., & Petitot, F. (2005). Un homme et une femme ne suffisent pas à faire un enfant. Entretien avec Maurice Godelier. *La lettre de l'enfance et de l'adolescence*, 1(59), 17–26. https://doi.org/10.3917/lett.059.0017

Beltsiou, J. (2016). *Immigration in Psychoanalysis: Locating Ourselves*. Routledge.

Benedek, T. (1959). Parenthood as a developmental phase: a contribution to the libido theory. *Journal of the American Psychoanalytic Association*, 7(3), 389–417.

Corin, E. (2012). Interdisciplinary ddialogue: A Site of Estrangement. *Ethos* 40(1), 104–112.

Delanoë, D. & Moro M. R. (2016) Les rapports sociaux dans le transfert culturel, essai de problématisation, *l'Autre*, 17, 203–211

Devereux, G. (1967/2012). *De l'angoisse à la méthode dans les sciences du comportement*. Flammarion.

Godelier, M. (2005). Il faut toujours plus qu'un homme et une femme pour faire un enfant. *Médecine/Sciences* 21, 99–101.

Goody, E. (1982). *Parenthood and Social Reproduction. Fostering and Occupational Roles in West Africa*. Cambridge University Press.

Grinberg, L., & Grinberg, R. (1986). *Psychanalyse du migrant et de l'exilé*. Cesura Lyon Éditions.

Grossi, E. (2018). Clinique politique et politiques de la clinique. Le cas des unités de soins psychiatriques "ethno-raciales" de l'université de Californie à San Francisco. *Genèses*, 111(2), 92–113. https://doi.org/10.3917/gen.111.0092

Lahiri, J. (2003). *The Namesake*. Harper Collins.

Laplanche, J. & Pontalis, J.B. (1967). *Vocabulaire de la psychanalyse*. PUF, p 492

Moro, M. R. (2011). *Psychothérapie Transculturelle de L'enfant et de L'adolescent*. Dunod.

Moro, M. R., & Moro Gomez, I. (2004). *Avicenne L'andalouse. Devenir Psychothérapeute en Situation transculturelle*. La pensée sauvage.

Racamier, P. C., Sens, C., & Carretier, L. (1961). La mère et l'enfant dans les psychoses du post-partum. *Evolution Psychiatrique*, 26(4), 525–570.

Rouchy, J. C. (1995). Identifications and groups of belonging. *Group Analysis*, 28(2), 129–141. https://doi.org/10.1177/05333164952282003

Sturm, G., Heidenreich, F., & Moro, M. R. (2009). Transcultural clinical work with immigrants, asylum seekers and refugees at Avicenne Hospital. *France. International Journal of Migration, Health and Social Care*, 4(4), 33–40.

Chapter 1

Parenthood in migration

How to face multiplicity

Marie Rose Moro, Olivier Taïeb, and Sara Skandrani

Culture and parenthood, in the meaning shared by psychoanalysts, psychologists, psychiatrists, paediatricians, philosophers, teachers, social workers, and policymakers, are challenges of the twenty-first century (Gauchet, 2004). It is tempting to suggest that the most important issue is for everyone to find their own style of parenthood, to transfer or pass on the bond, the tenderness, the protection of self and others. Oddly enough, the English parenthood has only recently appeared in other languages (French, Spanish, or Italian) as a neologism (such as parentalité in French). It is as if we had just realized how precious what we have in our hands was, and that parents all over the world possess it. We have seen parents, those who are vulnerable or find themselves in difficult or inhuman situations, worry so much about finding strategies to survive, mentally or materially speaking – that it becomes difficult or impossible for them to pass on anything but the precariousness of their surrounding world. Therefore, it is important to study migratory situations since these situations lead the parents to changes and in some cases to breakdowns that make the establishment of parent-in-fant relationships more complex. Indeed, migrations are nowadays part of modern societies, which are multiform and multicultural, and migration should be a focus of our clinical concerns. It is very important because once this variable is considered, the risk is converted into creative potential, for both the children and their families and for caregivers, as will be seen hereafter from a French experience in infant care set up in Avicenne Hospital in the Paris suburbs and Cochin Hospital in Paris[1] (Moro, 1994; 2020; 2021; Moro et al., 2008). Better understanding, better care, better provision for migrants and their children are the challenges for early prevention and clinical care today.

Parenthood

You are not born a parent, you become one. Parenthood is made of complex ingredients. Some of them are community ingredients and belong to the society as a whole; they change over time, they can be historical, legal,

DOI: 10.4324/9781003174684-2

social, and cultural. Others are more personal and private, they may be conscious or unconscious, they belong to each parent as separate persons and future parents, to the couple, and to the family history of each parent. What is played out here is the part that is passed on and the part that remains hidden, childhood traumas, and the way everyone has patched them up. There is also another set of factors belonging to the child, who changes the persons who gave him or her birth into parents. Certain infants are more gifted than others, some are born within an environment that makes things easier; others, due to the circumstances of their birth (prematurity, neonatal distress, physical, or mental handicap), have several obstacles to overcome, and must develop numerous, often costly, strategies to enter a relationship with the distressed parent. Many authors along with Cramer, Lebovici, and Stern have shown that the infant is an active partner in the parent-infant interaction, and thereby in the construction of parenthood (Lebovici, 1983; 1993). Indeed, the infant contributes to the emergence of the maternal and paternal identities when the parents are taking care of him or her by handling, feeding, and giving pleasure within a process of exchange of actions and feelings that are a central part of the first moments of life (Delaisi de Parseval & Lallemand, 1980).

There are very many ways of being a father and being a mother, as it has been broadly shown by sociologists and anthropologists (Devereux, 1968; Lallemand et al., 1991). Professionals must leave room for these potentials to emerge. Yet it is a difficult task which implies to refrain from any form of judgement on the "best way" to be a father or a mother. Indeed, it is tempting for any professional to think he knows better than the parents what the "good" parental behaviour is and what the child's needs and expectations are. Social and cultural elements contribute to the construction of parental functioning (Bornstein, 2002; Tamminen, 2006). Cultural elements have a preventive function and give the opportunity to anticipate the issue of how to become a parent as it gives a meaning to the daily ups and downs of parent-child relations and prevents distress from setting in.

Early on, cultural elements mingle and become profoundly entangled with individual, family, and social elements (Cauce, 2008; Koumaré, 2000; Serre, 2002; Moro, 2007). Pregnancy, on account of its initiatory nature, recalls our mythical, cultural, and fantasized belonging. How can we protect ourselves in exile? How can we have fine and healthy children? In some places, the pregnancy must be concealed, in others, certain fish should not be eaten, or certain tubers that soften when cooked. In other places, the husband should not eat certain sorts of meat while his wife is pregnant, or dreams must be kept and interpreted and the demands made complied with, because in dreams it is the child who is speaking (Lallemand et al., op. cit.). In exile, these elements belong to the private sphere and can find themselves in contradiction with new, outside, medical, cultural, and social manners of thinking. Then comes the moment of childbirth. Here again, there are many ways of giving birth, receiving the child, presenting him to the world, and thinking about his otherness and sometimes his distress. There are also all sorts of "trivial" things that are reactivated in situations of crisis, reawakening representations that may have remained dormant, or that were thought to be outlived.

In the name of a sort of empty universality and simplistic ethics, we professionals do not integrate these complex manners of thinking neither in the design of prevention and care provision, nor in our theorizing. The issues we approach rarely integrate the cultural dimension of parenthood, and above all we do not view these ways of thinking and doing things as being useful in establishing an alliance, understanding, anticipating, and providing care. We feel that the technique is unclothed, that it has no cultural impact, and that it is enough to observe a protocol for the action to be correctly implemented.

Yet several clinical experiences (Moro et al., 2008) show that once these different representations are shared, efficiency is patent. From a theoretical point of view, they renew our manners of thinking, lead us to "de-centre", and make our models more complex and to set aside our over-hasty judgement. Apprehending this otherness allows migrant women to experience the different stages of their pregnancies and parenthood in a non-traumatic manner and to become familiar with other ways of thinking and other techniques. The migration does entail the need to change. But ignoring otherness is not only to miss the creative side of the encounter, but also to take the risk that these women will never find their place in our prevention and health systems, and it also restricts them to the solitude of thought and living. Exchanges with others enable us to change; we need to build together, exchange ideas, and confront perceptions with those of other people. If not, people's thought tends to close on itself and its own mechanisms and this can lead to rigidity and withdrawal.

Psychic and cultural transparency

Besides these social and cultural dimensions, paternal and maternal function can be upset by manifestations of individual mental functioning, or by earlier suffering that has not found relief. It usually appears in a sudden and violent manner when the line of descent is being enacted: for instance, the various forms of post-partum depression, and even psychoses, leading to loss of meaning. The mother vulnerability in this period is well known and has been theorized, in particular, via the concept of "psychic transparency" (transparence psychique by Monique Bydlowski). What transparency means is that, in the perinatal period, the mental functioning of the mother is easier to read and perceive than it usually is (Bydlowski, 1991; 1997). The psychic movements are more readable, fantasies and phantasms are more sharable. Indeed, the alterations occurring during pregnancy are accompanied by a more ready, more explicit expression of desires, conflicts, and impulses. In addition, childhood conflict is relived, reactivated in particular by oedipal revival. Later, functioning becomes opaque again. This psychic transparency is less recognized in fathers, who also experience upheavals relating to the reliving of their own conflicts, to the re-enacting of their own status as a son, and to the shift from being a son to being a father. The perinatal period, thus, enables regression and expression that are quite specific to it.

Exile merely potentiates this psychic transparency, and this will be expressed by both parents in both psychic and cultural spheres. On the one hand, it is expressed in the psychic sphere by the reliving of conflicts and the expression of emotions. On the other hand, it is expressed in the cultural sphere in the same way but relies on cultural representations and ways of doing and saying things specific to each culture. All these cultural elements, which we thought belonged to the preceding generation, are reactivated and suddenly become valuable and alive. Thus, it is appropriate to suggest the concept of cultural transparency to address and represent what the parents are experiencing. Their relationship with their culture and their parents is altered.

Early prevention

In this reality in which different levels interact one with another, the psychological dimension has a specific position in terms of prevention and care. Prevention, indeed, starts with the pregnancy. Some mothers-to-be experience difficulties to think about their expected child. It is then important to help them to invest in and eventually welcome their future baby despite their solitude – which is social and, even more, existential. Sharing a culture makes it possible to anticipate what will happen, to think about it, and to establish protection. The culture is a base on which we can build a place for the child to be born. The setbacks in this construction of the parent-infant bond find cores of meaning within the experience of the social group, but these meanings are far more difficult to apprehend in a migrant situation. What remains as fixed elements in this case are the body and the individual mental makeup since everything else has become shifting and precarious. Women living in their communities but excluded from their own societies, equally isolated, also find themselves alone in the task of humanizing the child, a common task to all birth (Rabain-Jamin & Wornham, 1990). The child is a stranger that the mother must learn to know and recognize.

In the perinatal period, adjustments are needed between mother and infant, and also between husband and wife. Dysfunction in the relationship could occur and is sometimes unavoidable, but it is often short-lived if early intervention is possible. To intervene early, demands need to be recognized in their somatic or functional "translations" – these demands are often difficult to express because individuals do not know to whom address them and how. It is, therefore, important to learn how to recognize the distress and doubts of migrant women through small clues (somatic complaints, complaints concerning the child, requests for social assistance). Most of all, they should be allowed to say things, in their own language if necessary, through other women in their community.

Early prevention is available from the start of life in prevention centres, maternity wards, paediatric departments, infant welfare centres, and GP consultations. This perinatal prevention work is essential because the period is crucial for the child's development and for the construction of the child's place in the family.

Care represents an issue as important as prevention. Day-to-day difficulties of migrant or socially underprivileged families and their children are leading us to alter our psychological care provision techniques and our theories so as to adapt them to increasingly complex clinical situations (Réal & Moro, 1998). This also leads us to alter our own frameworks in order to adequately cater for these children and their parents and to refer them on to specialized consultations if necessary, within a network enabling links and to-and-fro movements between prevention and care facilities: this complementary functioning is essential. The aim is to enable the parent to move from the inside to the outside that he is afraid of, and to be what Michel Serres (1977) called the "weaver" working to seam together two worlds set apart by a sudden catastrophe.

The tree of life

Each of us, according to Serge Lebovici (1983; 1993), carries a trans-generational mandate: it can be said that our "tree of life" sends its roots down into the earth that has soaked up the blood from the wounds caused by the childhood conflicts of our parents (Coblence, 1996). Yet our roots, he says, can enable the tree of life to develop and blossom, if they are not too buried in the soil that they become inaccessible. Generally – and happily so – filiation, with its neurotic conflicts, does not prevent the processes of cultural affiliation. The child's tree of life, the mandate he is given via trans-generational transmission, thus brings the grandparents' generation into his or her psychic life through the childhood conflicts of his or her parents, whether it is pre-conscious or repressed (Lebovici, op. cit.). More contemporary conflicts, and in particular migratory trauma, can also take their place in this tree of life, and such events give new meaning, in the aftermath, to childhood conflict and traumas. This is the case for migratory traumas. When the weight of the transmission is too heavy, and translation too direct, filiation for the child becomes a "pathology of destiny" (Coblence, op. cit.). This is when there are "ghosts in the nursery" (Fraiberg, 1999). These are visitors that re-emerge from the parents' forgotten past, visitors that were "not invited to the christening". In favourable circumstances, the ghosts are driven away from the nursery and return underground. But in some unfavourable circumstances, these representations of the past in the present take over the field, settle there, and seriously affect the mother-infant relationship. Here is the therapeutic challenge: to create and co-create, with the mother and those around her – starting from the child as an interactive partner – the conditions to identify the ghosts, and rather than chasing them away to negotiate with them and, in a way, to humanize them. Once again, the task is to make something human even out of trauma, whatever its nature is, here breakdown arising from exile.

Pregnancy and childbirth in exile

Traditionally, childbirth is an initiatory moment in which the mother-to-be is necessarily supported by other women from the group: accompaniment, preparation for the different events, interpretation of dreams, and so forth (Moro, 1994, 2000). Migration leads to several breaks in this supportive process that constructs meaning. First, there is a loss of the accompaniment by the group, by the family, by cultural and social support, and an inability to give a culturally acceptable meaning to dysfunction, such as the mother's sadness, feelings of inability, or inharmonious mother-infant relations. In addition, migrating women are confronted with medical methods that do not allow traditional protective strategies. For these women, western medical practice can be violent, indecent, traumatic, and even "pornographic" (a word used by several patients). We became acutely aware of the scale of the violation experienced by the pregnant migrant women since the beginning of our work with them. The women referred to in our practice are migrants from the rural areas of North Africa, sub-Saharan Africa, or Sri Lanka. For city-dwellers, these effects are also present, but probably in a less explicit manner.

A case story: Medina

Medina, a Soninke woman from Mali had been referred for post-partum depression, apparently accompanied by elements of delirium, but this was shown later to be the cultural expression of a traumatic experience, following trans-cultural evaluation. There was no delirium, only trauma, even if its expression was unusual. Medina is a tall woman with a deeply sad look in her eyes. At our first encounter, she was wearing a bright yellow boubou and a cloth of the same colour covering her hair. On her serious face, there were ritual scarifications: a vertical line on the chin, two horizontal lines on the cheekbones, and a small vertical mark on the forehead. She spoke Soninke in a monotonous voice. From time to time, a few tears ran down her cheeks. She took no notice and went on talking about her complete incomprehension of what had happened to her while her son, Mamadou, was still in her womb. During the consultation, she had Mamadou on her back, he was two months old and her first child: Mamadou was very small as he was not feeding well, he was crying a lot and moaning painfully. Medina was not able to breastfeed him, he sucked the breast very feebly, and in addition, she was convinced she had no milk, or that her milk was not nourishing enough for the child. Medina had been in France for one year, where she had come to join her husband who has emigrated eight years before.

There are several moments that can take the form of genuine mental and cultural violations for these women from rural areas. But before any analysis is made, it is important to emphasize that what is violent is the fact that actions are performed without preparation. These technical acts are closely linked to the western cultural context. For those who do not share it, these acts, by their implicit content, become truly inductors of mental violation. Women can neither imagine nor anticipate them. The conclusion to be drawn is not that such acts should not be performed, which would be quite unacceptable both in terms of ethics and in terms of public health. To refrain from practising these acts would lead to exclude the women further from our healthcare system and would contribute to socially marginalize them. On the contrary, we have to ensure that these acts are efficacious and fulfil their purpose. To adapt our care and prevention strategies, we need to apprehend this otherness. Thus, instead of being an obstacle to interaction, it can become the opportunity for a new encounter.

Voicing the pregnancy

Traditionally, pregnancy should be hidden as long as possible, or at least it should be spoken of as little as possible so as not to arouse envy among sterile women, women who have not had a boy, women who have had too few children, or women who are outsiders. This explains the fear that Medina experienced when she went to see the social worker for her to complete the required pregnancy certificate forms. She felt threatened and unprotected. Anything could happen to her; she could even be "bewitched" and lose the child she was carrying. This fear was with her throughout her pregnancy, and even when the child was born, she was still terrified: the child was not protected, he could at any time return to the world of the ancestors; it means that he could die.

The ultrasound scan

In the hospital, things continued along the same lines for Medina. They took "photos" that showed what she had in her womb, that showed "what God was still keeping hidden" she said. For her, the scan was almost pornographic. Especially, because the medical team had shown her the images almost without comment, since she understood very little French. These images without words and without accompaniment were very violent. The practitioner performing the scan did not understand her refusing to look, he talked to her, encouraged her to look and not to worry... She closed her eyes to avoid seeing. He interpreted this refusal to look at the images as a difficulty investing herself in the child. In contrast, for other migrant women in the habit of asking for divinatory acts during pregnancy, such as the Mina or Awa women from Togo or Benin, the scan is sometimes associated with these practices, in which case it is felt to be familiar. Every situation is unique.

Childbirth

Then Medina gave birth, on her own, without an interpreter, with the virtually compulsory presence of her husband, who was brought into the labour room because things were not going well. A caesarean was envisaged but the husband was terrified, and he refused. Eventually, they waited a little, and Medina was calmed by bringing in the labour room another Soninke woman who had just given birth in the same ward. Then, she said, the child consented to come out "on his own". We now know the importance to allow for physiological labour every time it is possible, that is to say as long as the lives of the mother and the child are not at risk.

For Medina, there was the recurrent idea that the child she had born and that came into the world in these conditions was not protected, he was in danger, and so was she. In this case, it was the category "lack of protection of mother and child", and also its cultural consequence, vulnerability towards a "witchcraft attack", that was the right category for us to envisage, as was confirmed in subsequent work with Medina.

Medina did indeed begin to feel calmer following certain cultural acts that contributed to shoring up the breach, the inadequate protection: the couple asked their families in Mali to perform protection rites for their son Mamadou, so that the child was brought into the generational chain and the wider family. At the same time, we explored the mother's sadness with her, and her lost support, by bringing to life cultural representations that had lost their meaning because of exile and family conflict; in other words, the cultural prop was partly reconstructed in the therapeutic group: she had left Mali without her father's consent, and therefore, her first child was unprotected. This work of co-construction of cultural meaning was the first step for the construction of a framework.

In the second stage, the many losses that Medina had suffered were approached. Her mother died when she was born, and she had been brought up by her father's other wife. In addition, she was distressed and sad in her life of exile, separated from her sisters, one of them died before she could have seen her again. Supported by the group (Moro, 2003) and the framework offered, Medina went on to elaborate her sadness, she found meaning for everything that had happened during her all-too-lonely pregnancy, and she constructed a secure relationship with her son Mamadou. The protection of the maternal grandfather requested and obtained by Medina then took effect.

In the preventive sphere, it can be seen from this story, and many others like it, that there is a need to enable pregnant women to have a culturally acceptable representation of what is done to them. They can then build an individual strategy enabling them to shift from one world to another without having to relinquish their own representations – thus constructing a genuine métissage (the French word) or cultural hybridization.

In intra-cultural situations, through pregnancy and childbirth women put themselves in the line of mothers and grandmothers, thus find efficient support (whether family, medical of friendly). In a transcultural situation, women will no longer find the support required to shore up their internal disarray, this leads to a "potentiation of the mechanisms of confusion through exile" (Moro et al., 1989).

Other attitudes can be seen among mothers and need to be understood to be linked to the trauma of certain exiles, and the way in which this reactivates the previous conflict. There is first of all the apparent "opting out" of certain mothers: it is as if they were saying that the abilities are with someone else, with the foreigners. Then, they go on to over-hasty acculturation: everything that comes from me is bad, and everything good comes from outside. Or, conversely, there is the development of a cultural rigidity: women tend to return to practices that may be outlived in their original families, and there is, more importantly, a loss of their adaptive flexibility to any culture, and more rigidity in behaviour (Rabain-Jamin, 1989; Bornstein & Cote, 2004); there are above all thoughts that are secondary to a trauma that cannot be expanded upon.

Pregnancy and childbirth in a situation of migration reactivate the loss of a framework. When events are not carried by the group, their traumatic nature is enhanced. Thus, it is for childbirth, the time of a breach in the maternal shell, both mental and physical, which is often a factor that reactivates the sufferings of exile.

If there is a pathology of exile, the pathology cannot be positioned on the level of content, since it is all the same; however, this specificity can be sought in the functioning of the "containers", and the internal and external frameworks.

The infant

The infant develops within a cultural shell that pre-exists before his or her birth. What is the nature of the infant? Where is he from? These questions on the child's ontology have been with human beings through time and under all latitudes. The questions seek to apprehend the otherness of the infant by establishing him or her within ontological representations that are specific to each cultural group. The infant is a stranger who will have to be identified (ibid.).

These questions, and their answers, pervade the whole of family discourse. Overall, they try to determine whether the infant is a "virgin" being, or whether he has arrived already possessing his/her own abilities. In North Africa, it is sometimes said that the infant is an angel until his/her first chuckles – they say that the infant is pure if he has not opened his mouth, and if he dies, he will go straight to heaven. In India, in some families, it is sometimes said that the infant is a trans-migrant, loaded with baggage containing tendencies and experiences from his previous life (Stork, 1988). In certain West African countries, it is said that the infant is not human, he is a stranger from another world, a visiting stranger, who may leave again without notice if the world of humans does not please him. Thus, it is the infant that decides his own death, and this strange ability is significant of the infant's otherness. In so-called traditional societies where, infant mortality is still high, this ontological representation is an attempt to give an acceptable meaning to this unacceptable event. In other places, the infant will only really achieve human status when he has reached the age of talking and walking: the risk of mortality decreases markedly after two years old. In Mongolia in certain regions, it is only with the first haircut – between the ages of two and five – that the child shifts from an intermediate being to a human being (Fontanel & D'Harcourt, 1998). In Western Europe between the two World Wars, popular representations saw an infant carrying no trace of any sort, a dough or clay that was to be shaped; educational prerogative belonged to the parents, who were supposed to shape the infant in their own image. Later academic theory, with child psychiatrists such as Lebovici, Cramer or Brazelton, set out very different representations: the infant came to be thought to arrive in the world with a baggage of abilities that the adults had the task of bringing out (Lebovici, 1983). If this theory had such success, it is because popular representation had already noted, beyond prevalent discourse, the specific abilities of the very young infant.

The "enculturation" of the infant as defined by Margaret Mead in 1928 and 1930 is enacted through the body, care, and mothering, and also through education, speech, and implicit components of discourse (Mead, 1963; 1973). Enculturation is the incarnation of culture in each one of us. Culture embeds itself in perceptions and sensations as the child grows. In Niger, in order to be considered handsome, Peul infants should have a thin nose; among the Tuaregs, the mother will pull and pinch the child's nose, a symbol of honour. In West Africa, Bambara women massage their infants energetically so that later they will have "sure feet in the bush" and become brave hunters (Lallemand et al., op. cit.). Thus, each of these mothers implicitly passes on a fundamental value belonging to the group to her child. This enculturation is part of what Devereux (1970) has referred to as the cultural "envelope" or shell, a shell that clothes each one of us and forms a sort of second skin. Enculturation of the human child becomes a more delicate matter when it occurs in a cultural environment that is not the one in which the mother and those around her have grown up. The mother, undergoing the multiplicity of the worlds around her, is more prone to states of confusion, and even perplexity and this will make her function of "object-presenting" to the baby more difficult (Winnicott, 1979). The mother will in this case transfer her own perception of the world, a kaleidoscopic perception, sometimes pervaded with anxiety. Her classic function of guarding the infant from over-excitation is compromized; she has difficulty presenting the world "in small doses" so that the child is constantly at risk from encountering the world in a traumatic manner. However certain interactive patterns, even if altered by migration, retain coherence and are performed and passed on with sufficient serenity to enable good-quality mothering. For instance, this is what happens with massages performed on infants. Enculturation transits via specific interaction modes – the voice, the ways of looking and touching, kinetic stimulations. These patterns are variously implemented according to the cultural group into which the infant is born. Thus, mothers in sub-Saharan Africa and Asia do not talk much to their babies and avoid visual interaction: the voice and the eyes can be filled with evil intentions. There are various practices aiming to counter the effects of the evil eye or the evil tongue. It is easy to understand that in this cultural context the voice and the eyes are not the main channels for interaction. Our "quite natural" way of smiling and talking to babies is, thus, often seen as threatening by mothers from other cultures.

Naming the infant is the first step to humanization. In sub-Saharan Africa, to affiliate a child to the community and to the mother, the main task is to set the child apart from the "other world" he is supposed to come from: the superhuman and supernatural world of the ancestors and the spirits. Generally, when the infant is seven days old, the ritual of naming the child is performed, and this will consist in identifying which ancestor (or which spirit) is returning in the child. The infant is indeed a messenger moving from one universe to another, and correct identification of the ancestor will apprehend the message the child brings. It is when the ancestor has been correctly identified that the infant can embark on a process of humanization. There is then a breaking-off between the superhuman world and the human world. This breaking off is the sine qua non-condition for the infant to be able to develop harmoniously and finally settle among humans. In this mode of humanizing the infant, the primary separation is seen first as occurring between the ancestor and the infant. This separation enables the child to settle into the primary relationship with the maternal figure. In this logic, the infant is not at first in a symbiotic relationship with his mother. The child does not belong to the mother. If there is symbiosis, it is with the "other world", the world of the ancestors. So as long as this symbiosis is sustained, the child cannot become human and may present serious somatic or mental dysfunction, described by different etiological theories[2], such as the child-ancestor or the *djinna baby* (Moro et al., 2008; Moro, 2021; Nathan & Moro, 1989; Réal & Moro, op. cit.). Through the naming ritual and primary separation, a whole theory of the humanization of the infant can be seen as long as those receiving the child have not settled their accounts with their ancestors and forerunners, the child runs the risk of paying dearly. Psychoanalysis confirms this, studies on trans-generational issues. The naming rituals, as practiced in sub-Saharan Africa, are an attempt to guard against subsequent serious disorder by forcing each member of the community to see him or herself as part of a chain of generations, in a trans-generational interaction cleared of major conflicts that could hinder the child's development.

Conclusions: To be affected

The consequences to be drawn for day-to-day work with parents and future parents are considerable (Kotchick, 2002; Moro, 2003; 2020; 2021; Koniak-Griffin et al., 2006; Moro et al., 2008; Seeman, 2008). The task, for psychoanalysts, psychologists and psychiatrists, midwives and child nurses, obstetricians and nurses, social workers, and child education specialists, is to attempt quite simply to do their job better by adapting to these families from elsewhere. This work, sometimes seen as fraught with difficulty, once one becomes involved, proves rewarding and fascinating.

To be affected and "transported" by these parents and their infants is necessary to allow them to draw on their own resources.

Notes

1 www.maisondesolenn.fr
2 Cultural theories that give a collective sense to what is happening.

References

Bornstein, M. H. (2002). *Handbook of parenting*. Erlbaum.
Bornstein, M. H., & Cote, L. R. (2004). Mothers' parenting cognitions on cultures of origin, acculturating cultures, and cultures of destination. *Child Development, 75,* 221–235.
Bydlowski, M. (1991). La transparence psychique de la grossesse. *Études freudiennes, 32,* 2–9.
Bydlowski, M. (1997). *La Dette de vie, Itinéraire Psychanalytique de la Maternité.* PUF.
Cauce, A. M. (2008). Parenting, culture, and context: Reflections on excavating culture. *Applied Developmental Science, 12,* 227–229.
Coblence, F. (1996). *Serge Lebovici.* PUF.

Delaisi de Parseval, G., & Lallemand, S. (1980). *L'art d'accommoder les bébés : 100 ans De Recettes Françaises de Puériculture.* Le Seuil.

Devereux, G. (1968). L'image de l'enfant dans deux tribus : Mohave et Sedang. In *Revue de neuropsychiatrie et d'hygiène mentale de l'enfance, 4,* 25–35.

Devereux, G. (1970). *Essais d'ethnopsychiatrie Générale.* Gallimard.

Fontanel, B., & D'Harcourt, C. (1998). *Bébés du Monde.* La Martinière.

Fraiberg, S. (1999). *Fantômes dans la Chambre D'enfants.* PUF.

Gauchet, M. (2004). L'enfant du désir. *Le Débat, 132*(5), 98–121. https://doi.org/10.3917/deba.132.0098

Koniak-Griffin, D., Logsdon, M. C., Hines-Martin, V., & Turner, C. C. (2006). *Contemporary mothering in a diverse society. JOGNN, 35,* 671–678.

Kotchick, B. A. (2002). Putting parenting in perspective: A discussion of the contextual factors that shape parenting practices. *Journal of Child and Family Studies, 11,* 255–269.

Koumaré, B. (2000). Séré den: Quand le nourrir questionne la naissance et la mort. *L'autre, 1*(1), 65–68. https://doi.org/10.3917/lautr.001.0065

Lallemand, S., Journet, O., & Ewombe-Moundo, E. (1991). *Grossesse Et petite Enfance en Afrique Noire et à Madagascar.* L'Harmattan.

Lebovici, S. (1983). *Le Nourrisson, la Mère et le Psychanalyste: Les Interactions Précoces.* Le Centurion.

Lebovici, S. (1993). On intergenerational transmission. From filiation to affiliation. *Infant Mental Health Journal, 14,* 260–272.

Mead, M. (1963). *Mœurs et Sexualité en Océanie.* Plon.

Mead, M. (1973). *Une Éducation en Nouvelle-Guinée.* Payot.

Moro, M. R., Nathan, T., Rabain-Jamin, J., Stork, H., & Si Ahmed, J. (1989). Le bébé dans son univers culturel. In S. Lebovici & F. Weil-Halpern (eds). *Psychopathologie du Bébé* (pp. 683–750). PUF.

Moro, M. R. (1994). *Parents en exil.* In *Psychopathologie et Migrations.* PUF.

Moro, M. R. (2000). *Psychopathologie Transculturelle des Enfants et des Adolescents.* Dunod.

Moro, M. R. (2003). Parents and infants in changing cultural context: Immigration, trauma and risk. *Infant Mental Health Journal, 24,* 240–264.

Moro, M. R. (2007). *Aimer ses Enfants Ici et Ailleurs.* In *Histoires transculturelles.* Odile Jacob.

Moro, M. R. (2020). *Guide de Psychothérapie Transculturelle. Soigner les Enfants et les adolescents.* Inpress Ed.

Moro, M. R. (2021). *50 Questions Sur Les Bébés, Les Enfants, Les Adolescents. Comment Devenir des Parents Ordinaires ici et dans le Monde.* La Pensée sauvag.

Moro, M. R., Neuman, D., & Réal, I. (2008). *Maternités en Exil. Mettre des bébés au Monde et les faire Grandir en Situation Transculturelle.* La Pensée sauvage.

Nathan, T., & Moro, M. R. (1989). Enfants de djinné. Évaluation ethnopsychanalytique des interactions précoces. In S. Lebovici, P. Mazet, & J.-P. Visier (eds), *Évaluation des interactions Précoces* (pp. 307–340). Eschel.

Rabain-Jamin, J. (1989). La famille africaine. In S. Lebovici & F. Weil-Halpern (eds), *Psychopathologie du Bébé* (pp. 722–727). PUF.

Rabain-Jamin, J., & Wornham, W. L. (1990). Transformation des conduites de maternage et des pratiques de soin chez les femmes migrantes d'Afrique de l'Ouest. *Psychiatrie de l'Enfant, 33*(1), 287–319.

Réal, I., & Moro, M. R. (1998). De l'art d'humaniser les bébés. Clinique trans-culturelle des processus de socialisation précoce. *Champ Psychosomatique, 15*, 91–108.

Seeman, M. V. (2008). Cross-cultural evaluation of maternal competence in a cultur-ally diverse society. *American Journal of Psychiatry, 165*, 565–568.

Serre, G. (2002). Les femmes sans ombre ou la dette impossible. Le choix de ne pas être mère. *L'autre, 2*(2), 247–256. https://doi.org/10.3917/lautr.008.0247. www.revuelautre.com

Serres, M. (1977). Discours et parcours. In C. Lévi-Strauss (ed.), *L'identité* (pp. 25–39). PUF.

Stork, H. (1988). *Enfances indiennes. Étude de psychologie transculturelle et comparée du jeune enfant.* Le Centurion.

Tamminen, T. (2006). How does culture promote the early development of identity? *Infant Mental Health Journal, 27*, 603–605.

Winnicott, D. W. (1979). *L'enfant et sa famille: les premières relations.* Payot.

Chapter 2

The involvement of fathers in exile on the perinatal scene

Claire Mestre, Lia Fort-Jacques, and Estelle Gioan

The role of exiled fathers during the perinatal period raises issues about the way they are catered for and supported in our clinical practice, and the psychological elaborations necessary for them to become part of a trio: the mother, the father, and the newly born baby. These questions are the meeting point of different themes: the way French institutions cater for fathers in general, and migrant fathers in particular, the roles attributed to fathers by their culture towards their children, and how these roles evolve because of migration, and finally the psychic processes involved in becoming a father in a setting of migration.

The issue of the father's role in a context of migration should be set against the French context characterized by a social evolution of family, with, at the forefront, the feminist movement and its repercussions on marital relationships and the family, and by the place given to psychology in the field of human sciences. Fathers are now recognized in their many dimensions of status, function, and role, as English-language (Lamb, 2010; Lamb & Tamis-LeMonda, 2004) and French studies (Le Camus, 2002) have confirmed. Migration renders the issue of fathers in the perinatal period more complex, especially as they need to assert their legitimacy. Institutions have, thus, been destabilized by having to cater for exiled families and the need to make room for both parents. In a context where paternity references are evolving, fathers who have been confronted with exile have to face the need to adapt to the host culture, a more or less painful process.

The perinatal scene (Abécassis & Bidaud, 2014) opens a particular psychological window for men, who, when becoming fathers, can present disturbances linked to paternity, or can be called on to back up their companion if she is suffering from ill health. Fathers are becoming more and more the agents of their own parenthood and it is vital to provide specific support and care and to help them establish links with their child. However, it seems that the role of fathers has been marginalized in the perinatal care system, or even ignored when they are migrant fathers. This shortfall aggravates migrant men's dual vulnerability in becoming fathers: vulnerability towards the transition towards paternity and vulnerability resulting from exile.

DOI: 10.4324/9781003174684-3

To help exiled fathers when they become fathers, we need to understand how they apprehend this shift, psychologically and psychically. How do they experience their paternal implication at the time of the child's birth? This question calls for an exploration of paternity in the setting of migration and the attendant difficulties. Clinical situations collected during our psychotherapeutic and psychiatric care will give an idea of the difficulties and the elaborations of exiled fathers, anxious to take on the place that is given to them or that they want to lay claim to.

Institutions and the involvement of migrant fathers

The migrant families that we meet in our psychiatric and psychotherapeutic practice are in situations of distress because they have experienced exile[1], with the attendant uncertainties in terms of social and sometimes administrative issues. Furthermore, they are generally far away from their own families, which make them more vulnerable. Care professionals need to be attentive in the perinatal period, as it can be a real ordeal for both women and men. They find themselves in a situation with multiple issues. Indeed, the fathers' place at the baby's side is at the point of convergence of several issues: the evolution of the family under the impulse of the feminist movement, human science research on babies and parenthood, the role of professionals in the care of children, and the diffusion of these developments to the public via the media (Neyrand, 2005). Denial of the importance of the father has long prevailed, backed up to some extent by psychoanalysis which has given them a largely symbolic role. The father's place is at the heart of a struggle centred on the child's needs (and rights) and this struggle has been led by professionals and their institutions, human science researchers, and parents.

Lamb's (2010) concept of "paternal involvement" taken up again by Ramdé (2015, p. 4) can be defined as time devoted by fathers to direct interactions with the child, of a playful, affective and social nature, the fathers' availability for the child and their acknowledged responsibility in childcare, education, and their share in parental tasks. Two forms of paternal involvement can be observed in father-child interactions: direct involvement characterized by care, authority, and play, and indirect involvement characterized by a role of provider towards the child and the mother. Depending on cultures, one or the other form will take precedence. In French society, this involvement can be confronted with what the sociologist Christine Castelain-Meunier calls *matrifocal*, based on her research on the role of fathers around the child. "Supported by state interventions, the focus on the mother seems to have been well consolidated. The focus is recalled, for instance, by childcare professionals who often tell surprised fathers picking up their child: 'will you tell your wife that he took his medicine…', as if education was the women's monopoly and fathers were merely used to relay information and did not have an educational role in their own right" (2004, p.39). One of the consequences of this focus on the mother is paternal withdrawal, to the point of self-effacement, but, conversely, it can also generate the will to resist.

Paternal involvement is, therefore, at the centre of a social paradox: women have a privileged place at the child's side and this place is "scientifically" and socially consolidated, so that men need to show considerable resolve in finding their real role from the outset. Consequently, it is up to women to leave some space for their companion, and it is up to men to make use of that space. One obstacle nonetheless remains: "tradition", even if it is not homogenous across cultures[2], can deprive men of representations that identify them as paternal figures, affectively close to their children (Stork, cited by Neyrand, 2005, p. 321). Bourdieu's[3] notion of *"habitus"* is relevant here: habits are not easily changed from one generation to the next.

The notion of involvement enables us to highlight the willpower of the migrant fathers we support, their considerable efforts in "de-centring" themselves from their traditional role and in adopting new ways of doing things, and these efforts should be backed up by the institutions (Lamb & Tamis-Le-Monda, *op. cit.*).

Paternal involvement in a migratory context has not generated much research to date (Ramdé, *op. cit.*), and most studies were carried out on the other side of the Atlantic. Nevertheless, this involvement is seriously tested. Indeed, exile has an impact on an individual level, by undermining internal and external references and leading to marital issues (*ibid.*). Yayhaoui (1997), a precursor in the psychoanalysis of migrant fathers, and Marie Rose Moro (Moro et al., 2009) underlined how difficult it is for a man to be a migrant father, torn between the "family myth" and institutional ideology, with institutions not taking cultural differences into consideration. Indeed, it took a long time for institutions in France and Canada to take an interest in migrant fathers in the areas of childcare and education (Este & Tachble, 2008). These institutions, essentially run by women, often have pre-conceived ideas about migrant fathers and they also have their own issues in apprehending paternal involvement in their societies.

Social situations, such as social precariousness, where it is impossible to get work, can also lead to the loss of the father's provider status and a weakening of virility in the context of migration (Bergheul *et al.,* 2018; Touhami & Moro, 2019). It is on a disqualifying, if not violent, mode that fathers experience what is given them to understand the norms of the host country (Pachoud and Lhuillier, 2019).

Because of the small number of studies on the subject, different research programmes have been deployed in Quebec, one of which concerns support to immigrant fathers and another concerns father-child relationships, marital relationships, and paternal identity, with a particular focus on the perinatal period. The synthesis of these studies highlights the multiple issues facing migrant fathers. These issues concern the role of provider, the dis-integration of social ties, the reconfiguration of the couple relationship, a re-definition of the relationship with the child, and the conditions of access to institutional and community services. The present authors have observed that unemployed status and the lack of professional qualification led to changes in the paternal role, which impacts the affective and family spheres more particularly. Being the spouse's main support and being a playmate for the child are the new emerging roles that enable the paternal role to be centred on the family. Nevertheless, the authors have pinpointed the gap between the values of the country of origin and those of the host country. Furthermore, immigrant families are confronted with the isolation that can lead to the emergence of family tensions (de Montigny *et al.*, 2015). In this unstable migratory context, how can exiled fathers cope with the need to be present on the perinatal scene?

As care and prevention professionals in the Bordeaux transcultural con-sultations, we have been able to establish a few hypotheses on the psychic processes among migrant men when they become fathers.

Care setting and methodology

Our hypotheses on the psychic processes of migrant fathers are based on transcultural clinical practice calling on psychoanalysis and anthropology. They stem from the Bordeaux university hospital transcultural consulta-tions (Mestre, 2016), which have been deployed for over 20 years using a model experimented and theorized by Tobie Nathan (1986) and Marie Rose Moro (1998).

These psychotherapeutic consultations integrate the patients' first lan-guage and take place within a multi-disciplinary setup. In Bordeaux, the healthcare team comprises a main therapist and co-therapists with differ-ent qualifications: psychologists, anthropologists, interpreters, and trainees form a therapeutic group of three to five people around a clinical situation. This situation can concern an adult, a couple, a mother-baby dyad or a fam-ily. Patients are referred by health professionals from the social and edu-cational sectors. The transcultural consultation staff also liaises with the university hospital maternity department. The tool used for care provision and research is what Georges Devereux (1985) called *"complémentarisme"*, involving dual references, not used simultaneously however, to psychoa-nalysis and anthropology. This methodology is deployed on two levels, the individual and the collective (Laplantine, 2007), and uses culture, both the migrant culture and that of the professionals, as a vector of action, where culture is seen as constantly evolving and blending.

Anything that is heard or interpreted is also set against the life context, the administrative situation, and the patients' migratory trajectory. Their psychological difficulties are, therefore, not only seen as the fruit of their conflicts in infancy, but also of the restrictive, even hostile contexts in which they are evolving (Mestre & Moro, 2012). It is also important to include the migrant patients' project for psychotherapeutic care and to make sure it is not minimized and that system of domination in the host country society do not impinge on the care provided. Care provision, therefore, requires different levels of interpretation: psychic, cultural, social, and political, which cannot be achieved without intense group work, research, and analysis of practices.

Psychotherapeutic care sessions for women giving birth have enabled an understanding of the psychic processes required to become a mother, to care for and to learn how to have and hold a newly born baby; maternity in the context of migration and exile has now been well documented on a psychological and cultural level since Marie Rose Moro's first work (1994). In response to women's solitude and suffering and an accumulation of many vulnerability factors, we set out to create, alongside psychological care, collective venues to provide support in this highly vulnerable perinatal period. One of these is our "welcoming the newly born baby" workshop (Gioan & Mestre, 2016). The healthcare team is multidisciplinary, including a psychologist, a cultural mediator (or anthropologist), a psychomotor specialist, interpreters, and trainees. They provide support for women and their babies using cultural objects and mothering techniques from the host country and the country of origin to allow women to regain assurance in the "holding" of their baby, as this holding function has been compromised by an often traumatic and constraining history of exile. Our care calls on Winnicott's model with his concepts of the "transitional space" and "good enough environment" (Winnicott, 1969).

Winnicott's observations and theoretical proposals provide a sound framework, which has enabled us to relate the issues of a baby's birth in exile to the "environment" that is provided. Winnicott's theoretical contributions have enabled us to be attentive to what he called "environment" or "care techniques",[4] and to create an intermediate illusory, culturally rich space. For us, the father's presence on the perinatal scene has become self-evident, not only because parenthood is clearly shared, but also because of the faltering of certain mothers as a result of extreme suffering, and the fact that the fathers also come to these therapy groups. The father is, thus, part of this intermediate space that Bernard Golse (2017) called "espace à vocation paternelle", the paternal space.

Very early on, the paternal space and its functions have a protective and provider role for the mother-baby dyad, before taking on a more separating role. The father provides a sort of envelope, a container, a "holding" function. He takes part in baby care and plays the third role and is not just a "third party": "a father is not between a mother and a child. He is with the mother in her relationship to the child. There are three of them in the relationship. A father is not a third party, he is the third" (Clerget, 2015, p. 120). For migrant fathers, we will see that this relationship "with", even "united with" is particularly true. Third parties are defined by a framework; the "learned third parties"[5] relate to the professionals who encourage and support parental communication, exchanges, and participation, despite their difficulties, by using psychological and cultural ingredients, where culture is seen as at once their culture and ours.

The observation technique we use is clinical: how do the mother and father show interest in their child, how does the child interact with them and with us? It also takes its inspiration from Esther Bick[6]. The first observation is based on semiology and description, the second is more based on interpretation.

It's not a man's job

Among the clinical situations that have emerged from the consultations and the workshops we have led and/or analyzed, we were able to observe the migrant fathers' attitudes. These fathers became involved in their baby's care mainly when their partner found herself overwhelmed, depressed or psychologically absent. This was the case of Sliman[7], 36-year-old, husband of Aïssatou, 19-year-old, who was referred to the transcultural consultation by the maternity unit psychiatrist. The psychiatrist warned us about Aïssatou's psychological state. She was hospitalized in intensive care because of serious vomiting linked to pregnancy. The observations cited signs of "depression, suicidal ideation and prostration". Aïssatou was then five months pregnant and had already been hospitalized twice. She had lost a lot of weight since the start of her pregnancy. After the birth, we met the father, Sliman, who was all smiles: he proudly gave us the reason for their choice of name for their son, as it signalled filiation, lineage, and grandeur. They chose a protecting name from the Coran. They both come from a country in West Africa where they met a few years ago. Sliman is a philosophy teacher. Because of their different ethnic backgrounds, Aïssatou's family were hostile to their union. To oppose this choice and wash away their daughter's "dishonour", they had tried to organize marriages, which the young woman had refused with determination. Aïssatou became the target of serious maltreatment and decided to leave "to live in peace and live our love" in her own words. Tempted by suicide, Sliman, agreed to follow, despite his comfortable social situation.

Parents and baby came back to the consultation sessions three months after Loman was born, via the "Welcoming a newly born baby" workshop, to which they were invited. Sliman, who speaks for the couple, told us with a mix of sadness and rebellion how the baby had been placed in the meantime, even though relationships with the psychiatrist were good. The notification was filed, it seems, based on an evaluation of the mother's psychological state and their extremely precarious situation. Indeed, they were asylum seekers and were living in unstable accommodation.

Sliman never ceased talking about the wound inflicted on their lives and about his own position. "It is as if acid was poured over a body" he said. "They treated us like children" he added. Following a legal battle, Loman was reunited with his parents, and they called on a lawyer to denounce their "stigmatisation". Sliman noticed the effects of the abrupt weaning on Loman, who had been breastfed by his mother: the baby was "sad, indifferent, he drank much less and had much less appetite". The parents turned to a position of distrust towards the institutions: "they are befuddling us" he said. Sliman expresses himself with ease, using imagery made up of proverbs and quotes. The transcultural team supported the parents in their requests for protection, which failed and was rejected, because love did not have a place in the international convention[8] in charge of their case. Sliman, after giving an account of the injustice experienced in his country, and then in France, ceased to talk, feeling disqualified. Aïssatou left France with her son in a desperate acting-out. Sliman, forsaken, kept in touch with the team and attended all the encounters, which should have been for all three of them.

In what way does this story of failure give us warning signs regarding the wounded state of a father? Sliman became a father after having woven an alliance, not only formed on mutual love, but also on a resolution to combat a traditional social system that oppresses women. This marital link seems us to be the starting point of a commitment to a woman and later to a mother. Why did the institutions not take this commitment into consideration? Sliman was able to put into words all the difficulties generated by institutional ambiguities: the failure to hospitalize, the paradoxical injunctions... When asked about his involvement with the baby, he showed how firm his determination was to be with the mother and his will to do his best. He loved holding his son in his arms, but he had learned "on the job, by watching others" he said. It was an unprecedented situation compared to his culture of origin, it was complicated, it required courage and adaptation, because he concluded: "it is not a man's job". First a jovial but then a devastated man, Sliman had a heart-felt will to keep his role as a man and to pass his culture on to his child.

The couple's failure to provide care to their newly born baby was not in fact inevitable. Indeed, we were able to observe an Afghan father, Ashem, who despite his wife's hospitalization, with the help of a compatriot and recommendations from the healthcare team, was able to look after his newly born daughter (Mestre & Fort-Jacques, 2021). In both cases, the paternal role is one of an alliance with the mother, before the arrival of the child. Ashem, like Sliman, wanted to protect his partner from patriarchal laws. When they became fathers, they were both in a caring relationship with the child, even if it was imposed by circumstance: they consented, remaining active, and concerned with the child's development and with the transmission of culture.

Our observation of Sliman, with his history of an African father in exile, could apply almost in the same terms to other men, such as the father of Liam, a two-year-old Albanian child whose mother could not look after him because of serious depression (Allafort & Mestre, 2021). While the mother was undergoing psychotherapeutic care in our transcultural consultation, the child and Ahmet, the father, were seen in a parenthood workshop for young children and their parents, which opened in the Bordeaux "*Centre d'Accueil pour Demandeurs d'Asile*" (Asylum seekers' centre) where they were accommodated. This workshop was based on the methodology presented above.

Ahmet expressed concerns over his wife's psychological state and never left her on her own. He came to all the workshops during his stay, stating: "Normally speaking, it is not a man's job" he was attentive to the interests of Liam, who was learning to play under the benevolent and encouraging attention of the multidisciplinary team. The father would observe every gesture: cradling by one participant, consolation from another, caring attitudes towards the child. They were gestures and practices to be learned and which he could appropriate: cooking, caring, holding, things that he would never have done in his own country. He was, thus, able to relax, playing with Liam, and he started to make a little tractor out of playdough during one of the workshops. Liam loved tractors. It was an opportunity for his father to have his agricultural past resurface and pass this attachment and universe now long gone on to his son.

Thus, while we were able to observe the fathers' positioning in a care context where they were required to stand in for their partner and provide a completely new form of fathering, on what psychic work is this commitment based? Psychotherapy among men talking about their involvement in their role as fathers could shed some light.

A father at odds with his own father

Goodluck was referred to the transcultural consultations by his GP for psychological disturbances. He is Nigerian and has been living in France for six years. His partner lives in sheltered accommodation with her three children, and he only shares the odd nights with her, as he is not allowed to live there permanently. He, therefore, spends a lot of time outside during the daytime and sometimes takes part in voluntary work.

Goodluck and his partner had two children when we first met, a boy of six and a girl of three. He defines his relationship with his partner as a parental, and not marital, couple. He calls her "the mother of my children". Goodluck previously lived in Kano (Northern Nigeria). His mother died when he was a child. He said he grew up in town, raised by his father and one of his father's wives and his siblings. His father had three wives, and his mother had five children, of whom he is the second. He left home when he was 17 to train as a mechanic. He is illiterate. Concerning his migratory trajectory, Goodluck lived through inter-religious conflicts in his region (where Boko Haram has been spreading terror), and he fled after a religious attack by a Muslim group who destroyed a Christian church. His migratory trajectory extended over several years: he travelled through Niger, Algeria, Morocco, and Spain before arriving in France. He told us about serious maltreatment and multiple traumas. His trajectory was marked by two events: the announcement of his father's death when he was in Morocco and meeting his partner and the birth of his son in the Spanish enclave in Morocco. Goodluck is a Pentecostal[9]. He speaks Pidgin English and consultations were carried out in English with an interpreter.

Goodluck was calm at first but he was distrustful, and his internal tension could be felt. He tends to be withdrawn and wears a cap and a scarf. He is rather tall and strong, and his face is marked. He complains about being tired, about substantial memory problems, and strange sensations in his head. He mentioned having nightmares, visions of dead people, and "spirits" and voices. He recounted experiences of persecution, with dissociative elements. Goodluck was convinced he had undergone change because of the events he had endured.

It was decided that he should be seen in group consultation[10], so that his traumatic experiences and his anxiety might be heard in a containing context and so that he was provided support for an elaboration and co-construction of meaning of these raw psychic manifestations and the disjointed narrative of his life story. The interviews were spread out over several months, enabling an understanding of Goodluck's psychological disturbances. As for his position as a father, he talked about identifying himself with his father in terms of violence and his differentiation in terms of religious belief. He wondered about his filiation and the transmission of the surname, he mentioned the issue of paternal mourning and that of fatherhood confronted with his own model and with western practices.

Goodluck told us about scenes of fighting and dead people he had seen during his migration. The resulting hallucinations clearly generated anxiety: he said: "it is as if I was going to die, go mad". The voices he heard were frightening and called him by his name, telling him to harm himself, "to take a knife and stab myself with it" he said, "or to kill my wife and children" he added. He seeks to protect himself by keeping dangerous objects away. Goodluck also described internal tension, irritability, and impulsiveness in his relationship with others, so much so that despite his avoidance strategies and his tremendous efforts to contain himself, we were worried for his entourage and his children.

Nevertheless, violence was also connected to his father figure. Goodluck's description of his father was that he was an army man, invincible, feared by everyone and by himself when he was a child. He remembered how unpredictable he was. He said: "he was an evil man... as soon as you made a mistake, he would beat you, as soon as you saw him, you ran away... But he could be kind... He could be jovial... but the smallest of things happened, and it would ruin everything, he would destroy everything... People would say: 'he's mad'... He feared nothing, he was never afraid". In the family narrative, Goodluck's father had his own father's magical protection, which had allowed him to survive the Biafra war.

He, thus, identified with his father for his strength and anger, but he also acknowledged his kindness. "He needed help", he said, suggesting his father was ill. He confronted his paternity with that of his father, and when the announcement of his death was mentioned, he said he had been unable to say farewell: "My father would not have let me leave, because it was too dangerous". Paternal transmission takes on very contrasted paths: via violence, but also via an intention to protect.

Goodluck appeared invested as a parent and expressed appropriate paternal preoccupations. His experience of parenthood focuses on care and support, in the various household tasks, and in the children's education, with their wellbeing in mind. He said: "I do my best, I get them dressed, I pick them up from school, I do the cooking, I make them happy". These dispositions constitute a redefinition of paternal identity, which was originally on a completely different model. Indeed "the way children are raised here is very different. Over there, in Africa, there are times when you don't eat, you don't go to school... Adults don't take care of the children. I had to fight to have a family in acceptable conditions", he said. He observes what others do: "Europe is one hundred per cent good... to make the children happy...". When he was a child, the family atmosphere was not easy: he lived in a house with only one room, the father would bring money home and the women attended to the household tasks (shopping and meals). It became clear that Goodluck had not only survived his migratory journey but also his childhood.

When his last daughter was born, Goodluck was first happy, he and his partner had chosen a name for her after a beautiful dream he had had, but he became worried and was aware of the need to console a crying child but did not know how. To help his partner, he drew from his present environment (the host country) to compose his own way of becoming a father: "What I saw, what I see on television, other people... the more you see the more you learn". This is how he showed us his way of deploying creative potential. There was no undermining of his masculinity in the role he chose. However, his discourse is nonetheless punctuated by self-deprecation, low self-esteem: "When you're a father, it is hard not to be doing what ought to be done for our children, I want to do more". He felt wounded by the fact that he did not have money to give his children what they wanted, such as outings (turns on the merry-go-round for instance) or materials for school. He, thus, referred to a certain failing as a father, underlining at the same time the host country's concern for children: "In Europe, people help children a lot... but if a man finds it hard to fend for himself, then he finds it hard to fend for his children".

Goodluck also described times when he felt overwhelmed by his children's constant requests: "They make me talk, they make me run around, they upset everything, they spread everything around, I end up shouting". He tried very hard to hide his irritability and reported a sense of loneliness and isolation as head of the family. He said: "If I were at home, I'd be alright. Here, there is no-one to help, no father, no brother, no mother, no sister, no-one... If I have problems, I have no-one to go to". He, thus, pointed out the lack of community solidarity, and the fact that taking on parental responsibilities required him to have a job and an income: "In Europe, when you don't have work, you don't get help", he said. This generated sadness and anger in him. Goodluck was at that point close to breaking down.

Paternal space

Following the narratives by Sliman, Ashem, Ahmet, Goodluck, and others, it appears clearly that paternal involvement is based on a determination that defies traditional norms and requires intense psychic work. Each one of these men, in his own way, found the path to paternity adapted to a migratory context, albeit with the support of a benevolent healthcare team.

When a child is born, fathers in exile, like the mothers, experience severe isolation and a complete break with their references and the community they belong to. How relevant is it to transpose the notion of "co-mothers", suggested by Marie Rose Moro (1994), to that of "co-fathers" (Pachoud et al., Op. Cit.)? The term "co-mothers" is a reference to the women who are traditionally present at the mother's side, helping her in her new maternal duties, an accompaniment that is absent in the host country. It seems that while men also experience this lack of community presence, they feel they must "de-centre" themselves from their "traditional" mission to acquire a "maternal" stance, which should not be "their business". This stance, therefore, needs to be won over at the cost of innovation, possibly to the point of transgression. Fathers, thus, run the risk of being mocked in this new role that belongs to the feminine sphere[11].

The clinical examples given here have clearly shown that, despite all the social and cultural pitfalls, fathers in exile are capable of involvement, and migration can become an exceptional opportunity to experience it (Roer-Strier et al., 2005). In a Quebec study concerning the involvement of fathers during the perinatal period, more than half of the mothers who were interviewed considered that their partner would have been less committed to them and their baby in their country of origin. This adaptation, resulting from social pressures for the sharing of tasks and parental responsibilities, takes the form of genuine paternal involvement in the domestic sphere, a transgression that can have a cost. As a result, "roles intertwine, responsibilities overlap and parents are suddenly exposed to new social norms, disseminated by health professionals, especially if the social and family networks have broken down" (Battaglini et al., 2002, p. 173).

Do the psychic processes at work among the father's mirror those of the mothers? This question, which already exists in our own society, could be considerably expanded upon, so great are the recent changes and the influence of diverse psychological theories.

What Marie Rose Moro has said about the resurgence of cultural elements and of representations from former generations seems suited to exploring the psychological and cultural dispositions of fathers, and the way they position themselves. Indeed, the arrival of a child triggers a re-emergence, for both mother and father, of fantasized representations and family myths from the culture of origin, contributing to the construction of parenthood (Moro, 2004). Conflicts that have been endured by the fathers also emerge, linked to their own status as sons and their past relationship with their fathers, on which more recent conflicts are superimposed, as a result of their migratory trajectories and traumas, as was seen with Goodluck's psychotherapy.

Among the fathers, could the genuine desire to participate at all costs in their child's care from birth be easier for those who, like Sliman and Goodluck, have already experienced a break from their traditions and masculine filiation? Indeed, both Sliman and Ashem had already opposed the diktat of their patriarchal family, and their commitment as fathers is the extension of their solidarity with their partner.

Psychic work with fathers is nevertheless pervaded by considerable tension in maintaining their position of "co-mothers" at their partner's side, without relinquishing the need to be faithful to their culture, values, and codes, as was shown earlier in a study on West African fathers (Koné-Mariko & Mestre, 2018); this tension is prolonged throughout their migratory life trajectory with the education of their children (Pourtois et al., 2004).

During the perinatal period, committed fathers, thus, overcome their reluctance and draw from deep inside them new creative abilities to invent their own forms of fatherhood, another kind of motherhood, which preserves their virility and the values that define them[12]. Besides searching for the appropriate de-centring, most men in exile, unlike the mothers, generally do not have any fathering models, or very few, that they can appropriate, as their bodily memory is probably less developed than in mothers (Mestre & Gioan, 2014). Indeed, even if they were carried by their own mothers as children, they had few demands from their mother to help her care for the younger ones. They, therefore, must draw on models in the host country. As a result, they offer their arms, their voice, their songs to take over this paternal space, to hold the baby, and initiate gestures and attention that made them the third person on the perinatal scene, while at all times ensuring their virility is not undermined. Their desire to be present can be seen in the transmission of a name, a language, songs and rhythms, memories, and stories.

Conclusion

The paternal space can only exist if health professionals facilitate it and give up their gatekeeping role, which is still all too often opposed to the father's presence in infant care settings (Frascarolo *et al.* 2017). This opposition thrown in the face of fathers (whatever their condition, migrant, or non-migrant) can be exacerbated in the case of fathers in exile because of prejudice. The consequences can be catastrophic. Fathers who have already endured exile cannot on their own do what is required of them, especially when their partner's presence is uncertain because of exhaustion and suffering. They need to feel invited to deploy their paternal and fathering role, mingling psychological, social, and cultural ingredients from the host country and the country of origin, and to be encouraged to support their involvement as fathers. Several settings can be designed for this purpose: transcultural consultations and group workshops for migrant fathers, where they can feel less lonely in elaborating their real role as fathers. In these benevolent and favourable venues, which form genuinely "transitional communities" (Allafort & Mestre, op.cit.), where the care of the baby is shared, where the cultures of each participant intertwine, where friendly encounters occur, the psychic processes will be more finely apprehended, to form a basis for paternal involvement in exile.

Notes

1 The experience of exile is common in lots of patients we encounter, whatever their status: refugees, asylum seekers, illegal immigrants, etc., and whatever their reasons and their choices, willing or unwilling, for leaving; the term exile puts the emphasis on the experience and not on the administrative dimension, even if this is very important. The new place of living is not yet fully mastered and there is an effort to keep the former place of living present so as not to get lost.

2 Even though the perinatal period is generally a women's domain, it has been observed that men, for instance, in Madagascar, care for their children very early on and do so publicly: for instance, they can be seen carrying babies in the streets (personal observation).

3 In Bourdieu's definition of "habitus" (1992), the body also has a central role, as a container for the schemes of thought, perception, appreciation, and action.

4 This environment provides "a good care technique (my emphasis) 'good enough' for the child (1969, p. 201). This is how a child can grow; his centre of gravity is not initially individual: the individual will progressively form from a core, and the shell will be formed by the 'holding'" and the "general situation" or "general management" (ibid. p. 201).

5 A concept freely inspired from Michel Serres's philosophical work *Le Tiers Instruit* (1992). The "learned third party" concerns professionals (from the healthcare, medical, psychological, and social world) in relation to unprece-

dented situations, such those involving migrants. The learned third party uses his position to provide assistance, using his particular approaches to educating, teaching. It is an individual reflexive position along the lines of whoever is left-handed becomes right-handed, whoever is Gascon becomes French", i.e., the way he himself developed and learned from all horizons, including professional sources, how he was shaped and what disruptions he had to endure to open up and learn. It is the perception of the cultural mix within us. The learned third party is a mix, creating a mix of knowledge and practices. He does not give up on influencing others but also embraces surprise and astonishment in discovering other people's practices, languages, *habitus,* life trajectories, and pain.

6   Observation involving post hoc drafting. The written observation is read by a group of therapists and comments emerge.

7   All the names have been changed.

8   It is the Geneva Convention which protects people threatened by their own country.

9   The Pentecostal Church is an evangelical Christian trend that was implanted in Nigeria during the Pentecostal revolution. It is a religion that promotes a break from traditional beliefs in witchcraft and fetishism in the name of "delivery from the ancestral curse". This religious trend has been a factor of tension in the northern part of the country, where there is a major influence of Islam. Family values are promoted, especially in relation to parental responsibility (Fancello, 2008).

10   The group of therapists included Claire Mestre, Lia Fort-Jacques, an interpreter, an anthropologist, and psychologist trainees.

11   Here are two accounts to back up this viewpoint. The first one is provided by the filmmaker Eric Tellitocci, author of documentaries on lullabies from all over the world and used in exile. One of his protagonists, Aladji, born in Senegal, was invited to be filmed while cradling his child; he accepted the invitation, but unwillingly. Indeed, his friends were making fun of him saying: "he's playing at being a mum". Thus, Aladji in front of the camera sang a song starting in Soninke and ending in French. It was interesting to see that he agreed to it provided he could keep his cap on! The second account comes from a male anthropologist, also born in Senegal, with whom we worked. According to him, feminine spaces are approached away from the gaze of a diaspora community, concealed from the country of origin. See Tellitocci, E. [Film-maker] (2010, 2014, 2016). Les Berceuses [Film]. Les Films d'été.

12   In Aichatou Koné's work (2009), a man who was interviewed, Mr. Traoré said: "I remain faithful to my values, I am a man after all, I cannot do what a woman does, I am the head of a family, and these things I must not or cannot do. But it is true, we are in a foreign country and all the family has stayed back home, so sometimes, it is a bit too much for my wife, so I do what I can but without overstepping the mark". This account shows how paradoxical fathering can be.

References

Abécassis, M.-L., & Bidaud, E. (2014). La présence contemporaine du sujet masculin sur la scène périnatale: une dynamique familiale modifiée. *Le Télémaque, 46,* 103–117.

Allafort, C., & Mestre, C. (2021) Co-construire une "communauté transitionnelle" avec les familles exilées. *L'autre, Cliniques, Cultures et Sociétés, 22*(1), 71–80. www. revuelautre.com

Battaglini, A., Gravel, S., Poulin, C., Fournier, M., & Brodeur, J-M. (2002). Migration et paternité ou réinventer la paternité. *Nouvelle pratiques sociales*, *15*, 165–179.

Bergheul, S., Ramde, J., Ourhou, A., & Labra, O. (2018). La paternité en contexte migratoire: déstabilisation et redéfinition du rôle paternel. *Revue Internationale de L'éducation Familiale*, *43*, 91–115.

Bourdieu, P., & Vaquant, J.-L. (1992). *Réponses, pour une anthropologie réflexive.* Éditions du Seuil.

Castelain-Meunier, C. (2004). Tensions et contradictions dans la répartition des places et des rôles autour de l'enfant. *Dialogue*, *3*(165), 33–44.

Clerget, J. (2015). *Comment un petit garçon devient-il un papa?* Éditions Érès.

Devereux, G. (1985). *Ethnopsychanalyse complémentariste.* Flammarion.

Este, D., & Tachble, A. (2008). Perceptions and experiences of Sudanese refugee and Russian immigrant men as fathers in the Canadian context [Conférence]. *Father Involvement Conference 2008:* Diversity Visibility Community, Toronto (Canada).

Fancello, S. (2008). Sorcellerie et délivrance dans les pentecôtismes africains. *Cahiers d'Études Africaines*, *189-190*, 161–183.

Frascarolo, F., Feinberg, M., Albert Szitman, G., & Favez, N. (2017). La fonction de garde-barrière (le *Gatekeeping*) des professionnels envers les pères: une puissante influence sur le développement de l'enfant et sur la famille. *Médecine & Hygiène*, *3*(29), 185–198.

Gioan, E., & Mestre, C. (2016). L'atelier accueil du nouveau-né. In C. Mestre (ed.), *Bébés d'ici, mères d'exil* (pp. 215–226). Éditions Érès.

Golse, B. (2017). Père œdipien, père préœdipien: La construction de la place du tiers au cours des interactions précoces. In N. Glangeaud-Freudenthal, F. Gressier (eds.), *Accueillir les pères en périnatalité* (pp. 13–24). Éditions Érès.

Koné, A. (2009). *Les pères d'ici venus d'ailleurs: cas des hommes d'Afrique occidentale devenus père en situation migratoire.* [Mémoire, Université de Bordeaux].

Koné-Mariko, A., & Mestre, C. (2018). La paternalité à l'épreuve de la migration. *Spirale*, *1*(85), 115–127.

Lamb, M., & Tamis-LeMonda, C. (2004). The role of the father: An introduction. In M. Lamb (ed.), *The role of the father in child development* (4th ed.) (pp. 1–31). Wiley.

Lamb, M. (2010). *The role of the father in child development* (5th ed.). Wiley.

Laplantine, F. (2007). *Ethnopsychiatrie psychanalytique.* Beauchesne.

Le Camus, J. (2002). Le lien père-bébé. *Devenir*, *2*(14),145–167.

Mestre, C., & Gioan, E. (2014). Comment la culture vient aux femmes à la naissance de leur bébé? *Spirale*, *70*, 85–92.

Mestre, C. (2016). *Bébés d'ici, mères d'exil.* Éditions Érès.

Mestre, C., & Fort-Jacques, L. (2021). Les pères en exil sur la scène périnatale. *L'autre, cliniques et sociétés*, *22*(1), 38–48. www.revuelautre.com

Montigny, F. de, Gervais, C. & Tremblay, J. (2015). L'expérience de pères québécois de la naissance de leur enfant. *Recherches familiales*, *12*(1), 125–136.

Moro, M. R. (1994). *Parents en exil, psychopathologie et migration.* PUF.

Moro, M. R. (1998). *Psychothérapie transculturelle des enfants de migrants.* Dunod.

Moro, M. R. (2004). *Psychothérapie transculturelle de l'enfant et de l'adolescent.* Dunod.

Moro, M. R., Mestre, C., & Réal, I. (2009). Périnatalité: des mères et des bébés en exil. In T. Baubet, M. R. Moro (eds.). *Psychopathologie transculturelle* (pp. 169–189). Elsevier Masson.

Mestre, C., & Moro, M. R. (2012). L'intime et le politique. Projet pour une ethnopsychanalyse critique. *L'autre, Cliniques, Cultures et Sociétés, 13*(3), 263–272.

Mestre, C. (ed.). (2016). *Bébés d'ici, mères d'exil.* Éditions Ères.

Nathan, T. (1986). *La folie des autres: Traité d'ethnopsychiatrie clinique.* Dunod.

Neyrand, G. (2005). L'enfant, la mère et la question du père. In *Un bilan critique de l'évolution des savoirs sur la petite enfance* (2nd ed.). PUF.

Pachoud, D. & Lhuillier, G. (2019). Être père et repères en migration. *Le Journal des Psychologues, 365,* 71–77.

Pourtois, J.-P., Demonty, B., & Jouret, D. (2004). Souffrances affectives, cognitives et sociales des parents en exil. *Pensée Plurielle, 8,* 51–60.

Ramdé, J. (2015). Le rôle du père dans le développement socio-affectif et cognitif des enfants en contexte migratoire. *Alterstice, 5*(1), 3–6.

Roer-Strier, D., Strier, R., Este, D., Shimoni, R., & Clark, D. (2005). Fatherhood and immigration: Challenging the deficit theory. *Child & Family Social Work, 10*(4), 315–329.

Serres, M. (1992). *Le Tiers-Instruit.* Gallimard.

Touhami, F., & Moro, M. R. (2019). Les pères aussi se métissent dans la migration. Analyse transculturelle. *Enfances Psy, 81,* 34–41.

Yayhaoui, A. (1997). *De la place du père: Entre mythe familial et idéologie institutionnelle.* La pensée sauvage.

Winnicott, D. W. (1969). *De la pédiatrie à la psychanalyse.* Payot.

Chapter 3

Managing encounters with otherness

Transcultural approaches in a French maternity unit

Rahmeth Radjack and Marie Rose Moro

One woman in five who gives birth in France is a migrant[1] and the figures are roughly the same across Europe and in most of the world. Migration, especially if it is recent and if the couple or the mother is isolated, induces a sudden break from previous references. For a long time, transcultural clinical practice has focused on the perinatal period when parents and babies have to adapt to one another in a setting of migration. Based on the notion of "complementarisme" (Devereux, 1970) – i.e., the essential but non-simultaneous use of anthropology for the collective, and of psychoanalysis for the intimate – a transcultural approach can help professionals cope with the encounter with otherness they sometimes experience in certain situations where patients and therapists do not share the same cultural references. Transcultural care needs in maternity wards call on a great deal of creativity in terms of care, availability, and separation of the different spheres (social, psychological, and medical) whilst maintaining collaboration. Here, we explore three different approaches, which will be discussed in relation to the relevance of their indications and the temporality of care implementation during the perinatal period.

Our description concerns the transcultural work that is carried out at Port-Royal Maternity unit, one of the maternity units in the French capital city, possessing a state-of-the-art unit in neonatology, and certain specialized consultation services (HIV-positive mothers, mothers in a situation of vulnerability, etc.). This unit concerns both mothers living in the vicinity of the unit and mothers from the Paris suburbs. The population is, therefore, a social and cultural mix, and transcultural dimensions are regularly addressed by the medical teams. Indeed, is it not imperative to include, among the duties of a maternity clinician, the transcultural dimensions of the initiatory pregnancy period, especially if it is the first pregnancy on foreign soil? Usually, transcultural work is initiated in the second line, when standard care has not been sufficient for reasons of cultural misunderstandings, healthcare nomadism, inadequate follow-up in care provision or the cultural coding of certain symptoms (Goguikian Ratcliff & Diaz-Marchand, 2019; Moro, 2020). In this unit, referrals are sometimes first-line

DOI: 10.4324/9781003174684-4

resorts since cultural dimensions have such an important part in the perinatal period. Furthermore, it is well-known that the risk of psychopathology is greater among migrant patients, especially for pre- and post-partum depression, which affects 38% and 50% of migrant women, respectively, with a greater risk if the migration has occurred recently (Goguikian Ratcliff & Diaz-Marchand, op. cit.; Mestre, 2016; Stewart et al., 2008; Zelkowitz et al., 2008). Complex post-traumatic stress states are also overrepresented (Vandentorren et al., 2016). Finally, a greater number of at-risk pregnancies, Caesarean births, and premature births have been observed, particularly among populations from Sub-Saharan Africa (Urquia et al., 2015). This could be linked to insufficient access to prenatal care, representations of pregnancy follow-up that are different from those of the country of origin, communication barriers, and often precarious and inhospitable conditions on arrival in the country (Sauvegrain 2012; Sauvegrain et al., 2017; Azria, 2015; Azria et al., 2015). These higher caesarean section rates would seem to be related to factors affecting the smooth progress of labour and delivery (small pelvis size more frequent in Sub-Saharan African women, scarred uteri due to previous caesarean sections), leading to specific protocols transmitted between obstetricians without respecting the physiological slowness of labour in these patients (Sauvegrain, 2012; Saurel-Cubizolles et al., 2012).

Psychological vulnerability triggered by migration, together with an experience of isolation and sometimes of increasing insecurity, could hamper mothers' ability to dream, i.e., their ability to represent the child and to put words on the psychological content surrounding the baby (Bion, 1979). A transcultural approach can, therefore, aim to revive this ability to think and dream and anticipate the child to be born, by going back to the parents' cultural representations of this initiatory, perinatal period of the arrival of a child.

There are three types of approaches that are conducted at Port-Royal Maternity unit when a transcultural consultation is requested from our team: 1- pre or post-natal individual consultations can be offered, followed by 2- transcultural consultations with a group of therapists, offered for certain indications (Moro et al., 2005); and finally, 3- talking groups as a preventive approach: detection of situations requiring the implementation of care to actively avoid the development of psychopathologies.

Individual consultations with a transcultural positioning

Individual transcultural consultations can only be initiated after discussion with the first-level care team on the relevance and temporality of offering it. Indeed, a certain number of situations can be resolved via a standard approach by the psychiatrist (first-level approach). The idea is not to offer a transcultural approach to each migrant family in the maternity unit (they are too numerous and not all have a need for it). The issue of the language is not sufficient either (all that is required is to find an interpreter). To our minds, transcultural consultations should be offered when the standard approach is not sufficient or ill-adapted. When an individual interview takes place with a mother or a future mother, we remain a complement to standard care, starting the interview by targeting cultural issues directly: how is a child welcomed in the home country? In case of a pathological pregnancy or a maternal psychological pathology, how would the problem be described? What would be done? The approach is based on several transcultural levers. First of all, bridges between life "back there" and life here are built so as to avoid the risk of a migratory divide. Indeed, parents often tell their stories starting from the day they arrived in France. If we do not actively look for information about their pre-migratory history, it is impossible to have access to it. On a practical level, the networks of kinship and social belonging are reconstituted during the interview: which family members have stayed behind in the home country, who in the family is in France, what are their contacts (telephone, frequency), has the birth of the baby been announced? Are there any friends, people from the community, at hand? Is the parent able to speak his/her mother tongue? Even for the most isolated individuals, to encourage them to talk about family during a consultation, or to help them call them on the phone or to encourage them to do so, can help these people to feel less lonely, a feeling that is very deleterious during the perinatal period.

It is also our goal to attempt the elaboration of a narrative surrounding the child and to develop a form of parenthood narrative (Golse & Moro, 2017), thereby placing the child or the future child in the family history. The focus is also on the notion of a cultural mix or blend: help with the construction of self between the two cultural worlds of belonging, and the use of the creative wealth from both (without this appearing incompatible).

The interview is based on co-construction: the patient is given an expert role and a mother is invited to express herself the way she wants, to be fully heard, avoiding turning what is unknown into what is known, as in Devereux's definition of "decentering" (Devereux, op. cit.). This can be done through narratives such as: "what is usually done in your country to welcome a baby? What are the rituals at birth?" The mother can, therefore, become an ambassador for the collective or family knowledge that she wishes for and chooses. What is most important is the meaning for her of whatever cultural or religious practice she decides to honour, as migration is bound to trigger changes, choices, and mixing.

Finally, we aim to co-construct solutions: "even if we cannot do exactly the same as in the home country, something can be done, for instance, asking the family to carry out part of the ritual over there", or else over here, even if it is not on the day initially required, or carry it out symbolically and partially. Culture is a dynamic process, constantly changing, and certain adaptations in practices on foreign land are perfectly valid.

This approach often helps people to escape a feeling of powerlessness and enables skills to emerge despite a traumatic past.

These individual consultations are held in the presence of an interpreter, who is often used as a mediator, i.e., the interpreter can be asked to momentarily relinquish a strict translation function to facilitate the sharing of cultural representations and the emergence of a discussion. A mediator of this sort can sometimes help to shed light on cultural misunderstandings (about carrying the baby for instance, in a given cultural group, rules of precedence, etc.). Sometimes, differences in cultural representations are an obstacle to professionals' usual practice in their role of accompaniment during this specific period. The interview setting, with the mediating interpreter's help, encourages attention and allows representations to be shared, followed by negotiations. The interpreter should be actively used to create bridges with the home country or countries that have been travelled through, and to valorize parental skills, so that they feel more at ease to express themselves. His or her mere presence is valuable and can lead to changes in the narratives, hence the importance of resorting to them even if the family is able to partially master the French language. Families sometimes speak French well, but they nonetheless wish to have a translator to talk about things in the languages used during their various experiences. Indeed, the use of a mediating interpreter enables a third party to be introduced in the care provider-patient relationship, and indeed a two-way relationship can be considered strange in some countries where groups are preferred when talking about deep subjects. The use of the mother tongue lends itself to the expression of affects, much more so than a second language.

This first individual involvement with a translator is sufficient in many situations, which can be made clear via the mediating translator and by the therapist's transcultural stance. The therapist accepts and welcomes the cultural narratives that serve as a container for the intimate individual material relating to the present situation of the mother, that of the family and that of the baby.

Transcultural consultations with a group of therapists

The flexible transcultural system that we have described previously (Moro et al., op. cit.) can in certain perinatal situations provide an efficient therapeutic resort. Most often this involves a small group of co-therapists attending transcultural encounters with mother-baby dyads or parent-baby triads every month in addition to other forms of care provision.

It is a specialized consultation that enables an often very productive elaboration in a group context. The use of a group is closer to cultural representations of the provision of care and attention. A group also creates a containing environment for these migrants who have broken away from their cultural envelope. Co-therapists, who represent a professional and/ or cultural otherness, make suggestions through the main therapist. This group-based hetero-narrative favours self-narrative (ibid.). The system has several types of indications. For instance, it can be relevant when the emergence of a psychopathology is strongly linked to migratory histories, or when parents express difficulties in establishing a link between their culture of origin and the culture of the host country. This type of consultation can also be used when the representation of illness and disease in the culture of origin requires consideration. For example, the ontological representation of autism in West Africa can enable this singularity to be conceived by the parents as acceptable (and culturally coherent).

Sometimes, families call on aetiological theories with the arrival of a child, born in difficult circumstances, whereby the child, the most vulnerable being, is thought to have been attacked (witchcraft for instance), thus affecting the family in wider manner. Cultural protection should then be considered. Finally, this setting is indicated when cultural and linguistic differences make care provision difficult, when there are discrepancies, misunderstandings, preconceived ideas, issues of hierarchy, etc., and when the parents feel lost, powerless, and passive in the face of their child's suffering.

To support the parental function, co-therapists often become "co-mothers" or companion mothers, compensating in part for the lack of support due to isolation. Consultations enable cultural support in a space that is different from the ordinary contexts, with combined observation of the main therapist and the co-therapists, to co-create, co-conceive, and co-feel with the parents and the baby (Lebovici & Stoléru, 1983). Parents are mobilized, within the transcultural consultation to develop their own mix from the different ways of the home and host countries. They often have doubts over their own abilities when they are confronted with different styles of parenthood. The therapists support the parents' role along the lines of the "co-mother" image, and thus ensure shared holding and handling, with joint observation by the mother, the main therapist, and the co-therapists. In this transcultural space, the child is envisaged, put into words, and spoken for by others. The baby is a central partner in the co-construction of the narrative. An "auxiliary" co-therapist stays by his side, at the centre of the group, when the child is independent or near the mother if necessary, when the child is younger (Rizzi, 2015).

Clinical situation: Can a homeless woman with no co-mothers become a mother?

Aminata, a thirty-year-old young Malian woman from Bamako, was referred to us for transcultural consultation by a maternity unit psychiatrist. She had arrived in France two years earlier. She was currently living in a women's shelter where she was accommodated with her one-year-old daughter. She was pregnant for the second time, at twenty-two weeks' amenorrhoea, when a psychiatrist saw her during her hospitalization for risk of premature delivery and for cervical cerclage. The psychiatrist was concerned about the haggard and lost aspect of the patient during the obstetricians' explanations about what would become of her baby if she delivered prematurely. The psychiatrist started to consider the possibility of long-standing or transitory cognitive difficulties for this woman, wondering whether these difficulties derived from a depressive disorder or whether they stemmed from post-traumatic stress. However, she could only retrieve very little information about the patient's clinical history and her life history. Despite the presence of an interpreter, there was persistent doubt. The therapist, therefore, asked for our advice to understand the impact of the cultural distance in this encounter, which appeared to be leading nowhere. Furthermore, as Aminata was alone, her first child was initially placed during her hospitalization, with her consent, in a nursery. She, however, became worried that this placement would be permanent. Indeed, the educational team at the maternity unit had cast doubts on her maternal abilities from their observations of her interactions with her daughter. The educational team was invited to the first transcultural consultation. From this moment, it was clear that the transcultural context facilitated the encounter, the emergence of a migration narrative, hitherto silenced, and the resolution of cultural misunderstandings.

The first consultation in our system starts with the presentation of each of the participants and the patient, which entails more detail than in standard care provision (who is who? where does everybody come from? Therapists and patients introduce themselves and answer any questions). It is the first step towards a possible encounter, where everyone is identified. An educator from the initial team that refers Amina to us comes with her to participate to the transcultural consultation. What do mothers, recently arrived in France, understand of the roles played by the different maternity unit professionals (social worker, psychologist, psychiatrist, child psychiatrist, midwife, paediatrician, childcare professionals, etc.), especially if they come from countries where medical follow-up for pregnancy is less medical and not implemented so early? Explaining what psychological care or child psychology care in the perinatal period is all about, even with no prior psychopathology detected, requires clarity when this type of psychotherapeutic setting does not exist in the country of origin. A detailed introduction from each protagonist gives the mother the opportunity to introduce herself in elaborated form, giving her true identity, or the one she chooses to put forward at this particular time, as it is the one that matters for her. All participants, therefore, begin by introducing themselves, stating, if they wish, their profession and cultural identity. In Aminata's case, the introductions concluded with what she had to say, after the interpreter. Aminata stated that she was a Soninke, her mother was Gambian and her father was Malian. She described her relationship to languages very modestly: she speaks Soninke, Bambara, a little Wolof, and a little French today. The main therapist took the opportunity to underline the value of this multilingualism. Aminata became more self-assured in her posture and the tone of her voice. After that came explanations on the context of the consultation, a mixed setting between the home and host countries, a space of transition between the way problems are solved in groups in traditional societies, and the way care is provided in the West. The main therapist stated: "We work as a group and in certain countries like the one I come from, when there is an illness or when we are in mourning, we stick to a group. We gather round the tree of words to find together the strength to tackle life's complex problems". Aminata was familiar with this system of group processing and seemed at ease when talking in the midst of ten different professionals who were putting their heads together for her and with her, in a benevolent attitude and with no judgment. Aminata later adopted an active role in this co-construction, telling us how people lived in her country, in her cultural group, in her family, thus unravelling her singular history. After having asked the team who had referred her to us to present, in the simplest possible way, the issues that led to the consultation, her opinion was then heard. At that point, she said that the language barrier could have led to misunderstandings. We came to realize that beyond the issue of words, it was the confrontation between very different cultural worlds and a history marked by disruptions and traumatic events that could explain Aminata's withdrawal from her relationships with others and the avoiding nature of her contact.

Generally, the start of the first transcultural consultation is often oriented towards the patient's cultural identity and gives the tone of the consultation by tackling explicitly cultural issues with no taboo, thus showing that this dimension can be shared. The focus is on understanding and looking together for ways of resolving conflicts. The therapists' active participation in the group is valuable and has a containing function. Beyond the narratives, tone and context are very important. According to Guedeney (Guedeney & Guedeney, 2006) the perception that the patient has of the therapists' behaviour, particularly the tone of voice, and the way they approach patients, is at least as important as what they say. The pleasure experienced by the therapists and the accompanying educator who shares that pleasure is just as important, as is the circular layout of the group, which puts everyone on the same level.

Once a relationship of trust has been established, and this can be felt in the syntony that becomes established, the migration narrative can be broached. This is sometimes accompanied by psychological trauma. This was the case for Aminata, who was an asylum seeker. Here the professionals show they can accommodate this narrative and make something of it, transform the intense emotional load, and put forward the heroic value of the patient's life trajectory and courage. Aminata arrived via Morocco and Spain. It took her three months and "the journey was not easy" she modestly added. One of the co-therapists said that she must have been "very intelligent and brave to find her way and avoid obstacles". This suggestion aimed to change the accompanying educator's point of view and to share with Aminata a positive view of her trajectory. Could it not be said (and this is one of the assumptions in this programme) that any migration requires skills for adaption, cognitive abilities for organization, and courage to face adversity?

Aminata, with our help, continued the story of her life trajectory: she is the last in a line of siblings. She was "given" to her paternal aunt when she was very young and knew her mother very little. Her early childhood was spent in Senegal with her aunt. Even though she said at the start of the consultation that she had come from Bamako, it was quite clear that her trajectory was more complex, and that she did not appear to have been brought up in town. When her mother died, Aminata was taken to Gambia, "to another lady". We later found out that Aminata was to become the "little maid" of the house and very rarely went to school. In Gambia, she became pregnant and tried abort using traditional African medicine. She said with emotion that: "the child could not have survived, and I had the abortion at five months. When my father got to know, he came to fetch me from Gambia to take me back to Mali". Was it that period that was reactivated in traumatic mode when the obstetricians announced risk of termination of her current pregnancy at five months? In Mali, she lived with her father and his second wife who was "not very nice" to her. She did not get on well either with her siblings, as they had had a different education, and their relationship had deteriorated at the death of their mother. She described her experience of isolation, but at the same time, her strong desire to escape from it. Thus, Aminata took the initiative to set up in trade and started selling water. Once she had saved up enough money, she invested in the textile business: she acquired know-how in indigo dyes on clothes. She started planning migration to reach Europe "to flee from the great difficulties encountered in Mali". However, she also reported having the same difficulties here in France. Indeed, she met a Malian compatriot in France who extorted her money under the initial pretext of helping her in her administrative paperwork, as Aminata did not speak a word of French when she arrived. When she realized, she asked for her money back, but the man started to beat her. Very unhappy, she had no desire to stay in France. "I was disgusted", she said. She tried to sue the man, but to no avail, which discouraged her. Furthermore, she found herself homeless for a while and had to protect herself many times. "Men would offer me accommodation to have sex with me". She was raped during that period.

Today, she feels better because she has "a roof over her head at the women's shelter and the situation is not in any way comparable", she said. Her relaxed state could nevertheless be interpreted as a kind of affective discordance, particularly at the time of the temporary placement of her daughter. Why was it so easy for her to accept being separated from her daughter? The duration of the child's placement in a nursery was actually prolonged with Aminata's consent, as she now "readily" entrusts her child to others. For the time being, she can see her daughter, who is doing well, only twice a week, because she has to rest to avoid premature delivery. After the consultation, the therapist, to avoid any misunderstanding, told the accompanying educator that it is often culturally acceptable to leave a child with a stranger, if the child is thought to be better off. But the child remains the mother's child, it is not an adoption, it is a form of fosterage, which preserves parental authority (studied by anthropologists (Porcelli, 2011) as child mobility and fosterage).

The remainder of the consultation with Aminata focused on the primary maternal preoccupation (Winnicott, 1949), which Aminata talked about regarding her elder child. Her preoccupation was real. What could have also been a source of misunderstanding here was quickly explained: first of all, there was Aminata's depressive state on her arrival at the shelter. Once issues linked to material survival are solved, it is not uncommon to see the emergence, in the aftermath, of symptoms of a depressive or post-traumatic nature. Then one by one, sources of worry are resolved. In Aminata's case, the educator reported on the first worries that the shelter team had about "safety". The team had explained to her that she should be careful not to put her baby daughter on an adult bed or on her own, that she should be left in her cot, otherwise she could fall; but during the whole time she was at the shelter, they would find her on Aminata's bed, although she was starting to move about. Aminata would say she had forgotten, would then pick her up and put her in her cot. Further to this, her daughter fell out of a buggy twice because she had not been strapped in. The transcultural group then embarked on a de-centering exercise with the educator. Everything they required of her was new for Aminata. There are no cots in Africa. A child in the home country is carried close to the body. Is Aminata mistaken or are we the ones who do not understand the complexity of the situation? How can she acquire the notion of contextual danger? If we say: "this is not how it is done, it is dangerous! You do not know how to do it", her maternal abilities are questioned. We, therefore, wondered about what should be done so that the words that were said to her about the ill-adapted nature of what she was doing did not question her maternal abilities. Different ways of doing things need to be negotiated in different contexts, without casting any doubt on her role as a mother. The fact that the educator was working with us prepared the way for the transmission of transcultural skills to her own team, as always within this type of consultation. The notion of transcultural skills concerns all the required attitudes, knowledge, and abilities for the development of good-quality care among migrant populations (Domenig, 2007; Oppedal and Idsoe, 2015; Radjack et al., 2020). The accompanying professional is, thus, able to observe that elsewhere, pregnancies are cared for in different ways, and babies are carried differently. The educator seemed worried about the way Aminata carried her baby: "when she carries her baby, she is not held properly: she picks her up by the armpit". The therapist replied that there is not one child in Africa that has not been carried in this way, which Aminata confirmed, and which made everyone laugh, thus facilitating a contextualization process. Finally, concerning feeding: Aminata "kept giving her the bottle", despite the baby's frequent regurgitations. During migration journeys, mothers can no longer delegate the care of their babies. This two-way relationship with the baby alters the general balance in the exchanges and often causes mothers to worry about their ability to take care of their baby without the help of co-mothers. Thus, the bottle is often used to address the mother's worries about her ability to take care of the child without the assistance of the group (Camara et al., 2016; Rabain-Jamin & Wornham, 1990).

The cultural distance between Aminata and the women's shelter staff may have led to a series of cultural misunderstandings. The main therapist illustrated potential misunderstandings by using the image of the order used by Aminata to count on her fingers, which is different from one culture to the next. She was at the time referring to how old she was when she arrived in Mali, her point of reference being when she had been weaned off breastfeeding. Birth dates do not have the same importance in different cultural settings. Or again, therapists and co-therapists regularly use metaphors during their transcultural consultations, in their therapeutic suggestions and interpretations (Di & Radjack, 2020), because in certain languages, emotions or concepts are better expressed in the form of proverbs or metaphors.

The trustful relationship that we managed to establish with Aminata allowed us to broach her traumatic migratory narrative and help her escape the feeling of powerlessness. One of the co-therapists made the following empathetic remark: "It is hard to be abused by someone who is supposed to protect you, to then report it to the police and still not receive any protection. It is all more difficult and it can give you a feeling of despair. But there are solutions... So, when I listen to Aminata, I hear: 'I have been abused in my country, I have been abused by people of my own country abroad and I have been abused by the law in this foreign land'. But we are here to look for solutions of protection."

According to Bion (1979), the group is a container for the patient's raw emotions. By its ability to dream and to psychologically transform experiences, the group plays an initial (alphaizing) function of transformation and sublimation of anxiety, so that thought processes are re-launched (Bion, op. cit.; Fognini, 2004). The therapists' counter-transferences, both cultural (with the cultural diversity and otherness expressed by Aminata) and traumatic (related to traumas) (Feldman et al., 2017; Feldman & Mansouri, 2017) are discussed after each interview.

In situations of traumas, isolation, and disruption, the child is at risk of becoming the container of the parents' history rather than being the inheritor (ibid.). Whatever their nature, traumatic events are raw and are more likely to be incorporated than introjected. Their effect can be felt over several generations, like radioactive residues (ibid.) if they are not metabolized and transformed by the psyche. The clinician will be as much affected by the narrative as the baby. In a triadic situation, (mother-baby-clinician), the "radioactivity" is shared by all participants. The indication for a transcultural consultation following trauma takes on its full meaning. The group enables the traumatic countertransference to be diffracted, thus avoiding numbing. The affects felt by the co-therapists and the main therapist mirror what is experienced by the baby, in reaction to the mother. "There is no filiation without putting a history into words, without a narrative, without a narrative on filiation" (Golse & Moro, op. cit.). Putting the baby's history into words is paramount. Without the group it is sometimes difficult for mothers to achieve this, because of the massive nature of their worries, their numerous disruptions, exposing them to a risk of "mental blank", withdrawal, silence, and encryptment.

In the following consultations, we helped Aminata form her own cultural mix between ways of doing things in her home country and in the host country, and we assessed more precisely the interactions with her child in the nursery. In order to support parental roles, we need to become "co-mothers" within the transcultural consultations. We, thus, ensure a shared holding and handling of children with joint observation by the mother, the main therapist, and the co-therapists. As is often the case, we adopted a maternal attitude with Aminata herself, who had not experienced proximity with a mother or co-mother during this initiatory pregnancy period. This mobilization could be interpreted as a protective paternal countertransference and a "maternal attitude" as Lachal put it (2006) when he referred to Ferenczi's concept of maternal transference, where empathy predominates.

We also suggest another type of group that is situated upstream of the psychopathology, focusing on early prevention measures in this period of maternal life and psychological transparency (Bydlowski & Golse, 2001).

The talking group

This group is for any woman confronted with the issue of cultural diversity, whatever her origin. It addresses in particular isolated women who have recently arrived in France. The reconstruction of a female, maternal, social network enables this feeling of isolation to be compensated. A safe network is provided by professionals and other mothers or future mothers, enabling the expression and sharing of hitherto censored and restrained thoughts. Any migrant finds it difficult indeed to express to the host country how difficult life conditions are here, but this can be shared with other migrants who have gone through the same processes in France, even if their cultural origins are diverse.

Arrival in the group is managed smoothly and often in non-synchronized way. People enter and leave the group depending on their needs. Flexibility is indeed required to welcome and adapt to women who in the post-partum period want to end breastfeeding or baby care before joining the group, or those who are struggling to get organized among the multiple constraints and issues that affect them. There is a time for settling down, which is organized around drinks and snacks: water, for which the symbolic importance is strong and is a very frequent mark of welcome, coffee or decaf, herbal tea, orange juice, and cakes... as is the case with conviviality in numerous cultural traditions. This welcome phase is necessary before words can emerge. We also want to make sure that families in situations of great vulnerability are not starving or going short.

The group session is initiated by an introduction from each participant, parents, babies, and mediators, by the description of the role of this discussion group and by a brief overview of the previous session. The group is, thus, intended "to share narratives about the thousand ways of being parents" or "to exchange about the different ways of dealing with a baby, how to feed them, carry them, take care of them, love them, be with them, what the mother imagine or dream etc.".

The group session ends with a summary of all the themes discussed, and the feelings shared, or even the realization of a shared history. There is the possibility of coming again, but no obligation.

The positive effects of the talking group reside in the possibility for parents to lean on one another, focusing at the same time on their own particular trajectories. We were able to witness a few moments of enthusiasm for certain themes: for instance, the widely practiced period of rest after giving birth, a programmed isolation period of 40 days in several cultures, not solely in Muslim areas. In the words of Ben Mohammed (2010, p. 184) about North Africa, "the 40 days following the birth of a child are particularly dangerous for the mother and child. The tomb remains open during that time". The mother-child dyad is isolated, especially during breastfeeding, so as not to attract "the evil eye of envious women who might make the milk go dry". Other mothers have stated that in China too, the rule is "confinement" for one month after giving birth: neither the mother nor the baby can leave the house, except for medical appointments. And in this case, the mother has to cover her head. She must also avoid tiring activities such as reading or watching television and ideally, she must stay mostly bedridden. She must avoid washing her hair and, therefore, must settle for a quick sponge-down with hot water and lemongrass oil. At the end of the month, a big party is organized gathering all the family members.

Certain themes can be broached on our own initiative, when the group is new and inhibited, to show that traditions can be talked about freely, or to recall knowledge. The women in the group showed interest when I alluded to the Shamans' songs[2] described by Lévi Strauss (1949). Several stories on giving birth were shared in the group. First-time pregnant mothers were reassured, some of them talked about public documentaries that were very demonstrative regarding emotions and pain, which made them feel insecure. Fear expressed over the epidural anaesthesia was often stronger than fear over giving birth itself.

Certain themes mentioned by women have led to institutional repercussions: a reflexion on the creation of a talking group specific to parents of premature babies. We know that the risks of prematurity and low birth weight are significantly more frequent in a migrant population (Urquia et al., 2010) and that the experience of a neonatology unit stay aggravates the experience of isolation (Knipiler, 2017). A group is also to be started for parents who have experienced many disruptions and who often find themselves at a loss when they must go home without the baby, who must stay in the neonatalogy unit.

A particularly recurrent theme is Caesarean birth, which concerns several women, with epidemiological data from the international literature that once again shows that migrant women from Sub-Saharan Africa are twice as likely to give birth by Caesarean section (Merry et al., 2013). Concern is particularly prominent among these women because Caesarean birth is viewed as a cultural, religious, or sexual transgression. They risk being repudiated by their husbands, branded as sterile, and accused of the baby's malformations (Perrin et al., 2016). The issue of Caesarean births is regularly mentioned, and the mothers concerned come to this group in great numbers. Fathers tend to come only rarely.

Women have also mentioned the network theme (the role of the child protection institutions[3], medical care, the nature of a maternal unit, or a mother-baby unit). Sometimes, family situations reported by mothers or future mothers are astonishing and more easily elaborated and shared within a containing and secure group. Some women, thus, share traumatic events inside the group. The mediators then try to contain the negative emotions, they make room for the particular narrative by helping in the elaboration of a narrative that can be shared and could help the other participants. Some women can, thus, talk about themes that are seldom mentioned during individual interviews, such as their experience of placing their first child in the country of origin for protection, and the massive reactivation of the missing child during their current pregnancy (Prévost et al., 2021).

When the talking group is focused on situations of isolation and migration, it enables a two-way learning process on cultural representations and is a good preventive approach to decrease the risk of post-partum depression among migrant women, and of a confrontation with a reality that is potentially traumatic for them: Caesarean births, confrontation with the Western medical world and its practices, often experienced as violent. And the questions asked are numerous: "Why do we give birth lying down and not crouched or walking? Why are husbands invited to come into the birth rooms and not other women? Why can't I wear traditional protective objects around my belly or my ankles at the time of giving birth? Why can't I have the baby's placenta, my baby's real double? In my country, it is buried in a special place to ensure my child's good fortune..."

This group is a genuine transitional space, both culturally and psychologically. It enables mothers to explore different positionings, to play with representations and different manners of being towards pregnancies and babies, and to blend them. Tailored psychoanalysis in today's society has an important role to play in the creation and the development of innovating systems that integrate subjectivity and diversity.

Conclusion

Tackling the cultural dimension in maternity units is often taboo in France, despite the fact that it can be particularly important to take it into account during the perinatal period. The uncertainty of the different references resulting from migration and the loss of support of the cultural group can generate psychological vulnerability among mothers and fathers and interfere with parent-child interactions (Moro, 2020). The various transcultural approaches described here, which can be altered and adapted depending on needs, can encourage narratives, and help revive maternal psychological processes that have been halted and hampered by collective and individual traumas, the conflicts linked to migration, and the attendant damage. It is an invitation for a contemporary form of clinical practice, where the notion of the encounter during this perinatal period is so important for the future of the parents and children born in a host country.

Notes

1 Insee sources 2020.
2 His text concerned the incantation of a Shaman intended for Cuna women from South America, who experienced difficult birth deliveries. The song is a vivid epic where spirits are at war, echoing the itinerary between the uterus and the vagina, thus facilitating delivery by symbolic efficacy. "Difficult birth deliveries can be explained as a diversion by the soul of the uterus of all the other souls in the different parts of the body. Once these souls are freed, the soul of the uterus can and must continue its collaboration." This narrative, driven by the notion of a miraculous birth, appeases something in the pregnant woman and the child can, thus, be born (Lévi-Strauss, 1949, p 9).
3 Local paediatric care institutions run by the French public health service, to which any parent have free access until their child is six years old. These institutions provide prevention care.

References

Azria, E. (2015). Précarité sociale et risque périnatal. *Enfances & Psy*, *3*(67), 13–31.

Azria, E., Stewart, Z., Gonthier, C., Estellat, C., & Deneux-Tharaux, C. (2015). Inégalités sociales de santé maternelle. *Gynécologie Obstétrique & Fertilité*, *43*(10), 676–682.

Ben Mohammed, K. (2010). *Facteurs psycho-socio-culturels et dépression post-natale en Tunisie: exemple de la prématurité* [*Thèse*, Université Sorbonne Paris Nord et Université de Tunis].

Bion, W. R. (1979). *Aux sources de l'expérience*. PUF.

Bydlowski, M., & Golse, B. (2001). De la transparence psychique à la préoccupation maternelle primaire. Une voie de l'objectalisation. *Le Carnet PSY*, *3*(63), 30–33. https://doi.org/10.3917/lcp.063.0030

Camara, H., Radjack, R., Klein, A., Di, C., & Moro, M. R. (2016). Apprendre de la vie des mères. Approche transculturelle. *Journal de la psychanalyse de l'enfant*, *6*(2), 151–72.

Devereux, G. (1970). *Essais d'ethnopsychiatrie générale*. Gallimard.

Di, C., & Radjack, R. (2020). Des mots qui parlent bien aux maux. La fonction des métaphores dans la clinique transculturelle. *Soins*, 850, 31–34.

Domenig, D. (2007). Transkulturelle Organisationsentwicklung. In D. Domenig (ed.), *Transkulturelle kompetenz. Lehrbuch für pflege-, gesundheitsund und sozialberufe* (pp. 341–368). Huber.

Feldman, M., El'Husseini, M., Dozio, E., Drain, E., Radjack, R., & Moro, M. R. (2017). The Transmission of Trauma from Mother to Infant: Radioactive Residues and Countertransference in the Case of a Haitian Mother and Her Two-Year Old Son. *Child Care in Practice*, *25*(2), 215–226. DOI 10.1080/13575279.2017.1342600

Feldman, M., & Mansouri, M. (2017). Les paradoxes de la filiation d'une adolescence protégée. *Cliniques Méditerranéennes*, (1), 255–239.

Fognini, M. (2004). Perspectives et apports de Bion au travail clinique. *Le Coq-héron*, *177*, 144–166.

Guedeney, N., & Guedeney, A. (2006). *L'attachement: Concepts et applications*. Masson

Goguikian Ratcliff, B., & Diaz-Marchand, N. (2019). Avoir un enfant loin des siens: petits gestes, grands enjeux. In B. Goguikian Ratcliff & N. Diaz-Marchand, *L'accompagnement des familles: Entre réparation et créativité* (pp. 67–79). L'Harmattan.

Golse, B., & Moro, M. R. (2017). Le concept de filiation narrative: Un quatrième axe de la filiation. *La psychiatrie de l'enfant*, *60*(1), 3–24. https://doi.org/10.3917/psye.601.0003

Knipiler, T. (2017). Vécu et représentations parentales de la place de la famille élargie après une naissance très prématurée [Thèse, Université de Paris].

Lachal, C. (2006). *Le partage du traumatisme. Contre transfert avec les patients traumatisés*. La pensée sauvage.

Lebovici, S., & Stoléru, S. (1983). *Le nourrisson, la mère et le psychanalyste*. Les interactions précoces. Le Centurion.

Lévi-Strauss, C. (1949). L'efficacité symbolique. *Revue de l'histoire des religions*, 135(1), 5–27.

Merry, L., Small, R., Blondel, B., & Gagnon, A. (2013). International migration and caesarean birth: a systematic review and meta-analysis. *BMC Pregnancy Childbirth*, *13*, 27. https://doi.org/10.1186/1471-2393-13-27

Mestre, C. (2016). Bébés d'ici, mères d'exil. Ères, 2016. https://doi.org/10.3917/eres.mestr.2016.01

Moro, M. R., Réal, I., & Baubet, T. (2005). Consultation transculturelle en périnatalité: une psychiatrie de liaison pour les bébés et leurs parents migrants. In D. Bailly (ed.), *Pédopsychiatrie de liaison: Vers une collaboration entre pédiatres et psychiatres* (pp.35–41). Doin.

Moro, M. R. (2020). Guide de psychothérapie transculturelle. *Soigner les enfants et les adolescents*. InPress.

Oppedal, B., & Idsoe, T. (2015). The role of social support in the acculturation and mental health of unaccompanied minor asylum seekers. *Scandinavian Journal of Psychology*, *56*(2), 203–11.

Perrin, A.-S., Drain, E., Sarot, A., & Moro, M. R. (2016). Comment soutenir l'arrivée au monde d'un enfant de mère migrante dans une maternité française: entre urgence somatique et urgence psychiatrique, le temps de la reconstruction. *Neuropsychiatrie de l'Enfance et de l'Adolescence*, *64*(1), 31–35.

Porcelli, P. (2011). Le *fosterage*: entre enjeux psychologiques et culturels. *L'autre*, *3*(3), 278–288. https://doi.org/10.3917/lautr.036.0278 www.revuelautre.com

Prévost, C., Drain, E., Carbillon, L., Taieb, O., & Baubet, T. (2021). Être mère ici et là-bas, *une parentalité complexe. L'autre*, *22*(1), 61–70.

Rabain-Jamin, J., & Wornham, W. (1990). Transformations des conduites de maternage et des pratiques de soin chez les femmes migrantes originaires d'Afrique de l'Ouest. *Psychiatrie de l'enfant*, *33*(1), 287–319.

Radjack, R., Touhami, F., Woestelandt, L., Minassian, S., Mouchenik, Y., Lachal, J., & Moro M. R. (2020). Cultural competencies of professionals working with unaccompanied minors: Adressing empathy by a shared narrative. *Frontiers in Psychiatry*, *11*, 528. DOI: 10.3389/fpsyt.2020.00528

Rizzi, A. (2015). Importance des productions des enfants en clinique transculturelle. *Le carnet Psy*, *188*, 27–30.

Saurel-Cubizolles, M.-J., Saucedo, M., Drewniak, N., Blondel, B., & Bouvier Colle, M.-H. (2012). Santé périnatale des femmes étrangères en France. *Bulletin Epidémiologique Hebdomadaire*, *2-3-4*, 30–34.

Sauvegrain, P. (2012). La santé maternelle des "Africaines" en Île-de-France: Racisation des patientes et trajectoires de soins. *Revue Européenne des Migrations Internationales*, *28*(2), 81–100. https://remi.revues.org/5902

Sauvegrain, P., Stewart, Z., Gonthier, C., Saurel-Cubizolles, M.-J., Saucedo, M., Deneux-Tharaux, C., et al. (2017). Accès aux soins prénatals et santé maternelle des femmes immigrées. *Bulletin Epidémiologique Hebdomadaire, 19*(20), 389–95. http://invs.santepubliquefrance.fr/beh/2017/19-20/2017_19-20_3.html

Stewart, D. E., Gagnon, A., Saucier, J.-F., Wahoush, O., & Dougherty, G. (2008). Postpartum depression symptoms in newcomers. *The Canadian Journal of Psychiatry*, *53*, 121–124.

Urquia, M. L., Glazier, R. H., Blondel, B., Zeitlin, J., Gissler, M., Macfarlane, A., Ng, E., Heaman, M., Stray-Pedersen, B., & Gagnon, A. (2010). International migration and adverse birth outcomes: role of ethnicity, region of origin and destination. *Journal of Epidemiology and Community Health*, *64*(3), 243–251.

Urquia, M. L., Glazier, R. H., Mortensen, L., Nybo-Andersen, A. M., Small, R., Davey, M. A., Rööst, M., Essén, B., & for the ROAM (Reproductive Outcomes and Migration. An International Collaboration). (2015). Severe maternal morbidity associated with maternal birthplace in three high-immigration settings. *European Journal of Public Health*, *25*(4), 620–5.

Vandentorren, S., Le Méner, E., Oppenchaim, N., Arnaud, A., Jangal, C., Caum, C., Vuillermoz, C., Martin-Fernandez, J., Lioret, S., Roze, M., Le Strat, Y., & Guyavarch, E. (2016). Characteristics and health of homeless families: the ENFAMS survey in the Paris region, France 2013. *European Journal of Public Health*, *26*(1), 71–6. doi: http://dx.doi.org/10.1093/eurpub/ckv187. Epub 2015 Oct 28.

Winnicott, D. W. (1949). Le monde à petites doses. In D. W. Winnicott, (Ed.) *L'enfant et sa famille: les premières relations* (pp. pages 75–82). Payot.

Zelkowitz, P., Saucier, J.-F., Wang, T., Katofsky, L., Valenzuel, M., & Westreich, R. (2008). Stability and change in depressive symptoms from pregnancy to two months post-partum in childbearing immigrant women. *Archives of Women's Mental Health*, *11*, 1–11.

Chapter 4

Psychological approaches in perinatal health for refugees

An ethno-psychoanalytic perspective

Saskia von Overbeck Ottino

Introduction[1]

Across the world, becoming a mother is an event that is looked forward to and generally considered to be happy and full of promise, so great are the new life perspectives for each partner in the family. So true is this that when things do not happen in this manner, a parent can feel uneasy or even ashamed to express anxious ruminations, dark thoughts, or ambivalent emotions about the arrival of a baby. Indeed, the most anxiety generating or painful aspects of pregnancy and its outcome are often denied, or even taboo. In the universally idealized representations, a mother is "naturally" inclined to feel fulfilled by the birth of her child. Concerning migrant women, stereotypes are frequent. For instance, an "African mother" is seen as being "instinctively" a good mother, with, therefore, the risk that her suffering will not be identified.

While pregnancy is often a source of joy, also for refugee families, it is, however, important not to underestimate the numerous risk factors linked to traumatic experiences and migration, compounding individual factors. According to the scientific literature and WHO, 50% to 80% of refugees present psychiatric disturbances. More precisely, the fact of being a refugee multiplies by six the risk of postpartum depression and considerably increases the risk of developmental disorders among children (Kirmayer, et al. 2011; WHO, 2018).

Indeed, severe trauma has a negative impact on the course of pregnancy and the early parentchild relationship (Schechter et al., 2017). In addition, the loss of a familiar environment and the vulnerabilities arising from refugee status are not conducive to a secure enough environment to welcome a baby (Moro et al., 2008,; Overbeck Ottino von, 1998; 2011). While the psychic transparency (Bydlowski & Golse, 2001) peculiar to this period of life favours a fecund and structuring associative work for the mother-baby relationship, there is also the risk that it will give access to traumatic experiences hitherto contained in the struggle to survive during the migratory journey. This confrontation can lead to defensive reactions such as psychic

DOI: 10.4324/9781003174684-5

retreats (Steiner, 1993) or functional splits (Bayle, 2012) or even to depressive or posttraumatic decompensation. The newborn baby can then be exposed to traumatic break-in via a sort of emotional contamination, or because the mother is mentally absent, withdrawn into her own distress. In all cases, these experiences are damaging for the quality of early relationship and the psychomotor development of the child.

These mechanisms are in tune with what we sometimes feel by us in these situations: a sense of frozen connections, a vacuum between the baby and his parents, and between the parents and us. This feeling can contaminate the professional, when it should alert him to the relational issues at play, potentially damaging to the therapeutic alliance and implementation of treatment. While it is important to provide prompt support for these families, there is often a kind of tacit agreement on the notion that it is better to "wait and see", to avoid "stirring up the past", since the person is "not yet ready to see a psychiatrist" – a consensus on the need to freeze things rather than act.

It is very unusual for refugees to spontaneously ask for help in the prenatal period to explore their relationship with the baby to be born. Lost in a complex network of management and assistance, they often see psychiatry as a place "where you talk about things from the past that hurt", not as a place that could help them progress. Alongside, in the host country, the confrontation with a family in a situation of extreme distress can alter the sensitivity of an agent towards the present needs. He or she may, for example, adopt an excessively positive attitude, unconsciously to avoid contact with unbearable realities. In this case, the seriousness of the situation may then not have access to consciousness and, therefore, not be perceived.

These transferential and counter-transferential movements of withdrawal or avoidance, on the part of both the migrant and the professional, while inevitable and understandable, nevertheless threaten access to perinatal psychological care. Indeed, patient and professional alike are dealing with extraordinary experiences that can make them feel vulnerable and powerless. The confrontation with war, extreme precariousness, cultural differences, communication difficulties, and so forth can compromise individual abilities. Thus, in the face of patently obvious risk factors and events, normal reflexes are lacking, as if what should be perceived has been erased, denied, removed from consciousness for both the migrant and the host country actor.

In addition, the complexity of living conditions and asylum laws make the smallest initiative complicated and lead to mutual projections such as "my social worker does not want to help me" or "this mother is not organised". There can also be a consensus that things are "cultural", so that a too "Western" intervention would not be appropriate. Finally, the ambivalence towards the reception of refugees can be seen even in the rules imposed by the housing providers. For instance, for a refugee baby's cot will only be provided once the child is born. Whereas if a Swiss woman were to give birth without a bed ready for her baby, she would certainly be thought to be ambivalent...

To counter these trends and to help tailored to the needs of this population, it is necessary to strengthen a network of professionals familiar with and attentive to posttraumatic and cultural issues, able to encompass refugees, their accommodations and care facilities, as well as integration structures.

The place of culture in perinatal clinical practice

The terms migration and culture have different definitions. From a psychodynamic perspective, the term migration suggests that the change of place and culture implies a psychic work in connection with the loss of cultural and identity references, and the need to find links between the previous and the new cultural environments, to retrieve the full flexibility of the psychic functioning, and the feeling to live in the same world as the others. In this sense, culture is made up of ingredients that form a familiar environment: ways of doing things, ideals, taboos, ontological, etiological, and therapeutic representations, and so forth. Regarding the perinatal period, the issues are related to the representations of a given ethnic community about procreation, motherhood, the origins of the child, to collective projections onto the woman, the man, the parenthood, and to all the patterns of care and protection which surround this stage of life.

In most cultures, pregnancy and childbirth are extraordinary events, accompanied by the cultural group as an initiatory stage. At birth, the child is not always viewed as a human being. It may still belong to the world of the group's ancestors and be likely to return there. To maintain him in the world of the living, he must be held back, shaped, and made human. These stages are not managed haphazardly and according to whim, they are closely ritualized by the group. Pregnancy, birth, postpartum, and baby care are, thus, constrained by collective-cultural representations, where the prescriptions derive from a theory of the world, life, death, and illness that is specific to a given ethnic group.

For instance, in certain African ethnic groups, mothers massage their babies. These massages are rituals and intended to "knead" the child into human form to maintain him in the world of the living. When a mother massages her child, she is expressing her attachment and a certain number of projections that are her own. But cultural representations are also carried through these gestures: there are two worlds, that of humans and that of spirits; this other world can break in and take the child back; there are protective ritual acts delineating these two worlds. So, by massaging her child a mother will feel that she is a good mother. On the contrary, if she is prevented, or if, caught up in the losses of exile, she can no longer be that mother, she may feel unable to care for her child.

In any culture, the theories on the origins of the world and humans, or on misfortune and illness, which are cultural representations, can be seen as a way of giving cultural meaning to conflicts, anxieties, and fantasies that are universally human. From conception, the human child is, thus, wrapped not only by individual projections on the part of his parents, the parental projections, but also by cultural projections (Overbeck Ottino von, 2001) related to the ethnic group of his family. Thus, the ups and downs of the early parentchild relationship interweave with cultural correlates that pervade and give meaning to individual events. In clinical practice, these cultural ingredients can be mixed with more singular expressions: "My child is not sleeping well, maybe he is possessed by spirits". Sometimes it is the absence of any cultural reference that, like a photographic negative, reflects this lack: "Now I am here, I don't know how to manage my baby". These different ways of expressing the loss of a cultural container can be viewed as "appeals to culture", a need to retrieve an envelope for individual tribulations, a call for work on linking one set of references to the other.

In early relationships, culture acts as an envelope (Anzieu, 1987) making it possible, step by step, to contain the pregnancy and the emerging parent-child relationship, considering the personal and intergenerational upheavals underway. As an example, the umbilical cord and the placenta, as well as the process of naming the child, are particularly often subjected to ritualized procedures. These practices reflect a propping function, not by way of their technical function as such, but by their value as vectors of early attachment. Customs, thus, overlie psychic ingredients that are essential for the early parent-infant relationship.

In situations of exile, the subtle complexity of interactions between the "inside" of an individual parentchild relationship and the "outside" made up of the surrounding world, whether familial, cultural, or social, can fail and make the process of attuning to the child more problematic.

In clinical practice, the study of the difficulties related to the loss of the cultural environment suggests that the culture of belonging has a propping function by way of a to and fro between the psychic-inside and the cultural-outside and through this way contributes to the psychic development of the individual. In the area of early relationships, it supports exchanges between the baby, the parents, and the environment. Therefore, it is crucial in transcultural cases to foster the use of references from the culture of origin and work on linking the various cultural references present in the play.

First clinical case: Lila

Lila is a young Asian mother who has been in Switzerland for several years and has, thus far, felt quite at ease in her new country. She has learned French, found a job, made friends, and married a Swiss man. But since the birth of her child, things seem to be overturned: she feels lonely, as lost as on her first day in the country. Her baby is not feeding, is not thriving, and is developing slowly. She has no one to lean on, and she misses her family. Her husband is very caught up in his work, and in addition, she says, "there are things he can't understand". She no longer has the courage to carry the baby, who is drawing away from her. During the interview, the child does not react much, looking around him with little interest. The two of them form a rather sad, withdrawn pair. Facing Lila, I endeavour to broaden her horizon by talking about her family, the contacts she has with them, her mother's advice, the support she could seek from compatriots in Switzerland, or from her husband or mother-in-law. Gradually, as we come to talk about our familiarities and differences within one and the same space, Lila becomes more reactive and able to lean on me as a mother figure. She starts to recall memories of her childhood and recall baby care "at home". She rapidly regains confidence in her resources and her baby care skills. At the end of the session, she gradually comes out of her numbed state and starts to play with her baby.

The birth of a child far from home, especially for a first child, often reactivates the experiences of exile, even if the adaptation had been remarkable until then. This mother indeed says so: "I feel as lost as on the very first day". Alone with her child, she has difficulty recognizing him as her own. Should she see him as a child from her home country? But the references and the entourage are lacking to support her to do so. Or should she consider him as a child from here, and listen to the advice of the paediatrician or her husband? It is then she who feels foreign, and no longer knows what is good for her baby. In these circumstances, how could she feed and carry the child with the conviction of being a good enough mother, the essential ingredient for a harmonious early relationship, and an optimal development of the child? Our conversation, eliciting her original references, enabled her to retrieve resources she had set aside during her exile. It also enabled her to identify with the mother that I also am, discovering similitudes between her preoccupations and mine rather than strangeness. Thus, the two worlds, that of the country of origin and that of the host country, can now coexist rather than compete, without any hierarchy in values, leaving "here" and "there" to resonate and reveal fruitful complementarities. Lila can make her baby her own.

This example shows how a break with the family and the cultural environment renders the access to parenthood more problematic. Indeed, in exile, reference points may be missing in the daily real life, but also and above all for their containing, propping, and identity functions. It seems that while adaptation may be possible for a single individual, the inner feeling of belonging may not withstand the upheavals of motherhood. These mechanisms may then affect parenting skills and hence early attachment processes. Nevertheless, we can see how a brief intervention can revive the richness of the motherinfant bond.

Collective violence and the perinatal period

Refugee parents often cumulate a combination of pre-, per-, and postmigration vulnerabilities. They have fled a country at war and experienced ordeals during their journey. Once they arrive in Switzerland, the asylum procedures can be long, arduous, and source of further vulnerability.

The violence endured by refugees in their country is often extreme and highly organized. It affects the whole family and sometimes the whole country. It has real consequences, as the loss of many loved ones and numerous physical and psychological injuries. The political, cultural, and social situation is sometimes such that all that can be done is to flee, most often losing everything. The violence has quantitative aspects (duration, intensity, concrete consequences) and qualitative aspects (deliberate violence inflicted by another human being, violation of physical/sexual integrity) all of which generate trauma (Overbeck Ottino von, 1999; 2007). Indeed, the adult world becomes insane, the bad object of the infantile terrors makes flesh and sadistic impulses run out of control. The environment no longer fulfils its containing function. The break-in strikes the foundations of identity: "I no longer knew who I was"; the Ego functions: "I no longer knew what was right and what was wrong"; and takes form in the body: "I couldn't feel anything, I was a stone, a machine with reflexes". The feeling of vulnerability is extreme and verges on neoteny. Thereafter, once out of danger, patients often describe a feeling of metamorphosis of identity: "I am no longer the same", very often confirmed by people around them: "I don't recognise my husband anymore". Many describe the feeling of the loss of the illusion of a good enough world, and thereby the loss of the sense of the continuity of life. Many also express forms of survivor's guilt: "I should have been the one to die"; "How can I live here when my family is suffering so much there?"

The symptoms of Posttraumatic Stress Disorder (PTSD) are the visible witnesses to the inner upheavals caused by the trauma. They reflect the loss of control of the inner world, in both thought (intrusive memories, flashbacks), behaviour (impulsiveness), and somatic functioning (somatization, insomnia, nightmares). Avoidance behaviours, dissociative amnesia, or blunting of affects seem to be ways of avoiding (or coping with?) the compulsion of repetition of the trauma through forms of psychic retreats. The feeling of being suspended between life and death can persist even out of danger and can lead to hypervigilance. Further to this, the feeling of being more dead than alive, intensified by the often multiple bereavements, is expressed via various psychiatric symptoms (abulia, numbing of affects), and through culturally eloquent symptoms (feeling of cold limbs "as if they were dead", or shuddering signalling the "visit" of a dead person). There may also be dreams where the dead communicate with the living, offering both psychoanalytic, and cultural interpretations.

In perinatal clinical practice, it is particularly important to detect these posttraumatic disorders because of their damaging consequences on the parent-child relationship. The arrival of a baby in this sort of context, even when it is desired, is a source of anxiety and distress. The migrants must manage alone, far from home, in a new world. The conditions of life in refugees' shelters can enhance the feeling of instability. In addition, a transgressive pregnancy outside marriage, which is frequent among refugees, can lead to feelings of shame and guilt, and the fear of repudiation by the family back home. Compounding the posttraumatic symptoms, these concerns can show up in ambivalence towards the pregnancy, or also in alterations of the capacity for maternal reverie (Bion, 1962) and of the primary maternal preoccupation (Winnicott, 1958).

The parents, mother, or father, absorbed by their own problems, will have difficulties to tune to their child and connect to his needs, with all the consequences on his development.

The accumulation of risk factors among refugees in the perinatal period is often underestimated, including by the refugees themselves. When they seek asylum, they think they have at last reached their goals, safety, and peace of mind. After flight and the migration journey, they have an idealized expectation that everything will be fine by now on. In addition, they often hope to "draw a line under the past": "It's behind me, I don't want to talk about it anymore". But with this relative calm, instead of disappearing, the memories are liable to invade the psychic space. Sometimes it is the questioning of the right to asylum that reactivates posttraumatic stress. Indeed, we frequently observe depressive withdrawals or behavioural discharges. Asylum and its rules then often become the epitome of all evils, as if it was less "dangerous" to incriminate concrete elements "here" than to be invaded by the unbearable memories of "back there". During pregnancy, the suffering can also express itself in various ways in the body.

These symptoms can be very disconcerting and do not always generate empathy. The professional in the host country, faced with complaints, irritability, or somatization in a future parent, can indeed have feelings of powerlessness, or again can start to feel that the migrant is "asking too much", has too many requirements, or is manipulative. These are all unconscious ways of reversing the responsibility in the situation, whereby agents detach themselves emotionally. These effects need to be detected, since they are clearly damaging to the attention and empathy that the refugees need.

Second clinical case: Fatou

Fatou fled the violence in West Africa. She is referred to me by the neonatology department. The paediatrician is worried about her, finding her withdrawn and absent. She was repeating she was afraid not to be able to love her baby. Fatou just gave birth to an albino girl. A nice pink baby calling comments from my colleagues. During the first interview, she is prostrate and keeps adjusting a cap on her child's head. She does not say much apart from the factual aspects of her arrival in Switzerland and her hasty, premature delivery. She says not a word about the violence undergone. In response to her silence, I focus on the baby, the sole port of entry open to me, and say: "In your country people say a lot of things about albino children..." As she nods but remains silent, I continue cautiously: "I don't know how you feel, but they are often children that worry their parents; one does not know if one should rejoice or be afraid, one does not know if they bring fortune or misfortune..." She acquiesces again, I continue. "People also say they are children of the water spirits. In any case, they are children that we are afraid to losing (die) and that need to be protected (by rituals)". At this juncture, she takes up the conversation: "Yes it's true, people say they are children born from spirits, they frighten us, people say they will die, that's why I can't love the baby, I'm afraid she will die". I ask her: "Have you known any in your country?" She responds: "Yes, a cousin, but he didn't die. Maybe they don't all die". I pursue: "No, they don't all die". But in your country, I think that when something like that happens people wonder: "why did it happen to me?". Fatou becomes more animated: "That's exactly what I thought. You know, she's not my husband's child. Two years ago, back home, my husband was kidnapped, and I never heard of him again, I don't know if he is in prison, or dead, or if he has gone away somewhere... Later I met another man, the baby is his child. When I saw this baby all pink, I immediately thought this is the child of my sin". Fatou opens up and is able to recount the trauma experienced and the emotions felt: fright and confusion, and the pain of losing her husband. The child could have been fantasized as his, and thus compensate for the sadness of the loss. Basically, the albino child underlines what she feels as a fault, while at a latent level he seems to embody Fatou's desire to live, to survive her husband, and to differentiate from him. This strange little girl requires a clarification of the current mourning processes and accession to accepted and happy parenthood. Fatou can start to look at her with other eyes than that of wrongdoing. She can finally invest her for what and who she is. More at ease, better contained in her cultural references, Fatou relaxes. She tenderly removes her daughter's cap, revealing wonderful blond hair, and asks me lovingly: "Isn't she pretty? You know, I am so afraid of not being a good mother, I'm all alone here and I have been through awful things".

Technically, it was essential to take up the cultural thread of associations and the representations aroused by an albino child, to gain access to the singular psychic conflicts and the trauma experienced. This work contributed to broaden the psychic space towards collective-cultural dimensions, to reduce the splitting, and to render the conflicts in play more comprehensible.

Every culture has its theories on life, death, and illness, and it can be essential to refer to them to restore the flexibility of psychic functioning.

In certain posttraumatic situations such as that experienced by Fatou, this can be the only way in. It is as if we need to work on collective issues before tackling the singular, individual trauma. Here, the anxieties linked to the albino girl condensed cultural concerns about the child (born from spirits and to be protected by rituals) and individual sufferings (the guilt of having set aside an absent husband in favour of a lover), both aggravated by the distancing from family and cultural references. Linking the two spheres, making it possible for these different representations (cultural and individual) to coexist enabled Fatou to retrieve a thread of life, with its emotions, finding meaning in the different references present, and to restore her maternal functions with her child. The work with Fatou is not yet complete. It will be necessary to address more deeply the trauma experienced as well as certain projections on her daughter resulting from the burden endured. Indeed, in such situations, the baby is often expected to replace the absent ones, to restore a shattered parent, or to carry the hope of a better life. At the risk of not being connected to its primary needs. Therefore, it is important and often urgent to help parents to simply meet their child and not the object of grandiose projections.

Therapeutic tools: MEME, a specialized transversal unit

Geneva has been known in the past for its developments in the area of perinatal care, with figures such as Julian de Ajuriaguerra, Dan Stern, Bertrand Cramer, Francisco Palacio, or François Ansermet. These influences fostered the instatement of a network for the management of pregnancies with psychosocial risk factors, including gynaecologists, midwives, social workers, paediatricians, psychiatrists, and child psychiatrists within the Geneva University Hospital. Weekly meetings gathering all the partners are held to present situations and react to the needs in a coordinated manner.

Yet despite this system, which is accessible to all, refugee women who are at risk are often not detected, or only at a late stage, at the time of childbirth, and in this case, things need to be decided on and implemented in a hurry. Likewise, posttraumatic and crosscultural issues are only rarely broached.

To compensate for these shortfalls and more generally to respond to the difficulties for refugees to have access to mental health care, we have set up the MEME unit: Santé MEntale Migration et Ethno-psychanalyse, which is part of the Geneva University Hospital. The acronym MEME has several meanings. It can refer to a notion of sameness ("le même" in French means "the same") as opposed to otherness between humans. But more interestingly it echoes the concept of meme proposed by Richard Dawkins in "The selfish gene"[2]. A meme, by analogy with a gene, is a (nongenetic) replicator responsible for the transmission of behaviours or cultural elements, enabling a given culture to evolve, a bit like humans do. This polysemy of the word MEME is a good reflection of our setting, which intends to promote the meeting with both sameness and otherness, as well as psychic growth in a crosscultural perspective. The system was set up in 2016, alongside the considerable influx of refugees in Europe and in Geneva in particular, with the aim of facilitating access to mental health care. Indeed, although the literature reports psychiatric disorders in more than 60% of them, our care facilities remained underused. We, therefore, developed a screening strategy for psychological difficulties, in collaboration with the network partners: agents in the accommodation centres, social workers, GPs, pediatricians, teachers etc...

We then targeted three risk prone groups in child psychiatry:

- Unaccompanied minors, with systematic early screening and psycho-therapeutic follow-up.
- Families with young children, with a psychologist and a social worker working in close collaboration with reference paediatricians.
- Pregnant women, with a psychologist working in collaboration with gynaecologists and midwives in the hospital.

The centralization of health check-ups and care in the Geneva Hospital for all refugees arriving in Geneva did a lot to facilitate the implementation of these psychiatric resorts. The MEME unit is completed by an ethno-psychoanalytical consultation open to all families followed in the child psychiatry department. The purpose of this setting is to identify clinical risk situations, to promote early psychological assessments focused on the issues of migration and trauma, and to offer brief interventions or, if required, to refer to care within the Geneva network.

Concerning perinatal issues, close links between the MEME unit and shelters, GPs, and obstetricians facilitate the identification of needs for assessment and care, as soon as possible in the prenatal period. Most often we provide pre-, peri-, and postnatal follow-up, with weekly to monthly interventions, in our unit or at home, depending on the needs. A psychologist conducts assessment and psychotherapeutic interviews, a social worker proposes psychosocial support for particular aspects of a refugee's daily life, and a senior psychiatrist conducts family interviews and coordinates with the network. The unit is tightly connected to the institutions of the local network: healthcare, social, legal, and associative, to make the best use of available resources and help families find their way around the very complex offer. We work of course with cultural mediators and interpreters, who are familiarized with our specific approaches.

The cross-sectional and interconnected nature of our unit is particularly valuable. Thus, any protagonist in the network can signal a situation to seek our opinion or intervention, which we can initiate on the spot if required. Likewise, for particularly worrying cases, meetings can be convened with all partners to discuss the best course of action.

This flexibility of action is important, because we have observed that the families at greatest risk are often those the least inclined to ask for help and those that are the most reluctant towards care. As time for a baby is not time for an adult, waiting can be damaging for his development. This is particularly true because the earliest interventions are also the most efficacious for the course of the pregnancy, the development of the parent-child relation, the flexibility of parental projections, and the tuning of the different cultural references at play. More important still, the ability to assess risks and to anticipate often avoids emergency interventions at the time of childbirth.

Third clinical case: Zahra

Zahra was alone when she left Eritrea. She fled from a violent husband, leaving her little boy behind in the care of her mother. She thinks only of him. On the road, she met a Sudanese man "He was kind". They continued the journey together, and Zahra was pregnant when she arrived in Switzerland.

Her doctor was concerned about her because she had nothing to say about the pregnancy. Her belly grew bigger, and she appeared dazed, even terrified. We discovered that her family knew nothing, neither of the relationship, nor of the pregnancy. "I'll tell them later". During the first interview, she was immobile, bent over her belly, silent. I was wondering how this baby would find his place in the minds of these two parents, and his place in the world of exile. I also wondered about this woman's experiences in her home country and during the journey.

Many women flee domestic violence, forced marriage, and war with its dangers on their own. "It's a man's journey" Zahra will tell me. It is not uncommon for them to meet with a partner, who in some cases then travels with them. But pregnancies can also result from sexual violence, and this of course complicates matters. On the contrary, when the encounter is a fruitful one, it is in a way the life instinct that takes over. The child to be born is seen as a problem, but also as a promise for the future, an antidote to loss and solitude, and potential support. As caregivers, it is important to value the positive aspects of this new coming child but without trivializing the issues at stake: loss of references, pain of exile, guilt linked to life choices, etc... The elaboration of these psychic conflicts will depend on the quality of the relationship with the child and the weight of projections onto him.

Zahra and her companion are accommodated in two different shelters. They are not married and do not yet know where the relationship is taking them. In the follow-up in our MEME unit, we first include Zahra in the group of psychosocial risk pregnancies within the obstetric outpatient unit, with the agreement of her GP. This means she will have closer surveillance during her pregnancy, facilitated access to a social worker and a midwife as well as regular pre, peri, and postnatal psychological support.

As a child psychiatrist, it can be difficult to convince the network of the importance of antenatal follow-up: "The baby has not even arrived, how can you do anything?" Yet for Zahra, it is urgent to broach the question of her investment in her pregnancy and in the baby to be born. It is also important to explore her family and cultural references, the trauma experienced, the place of the child she has left behind, and the impact of a "transgressive" pregnancy on her psychic economy. Similarly, the place of the future father needs to be explored and attention should be paid to his own experiences. This is designed to ensure that the pregnancy and the birth will take place in the best possible conditions and that the child will receive care and the most favourable projections possible as soon as he arrives. We, therefore, have to raise awareness in the network of health and social professionals. Many are not familiar with situations such as that of Zahra, where war trauma, cultural gaps, loss of references, and social vulnerability intermingle. Lack of knowledge about asylum, as well as feelings of strangeness and powerlessness in the face of situations to which it is difficult to identify with, can generate defensive reactions, usually unconscious, leading to prejudices, the minimizing of difficulties and challenges, and even reactions that amount to neglect. Yet, for the baby to be born, each week counts.

Zahra courageously crossed land and sea but appears to have lost her soul on the way. She has left her heart with her mother and child in Eritrea, and her fears somewhere along the road of exile. She would like to look positively on her meeting with a kind man and the promises of her pregnancy, but these sources of happiness also open onto forbidden grounds. And while she desires to be able to love and wish to forget the past, Zahra is also willing to be freed from the violence and injustices endured. She is angry with her family and resents their failure to support her against her violent husband. Hence, her transgressive pregnancy also carries a movement of revolt. Through the sessions indeed, we discover an ardent, determined Zahra, wanting to "live her life". But she is afraid of losing her family by attacking their cultural references too hard. She is afraid that her anger could boil over and destroy everything. So, we accompany Zahra through her history of violence, but also of desires and precious memories, to find more ambivalent links with her past, her culture, and her family.

Zahra's treatment consists of:

- Joint social and psychological follow-up to intervene in the daily environment, leaving room for the emergence of emotions. We work systematically with an interpreter.
- Contacts with legal and asylum services in charge of the case. With medical certificates, we can support her asylum application by attesting to the psychological consequences of the violence experienced and confirming the need for the child's development of having both parents with him and be born into a secure environment.

- Socialization activities by referring Zahra to group activities and French lessons. The baby will be welcome there as well. Zahra is illiterate and her results are poor, but she is there every time, very keen to learn. She has always dreamt of going to school, and the idea of at last being there delights her. Results will follow.
- Regular contacts with the GP and follow-up in the maternity unit, in particular with the midwife.
- Interviews with the couple. The future father is fairly reserved, but supportive towards Zahra. There is scope for work with him too, but for the moment it is above all Zahra who seems open to an intervention probably partly as a result of the psychic transparency of pregnancy, making it a favourable period for psychic work.

Gradually, Zahra opens up. Thanks to the collaboration of the interpreter, we alternate the focus between Geneva and her village in Eritrea. We learn of certain childhood pleasures, soon doused by the pain of having left her son back there. She would like to bring him here, but the process offers little hope if Zahra is not financially independent. The perspective does, however, give a place to her son in our sessions and reduces her feelings of guilt at having a second child. Zahra begins to set up a corner of her room with things for the baby. She can tell her family about the pregnancy and feel their support. The baby will be a girl. "It is fine, my son prefers it to be a girl", she says. We wonder if he will then be less afraid of being replaced and forgotten. Zahra laughs: "I prefer girls also!" We are now able to talk about feminine complicities here and there.

At the birth of the baby, a fine little girl, Zahra and her companion seem more serene and ready for the child. Her name is reassuring, meaning "protected by God", and sounds familiar in the cultures of both parents. With the help of the interpreter, we explore the various lullabies from Eritrea and here. This brings us together and makes us laugh. Zahra is happy with her baby and sends photos to her mother and son. The two parents join to organize the celebration of the 40th day to welcome the child. The celebration was so joyful that the accommodation centre was taken over by all the people who came to gather around the new family. Zahra and those she loves are no longer alone.

The value of psychoanalysis in the perinatal clinic with refugees

Some professionals are doubtful about the usefulness of psychoanalysis in clinical approaches to migrant patients. I, however, consider that the psychoanalytic corpus offers ways to envisage and welcome complex situations and to cope with the crosscultural and trauma issues which always arise. Indeed, extended in its concepts (Kaës, 2015), psychoanalysis can broach the effects of cultural background and migration on psychic dynamic, as well as the impact of extreme trauma. It also offers the ideal tools to identify and overcome reactions of the countertransference type which can be damaging for the therapeutic relationship with refugees.

Georges Devereux, the father of ethno-psychoanalysis, proposed the concept of the ethnic unconscious (Devereux, 1980), which is very useful to represent the place of cultural-collective components in psychic functioning. Very briefly, the ethnic unconscious is derived from secondary processes and is made up of what a given culture imposes in terms of repressions according to its fundamental values. Indeed, a given culture will choose certain fantasies that can be expressed, and how they can be expressed, and others that must be repressed. This part of the unconscious is transmitted in the same way as culture, through a kind of teaching. Thus, each generation teaches the next to repress certain elements rather than others and to express some and not others. Therefore, the members of the same group have a certain number of unconscious conflicts in common.

The cultural impact on psychic functioning, thus, occurs at the level of secondary processes and thereby participates in psychic life as a whole, in both its dynamics and its economy. The influence of cultural representations on psychic functioning inscribes singular experience within a certain vision of the world, namely, that which is shared by all the members of a given ethnic group. An apparently personal experience will present familiar aspects to whoever belongs to the same group and will, thus, become shareable. The same experience, on the contrary, may seem strange for a foreigner, and especially if it expresses fantasies that are in principle repressed in the latter's culture. This experience might even provoke a psychic shock in the form of a return of the repressed.

This last consideration is very important in the therapeutic relationship. Since values, ideals, and taboos are not subject to the same pressure from one culture to another, patient and therapist do not only meet as individuals different from each other, but also as individuals different culturally. So, to say, there is a meeting of two different ethnic unconsciousness. If certain fantasies expressed in the culture of one of them are repressed in that of the other, this meeting may provoke an experience of the return of the repressed in the latter. This may then result in an uncanny type of experience as described by Freud (von Overbeck Ottino, 2008).

For Freud, the uncanny (Freud, 1919), despite what is often assumed, is not the result of a confrontation with the unknown, but the resurgence of something that was repressed, which was originally familiar. For him, the domains where we are still close to primitive functioning, as in our relationship with death, and situations where the boundaries between fantasy and reality tend to blur, are particularly prone to the appearance of the uncanny. In work with refugee patients, the confrontation with archaic material of this type is common: dealings with the dead, witchcraft, regressive aspects linked to the losses of exile, confrontation with extreme violence or sadism etc. And in addition, as explained, the exposure to fantasies that are present in the patient's culture and repressed in the therapists. In my view, these mechanisms and the confrontation with the experience of the uncanny are the source of many of the countertransference reactions observed in clinical practice with refugees and explain the frequency, the intensity, and the unconscious nature of them.

Group psychoanalysis gives a clearer picture of the articulation and resonances between individual ingredients and cultural components of the psychic functioning. For Kaës (2007; 2009), the group of affiliation precedes the subject, wraps, and shapes him through unconscious alliances. These alliances, halfway between the subject and the group, are a sort of cement for the group and a major vector of psychic transmission between the generations. Kaës describes three distinct psychic spaces: the singular (individual) space, the group space, and the space of linking between the subject and the group. These spaces operate with the same psychic material, but each one has its own metapsychology. Distinct associative chains emerge from them, but they are always in resonance with each other. This dynamic representation of the relations between the subject and the group is very useful for depicting how we are inhabited both by our personal psychic reality AND by the psychic reality of the cultural group to which we belong. This representation of a double associative chain, a group chain and an individual chain, is very fruitful for our discussion, if we liken the cultural space to a group psychic space. In ethno-psychoanalytic practice, by evoking cultural representations in addition to individual elements, we stimulate the interferences between the cultural and the singular associative chains. This work on the links and resonances between collective-cultural elements and singular offshoots can promote the emergence of hitherto silent associations and support the linking processes undermined by the ruptures of exile. We have seen this in detail with Fatou.

Cultural ingredients are, thus, at the origin of ethnic unconscious material whose movements are situated somewhere between the inside and the outside, between the singular and the collective. Following Winnicott, who sees the cultural experience as an extension of the transitional space (Winnicott, 1967), we can think of the ethnic environment as a transitional space between the subject and the group of affiliation, which offers him support in dealing with his daily tribulations. It is an intermediate psychic formation in which "cultural psychic reality" must be shared by the members of a group so that its "cultural objects" are operative at the narcissistic and object levels. Confession, for example, is only relevant within a group of practising Catholics. So, for each of its members, it will assume group AND individual dimensions. To pursue with Winnicott, by analogy with *the good enough mother* (Winnicott, 1973), we can envisage a good enough cultural environment offering a collective psychic envelope to provide cultural support to the individuals of a given ethnic group in their psychic evolutions.

And just as we are familiar with parental projections, essential for the child's development, I put forward the notion of cultural projections (Overbeck Ottino von, 2001) which shape the child, and subsequently the adolescent and the adult, according to the values and fantasies of a given ethnic group. This means that a Swiss child is different from a young Afghan, not only because he does not have the same parents, but also because he has grown up in an environment with different values, taboos, and group fantasies. Even before his birth, the cultural group will encourage the expression of certain fantasies and the repression of others. These processes are not just a matter of surface varnish or of different ways of life. It is an influence that contributes to the development of psychic functioning, at both conscious and unconscious levels, as does the impact of parents.

Thus, parents and children are enveloped by cultural representations that give meaning to the major events in their lives, be they happy or unhappy ones, or offer them therapeutic solutions in case of illness or misfortune. Culture maintains the subject in a familiar environment with its rules and its fantasies, but also its structuring and containing functions. Mourning rituals, for example, provide support for the work of mourning. Not being able to bury loved ones or not being able to bury them in a familiar way is likely to make the process of getting over a bereavement more difficult. As a contrast to this, a ritual, which generally follows the psychic stages of mourning, structures, supports and facilitates the mourning process. Similarly, feeling attacked by the evil eye or possessed by a spirit expresses a sense of illbeing (in other words a psychic conflict) in a broader dimension, at the level of the group of affiliation. The latter may respond by recognizing the disturbance and by proposing an appropriate ritual, which can also have a beneficial effect at the individual level.

In exile, this envelope, this cultural transitional space, is lacking and may lead to an impoverishment of psychic functioning which impedes the fluidity of the associative chains and the work of linking, thereby making the resolution of life crises or psychic conflicts more difficult. This shows the importance, already underlined in the clinical cases, of promoting links between the different cultural spaces.

Likewise, in the therapeutic encounter with a patient coming from a sufficiently different culture from that of his therapist, the function of a third-party played by a common cultural envelope can be missing. This lack can on both sides lead to a stiffening of the relationship or to paranoid reactions towards the uncanny. Very often also, both partners tend to cling to the manifest of the discourse, losing its latent dimensions.

Indeed, clinical work with refugees becomes even more complex if we consider the intercultural encounter, as an encounter between two ethnic unconsciousness for Devereux and between two group-cultural psychic spaces for Kaës. Referring to Winnicott, the meeting with the "cultural other" is an encounter that is not enveloped by a common cultural transitional space.

As we have seen, it can lead to the confrontation with forms of the return of the repressed and experience of the uncanny. Caught up in these strange and upsetting movements, the protagonist in the host country can have difficulty keeping on course and defining his place, role, and action. This is all the more true if he is not familiar with the issues specific to the refugees, or if he works too much on his own. He may then, like a vulnerable parent, lose his ability for empathy as well as his clinical skills, and disconnect from the needs of a family in distress.

Conclusion: Advocating for routine perinatal assessment in refugees

In encounters with future refugee parents, in addition to the usual concerns, ethno-psychoanalysis has the following to offer:

- Tools to think about the place of culture in psychic functioning with the concept of the ethnic unconscious
- Opportunities to represent the dynamics of collective-cultural components by way of cultural associative chains resonating with singular associative chains
- Theories to envisage culture in its role as a psychic envelope or potential space between the self and the surrounding world
- Ways to position trauma in a cultural and social context
- Arguments to apprehend transference and countertransference movements coming into play in intercultural encounters.

Ethno-psychoanalysis can, therefore, help to approach the complexity of perinatal situations among refugees, unfolding in the throes of migration, trauma, daily realities of asylum, and the countertransference impacts on professionals. The challenges are considerable, and we need to develop care strategies able to consider this complexity and favour early interventions. This will condition the welfare of the refugees of tomorrow and probably more broadly of our society at large, if we consider that its quality can be measured by the way it treats its most vulnerable individuals. And indeed, who is more vulnerable than a baby?

Notes

1   In writings on the perinatal period, the father is not generally given the same attention as the mother, although his place in the child's life is also central. Among refugees, the different issues raised also concern men and can have an impact of their role as parents. They, therefore, need to be correctly accompanied at this stage in life. In the article that follows, for reasons of simplification, I will not, however, systematically mention mother and father.
2   Dawkins (1976).

References

Anzieu, D. (1987). Les signifiants formels et le MoiPeau. In Anzieu, D., Houzel, D., et al. *Les Enveloppes Psychiques*. Dunod.

Bayle, G. (2012). *Clivages. Moi et défenses*. Puf.

Bion, W. (1962). *Learning from experience*. William Heinemann.

Bydlowski, M., & Golse, B. (2001). De la transparence psychique à la préoccupation maternelle primaire. Une voie de l'objectalisation. *Le carnet psy, 63*, 30–33.

Dawkins, R. (1976). *The selfish gene*. Oxford University Press

Devereux, G. (1980). *Basic problems of ethnopsychiatry*. University of Chicago Press.

Freud, S. (1919). *Das unheimliche*. GW XII.

Kaës, R. (2007). Un singulier pluriel. In *La psychanalyse à l'épreuve du groupe*. Dunod.

Kaës, R. (2009). *Les alliances inconscientes*. Dunod.

Kaës, R. (2015). L'extension de la psychanalyse. In *Pour une métapsychologie de troisième type*. Dunod.

Kirmayer, l., Narasiah, l., Munoz, M., Rashid, M., Ryder, A., Guzder, J., …Pottie, K. (2011). Common mental health problem in immigrants and refugees: general approach in primary care. *CMAJ, 183*(12), 959–967.

Moro, M.R., Neuman, D., & Réal, I. (2008). *Maternités en exil*. La pensée sauvage.

Overbeck Ottino von, S. (1998). Bébés en exil: à quel sein se vouer? La complexité des relations précoces en situation migratoire. *Petite Enfance, 66*, 46–52.

Overbeck Ottino von, S. (1999). Violences collectives et travail psychothérapique: nécessité d'une intégration des aspects individuels, familiaux et culturels. *Psychothérapies*, 194, 235–245.

Overbeck Ottino von, S. (2001). Mémoires d'exil: des projections parentales aux projections culturelles. *Tribune Psychanalytique, 3*, 51–66.

Overbeck Ottino von, S. (2007). Violences extrêmes: Le poids de la réalité à l'épreuve de la causalité psychique. *Psychothérapies, 273*, 127–138.

Overbeck Ottino von, S. (2008). Inconscient et culture: Psychothérapie complémentariste. *Actualités psychosomatiques, 11*, 109–128.

Overbeck Ottino von, S. (2011). Tous parents, tous différents. Parentalités dans un monde en mouvement. *L'autre, clinique, cultures et sociétés, 123*, 304–315.

Schechter, D., Moser, D.A., Aue, T., GexFabry, M., Pointet, V., Suardi, F., & Rusconi Serpa, S. (2017). Maternal PTSD and corresponding neural activity mediate effects of child exposure to violence on child PTSD symptoms. *PLoS One, 128*, e0181066.

Steiner, J. (1993). *Psychic retreats*. Routledge.

WHO (2018) *Report on the health of refugees and migrants in the WHO European Region*.

Winnicott, D.W. (1958). *Through pediatrics to psychoanalysis*. Tavistock.

Winnicott, D.W. (1967). The location of cultural experience. *Int. J Psychoanal, 483*, 368–372.

Winnicott, D.W. (1973). *The child, the family and the outside world*. Penguin.

Chapter 5

Immigrant mothers[1]

Pratyusha Tummala-Narra and Milena Claudius

Immigrant mothers

The mother or mother figure is central to the psychic life of people across cultures. In psychoanalysis, infant and child development rests on the experience of being cared for and loved by a maternal figure (Ferenczi, 1909; Freud, 1905). Attachment theory and research have emphasized the influence of the quality of the mother-child dyad on the child's well-being, drawing attention to the interface of the internal and the external (Bowlby, 1983; Main & Solomon, 1990; Malberg & Mayes, 2013). Further, research on attachment and neuroscience has advanced understandings of how early social interactions with one's mother influence experience of the self and of others, the ability to soothe oneself, and the quality of relating with others (Beebe, 2014; Beebe & Lachmann, 1988; Stern, 1985). Although the maternal figure has been viewed as playing a key role in the well-being of human beings, the internal life of mothers has not been adequately recognized or addressed in developmental theories. In fact, for over a century, psychoanalytic and non-psychoanalytic theories have perpetuated a decontextualized view of mothers and the mothering process. Mothers have almost exclusively been seen as containers of a dichotomized ability to give life (e.g., loving) and to destroy it (e.g., rage) (Jung, 1959; Rytovaara, 2014). It has also often been the case that the psychological experiences of mothering are overridden by a societal-wide dismissal or silencing of what are considered to be unacceptable or uncontained maternal affects (e.g., fear, anxiety, sadness, and aggression). More recently, some psychoanalytic scholars have challenged these decontextualized and objectified perceptions of women, and more specifically mothers (Benjamin, 2005; Brown, 2005; Harris, 2005; Smith, 2003; Stern, 2005). These theorists call attention to the complex intrapsychic experience of mothering, the vulnerability and the resilience of mothers, and to the social, political, and economic structures which influence the layered experiences of mothers.

In this chapter, we focus on the subjectivity of immigrant mothers as shaped by the interaction between the individual and social context. We

DOI: 10.4324/9781003174684-6

believe that immigration jettisons important pathways to parenting and development that have significant consequences on parents and children. As such, we argue that a psychoanalytic lens that integrates contextual understandings is critical to addressing the intrapsychic and interpersonal lives of mothers who either immigrate to the U.S. and of women who become mothers post-migration in the U.S. We review the literature concerning the context of immigration, including the experience of marginality and traumatic stress among immigrant women, which has a significant impact on the lives of many immigrant mothers. We then explore the internal life of mothers and the complicated ways in which immigrant mothers negotiate the mothering process and their identities in the face of cultural change and upheaval. We also provide a brief case vignette to illustrate the complexity of mothering in an immigrant context.

Context of immigrant mothers

Immigrants comprise 13 percent (41.3 million) of the total 316 million residents in the U.S., and over one-quarter of the U.S. population identifies as either first- or second-generation immigrants (Migration Policy Institute, 2015). By 2050, approximately 50 million people will be the children or grandchildren of first-generation immigrants (Passel & Cohn, 2008). Over the past three decades, an increasing number of women, both, single and married, have migrated to the U.S. in search of a better life. In fact, more women (51% of foreign-born population) than men are migrating to the U.S., contributing towards a global trend of a "feminization of migration" (IOM, 2006). While female migration to the U.S. has been consistently high since the 1960s, contemporary immigrant women are more often migrating autonomously and independently of men to meet economic demands as opposed to joining their partners or seeking family (APA, 2012; IOM, 2006; Sam, 2006). Unlike previous waves of immigration from Europe, the Second Great Wave of immigration to the U.S. has been described as unprecedented in regard to the diverse racial and ethnical backgrounds of immigrants. For example, in 2012, more than 25% of foreign-born women emigrated from Mexico, followed by women from China (6.1%), the Philippines (5.3%), and India (4.5%). The educational attainment of foreign-born women varies according to country of origin: More than 25% of women immigrants have a Bachelors' degree or higher. Women from India, Philippines, and China tend to be most educated, while women from Central America arrive with less educational privilege. Foreign-born women comprise about 15% of all employed women in the U.S., working across occupations, with one-third in management and about one-third in service professions (American Immigration Council, 2014). Foreign-born women (first generation) tend to give birth more often than U.S. born immigrant-origin women (second generation): Whereas in 1990, 15% of new mothers were foreign-born, in 2004, 24% of all women who gave birth to a child had arrived in the U.S. from another country (Livingston & Cohn, 2006).

While existing research on immigrant parents focuses primarily on mental health risks associated with mothers (Ahmed et al., 2008; Zelkowitz et al., 2008), little is known about immigrant women's wishes and hopes in becoming a mother in the new country. Multiple layers of the ecological context of immigrants, including individual factors (e.g., woman's age, socio-economic status, race/ethnicity, dis/ability, sexual orientation, documentation or authorization), meso-level factors (e.g., family traditions, community), and macro-level factors (e.g., discrimination, sexism etc.) influence women's choice in and decision to migrate to the U.S., and their subsequent adjustment (Bronfenbrenner & Morris, 2006; Marks et al., 2014). Migration, in general, is often triggered by adverse circumstances, including political/ ethnic violence and oppression, wars, famine, poverty, economic hardships, and natural disasters (Sam & Berry, 2006). As a consequence of limited social and economic opportunities, people move from one geographical area to another, often with the hopes of prosperity. In many cases, migration is not felt to be a choice but rather necessary for survival, as in the case of refugees. Additionally, researchers and clinicians have increasingly called attention to the problem of forced migration, such as in the case of human trafficking for commercial and sexual exploitation within the hospitality and care sectors (APA, 2012).

The layered context and circumstances surrounding the decision to migrate to another country shape women's intrapsychic experiences of mothering. However, for immigrant mothers in contemporary U.S., psychic life is typically invisible to the public eye, as a unique set of contextual stressors can impinge on the mothering process. While mothering can be an intense and sometimes overwhelming experience for women from any sociocultural background, mothering in an immigrant context contains additional layers of complexity. Immigrant mothers (first generation) face language and communication barriers, and both first- and second-generation immigrant-origin mothers can face social isolation, as they traverse across multiple, conflicting cultural systems of thought regarding parenting (Tsai et al., 2011; Tummala-Narra, 2004). The acculturation process for immigrant (first generation) and immigrant-origin mothers (second generation) is determined by the influence of multiple contexts, such as home, neighbourhood, physical and psychological distance from country of origin, access to support networks, and work environments (Akhtar, 2011). Acculturation is also multidimensional as immigrants adopt new language, behaviours, and identities (Birman & Simon, 2014). There is ample evidence for the positive impact of a bicultural identity among immigrants who maintain a connection with their heritage cultures and adopt the new culture (Berry et al., 2006; Birman & Simon, 2014; Feliciano, 2001; Marks et al., 2014).

While the multiple contexts within the ecology of immigrant mothers in the U.S. influence each other, a profound sense of isolation can develop due to marked environmental and cultural changes that affect mothers and their families (Levi, 2014; Marks et al., 2014).

Issues of gender and power within the family

Migration to the U.S. may be experienced by women, especially those migrating from countries of origin with less egalitarianism relative to that in U.S., as an opportunity to access an increased sense of choice and freedom in education and employment, increased sexual freedom, and new ways of defining the self (American Psychological Association, 2012; Tummala-Narra, 2013). The issue of egalitarianism should be understood as one that is intertwined with cultural transition. The timing of marriage and partnership can impact the ways in which immigrant women experience gender roles and power within their relationships. Specifically, women who marry a long period of time prior to immigration and are a part of a mutual decision to migrate may find it easier to adapt to the challenges of cultural change and adjustment in the new country, and negotiate changing gender role structures in collaboration with their spouses. On the other hand, women who marry soon before migrating may initially experience less anxiety in relocating to another country with their partner, but may in the long term find that they struggle with mourning loss and separation from the country of origin, complicating power imbalances in the marital relationship (Akhtar, 2011). Immigrant women often find themselves challenged with changing gender roles and conceptualizations of family life that stand in sharp contrast with those in their heritage cultures. Shifts in gender roles with the family, such as that evidenced in women and men working outside the home without the help of extended family members, may place immigrant women at risk for marital conflict and violence at the hands of their spouses or partners (Ahmad, Riaz, Barata, & Stewart, 2004; Morash et al., 2007; APA, 2012). The extent to which mothers experience stress stemming from shifting gender roles relies in part on extended family and friends, who either validate or exacerbate the conflicted experiences of mothers. For example, a 44-year-old Greek American client and mother of three daughters reported that when she permitted her daughters to engage more socially with friends, her parents and her in-laws would actively discourage her attempts to adopt new cultural behaviours. Such interactions can produce overwhelming conflict in the negotiation of motherhood.

It has been noted that the unequal distribution of power between men and women both in the country of origin and in the new country pose challenges to the negotiation of childrearing practices among immigrant mothers and fathers (Kim et al., 2006; Tsai et al., 2011). Tsai et al. (2011), in fact, called attention to the ongoing discrepancy between declarations made by the United Nations and the World Bank that accessing safe motherhood is a human right, and the realities of unequal power, financial hardship, lack of social support, and discrimination faced by immigrant mothers. For many immigrant mothers, although the family can be a seat of patriarchal power, it is core to survival in the new country and a powerful source of protection from racism and classism in broader U.S. society (Moon, 2003; Parrado & Flippen, 2005). The fact that family can be a source of support and stress can contribute to mothers' vulnerability of devaluing and idealizing the country of origin and the adoptive country at varying times, which shapes the negotiation of bicultural identity (Akhtar, 1999; 2011).

Trauma and marginality

While migration provides tremendous opportunity for women's growth, greater autonomy and gender equivalence, immigrant women have also been subject to systems of oppression, including racism and sexism (Tummala-Narra, 2013). Importantly, many women face traumatic experiences at varying points in the migration process (pre-migration, in transit to the new country, and post-migration) (Perez Foster, 2001). Women's experiences of physical and sexual violence have been identified as a public health crisis on a global scale. Many immigrant women and girls endure silence and isolation concerning violence within their homes, ethnic and/or religious communities, and within broader mainstream society. Challenges with language and communication, lack of knowledge of or access to resources and services, and cultural beliefs concerning violence against women can serve as barriers to seeking and receiving support (APA, 2012; Tummala-Narra, 2011). For mothers who have a history of being traumatized emotionally, physically, and/or sexually, the experience of raising children in a new country can intensify the mother's internal affective experiences and her relational experiences with her child (e.g., attunement and responding to the child), all of which can be overwhelmed by concerns for children's safety and complicate negotiations of autonomy and independence of her children. In particular, many immigrant mothers struggle with parenting in isolation, away from extended family support, intensified anxiety about losing their children, and about losing a sense of parental authority (Ackman, 2012; Levi, 2014).

In addition to physical and sexual violence, experiences of racism, sexism, homophobia, classism, and ableism, further contribute to the marginalization of immigrant mothers. For many immigrant mothers, the experience of becoming raced in a new country, while often unexpected, has important consequences for their intrapsychic and interpersonal lives. Specifically, many women are perceived as the racial other, as racial labelling and categorization immediately place them at a risk for marginalization. A Jamaican mother of two sons living in the U.S. stated in a session, "My kids say that we are African-American. We are Jamaican, not African-American. Still, they keep on me. Maybe, they are losing their identity". This mother expressed her fears regarding her sons' loss of identifications with their Jamaican heritage, alongside her frustration with having little control over how they were defined racially by others outside of her Jamaican community. Another mother who emigrated with her daughter from Bangladesh described her helplessness as she witnessed her 13-year-old daughter become increasingly influenced by mainstream American ideals of beauty. She stated, "She (daughter) just wants to be like the thin like the blonde girls on TV. She wants to wear things that show her body too much. I show her pictures of Bengali women to show how pretty they are, but she likes to be like the White girls here". In this case, racially charged messages about women and girls contribute to mothers' conflicts concerning their children's and their own identifications with the heritage culture and the adopted culture. They also present an impossible dilemma of never being able to realize the hope that children will someday be fully accepted and valued in mainstream society or achieving an ideal of Whiteness (Eng & Han, 2000).

The marginalization of immigrant women is further evident in racial, ethnic, and religious discrimination. There is ample evidence that these forms of discrimination are associated with mental health problems, including depression, anxiety, substance abuse, and suicidal behaviour (APA, 2012; Takeuchi et al., 2007). Over the past two decades, there has been mounting anti-immigrant sentiment in the U.S. and elsewhere centred on the increasing rates of immigration from Africa, Asia, Caribbean, and Latin America. Contemporary immigrants are often branded as criminals, terrorists, or people who are taking away jobs from "Americans". Xenophobic responses to immigration create contexts where immigrants experience anxiety about their sense of safety and belonging (APA, 2012). Further, immigration policies in recent years have posed a tremendous danger to the physical and psychological well-being of mothers and their children as forced separation through deportation has continued to persist (Comas-Diaz, 2010; Miranda et al., 2005). One clear example of this problem is evident in the experiences of Central American immigrant women who make arduous journeys to escape poverty and violence and search for employment in the U.S. to support their families in the country of origin (Paris, 2008; Suarez-Orozco, Todorova, & Louie, 2002). These women, most of whom hold unauthorized or undocumented status, live in fear of authorities and of being separated from children who are born in the U.S. Other women are separated from their children who remain in the country of origin with extended family. This latter group often sends money to the extended family and children and engages in plans to reunite with children. These mothers cope with significant anxiety regarding the safety of their children and guilt about not being able to directly care for them (Paris, 2008). Each of these circumstances poses risk for depression, anxiety, and other psychological concerns, especially when mothers are unexpectedly and abruptly separated from their children. Further, prolonged separation from a child often contributes to marked ambivalence within the child upon reuniting with his/her mother (Phoenix & Seu, 2013).

The mothering experience in the context of immigration

The internal life of the mother

In order to understand the nuances of the experience of immigrant mothering, it is necessary to consider aspects of the maternal experience that are shared across cultural contexts. Although traditional views on motherhood and parenting more broadly have been challenged, and fathers generally have become more involved in childcare in many regions of the world, mothering continues to be associated with the conception of women as primary caretakers (Ruddick, 2005). It is important to note that mothers are often transmitters of cultural values, traditions, beliefs, and modes of behaviour, even in cases when fathers are highly involved with parenting. As such, for many women, mothering is a critical part of their identities (Tummala-Narra, 2009). Exploring the internal, affective world of mothers as shaped by contextual realities is at the core of understanding the reactions and behaviours of mothers. A number of scholars have written about the essential need that mothers have toward protecting their children from harm. Janna Smith (2003) has underscored the ways in which mothers' emotional lives, on both conscious and unconscious levels, centre on the physical survival of their infants and children. Daniel Stern (2005) further noted the importance of older, more experienced mothers for women who are new to motherhood, particularly as they help new mothers bear fear and anxiety about the infant's survival. While early theories dismissed these embedded fears for the child's survival as neurotic, pathological, or emblematic of the mother's narcissism, contemporary psychoanalytic theorists have highlighted the fact that the mother's preoccupation with the child's safety and her vigilance in safeguarding her child is an essential, organizing principle of motherhood that promotes the child's development. Stern (2005) described the "motherhood constellation" as one which is analogous to falling in love. He suggested, "Most mothers either fall in love with their babies, or want to, or wish they could, or regret that they have not" (Stern, 2005, p. 4). By likening the mother's psychic experience with falling in love, Stern emphasizes the intersubjective quality of the mother-infant relationship which is composed of mutually created and understood language and symbolism.

While a mother's love and desire to be with her infant or child are an essential aspect of her internal experience, a mother has needs and desires that are independent of her child's needs. Sara Ruddick (2005) has written eloquently about the ways in which a mother can experience the pleasures and agonies of her children as her own, and at the same time a desire to pursue ambitions unrelated to her children. Ruddick aptly pointed out that women's conflicts between maternal and nonmaternal desires are natural to the mothering experience. The decontextualization and pathologization of these intrapsychic conflicts are manifested in dichotomizing mothers as "stay at home mothers" and "working mothers" (Ruddick, 2005). Further, economic circumstances often dictate whether mothers have a choice in working outside the home. However, mothers who must work to financially provide for their families are often assumed to be burdened with having no choice but to work, and mothers who do not have the same financial demands are often seen as ungrateful for having choice in working outside the home. In either case, the mother's desire is dismissed and distorted.

Maternal aggression is another aspect of intrapsychic experience that requires attention. On a societal level, there is little tolerance for women's and mother's aggressive feelings. Perhaps, one of the most stigmatized acts of aggression that has received a great deal of public attention in the U.S. is abortion. In a recent legal case in 2015, a 33-year-old Asian Indian woman, Purvi Patel, was arrested for feticide in Indiana. Ms. Patel had sought medical attention in a hospital due to severe bleeding, after which her physician observed that she had a protruding umbilical cord and then informed the police due to suspicions of child abuse. Although Ms. Patel reported that she had miscarried and left her stillborn child in a dumpster due to suffering a state of shock following the miscarriage, she was suspected of taking illegal abortion medication and found guilty of child neglect and of killing her foetus and sentenced to 20 years in prison. Ms. Patel is the first woman in the U.S. to be sentenced to prison for such an action, raising both antipathy for her behaviour and immense fear among women, particularly women of colour, with regard to the public's protection of their human rights. Perceptions of maternal aggression in this example, albeit an extreme and tragic one, reveal the problematic ways in which women's and mothers' aggression is unaddressed in contemporary society. Rather, this dimension of internal life remains unacceptable and punishable, without inquiry into the deeper, structural problems associated with aggression.

Maternal need and desire are further problematized in constructions of the mother as a unidimensional figure that exists only for the other (e.g., child). Jane Lazarre (2005) noted the problem of idealized images of the mother as superhuman, or of generalizations of all mothers as having the same character, temperament, and needs. In response to the question, "What do mothers want?" she wrote on part of her response as follows: "For people to remember, or learn, that we are daughters too, foolish rather than wise at times, sometimes weak when we would so love to be strong, moved by desire and self-doubt at every age just as when we were girls, unable to fix things at times, and at times—as much as we would love to do so—unable to provide" (Lazarre, 2005, p. 218). Complex, contradictory feelings of competence and self-doubt lie at the core of maternal experience. Yet, discourse that promotes the myth of the perfect mother or superwoman who provides perfect attunement to her children and attends to the needs of others within and outside of her family detracts from the real, lived experiences of mothering. Further, this type of destructive discourse produces in the mother an illusion of control over her children's lives, specifically that if she conducts mothering in a particular way, that she can ensure her children's safety, well-being, and success.

Forming a maternal identity in a new land

Immigration adds several layers of complexity to the internal life of mothers. Mothering in a foreign land brings about unique challenges in family dynamics, attachment, and identity formation (Tummala-Narra, 2004). Becoming a mother invokes memories of one's own childhood, parenting figures, and cultural traditions. For first-generation immigrant mothers, these memories can be associated with the wish to reconnect to one's ethnic heritage and a nurturing, idealized image of a parent (Tummala-Narra, 2004). Moreover, in the process of maternal identity formation, the physical and psychological separation from one's own mother can be intensified as new mothers begin to identify as both – mother and child (Chodorow, 2000; Tummala-Narra, 2009). The process of becoming a mother is also characterized by a range of coexisting emotions experienced during and after childbirth: Immigrant-origin mothers may experience an altered sensibility, feeling a profound loss and tremendous possibility at once. Intensified feelings of mourning the loss of the mother country may be reflective of a realization of the discrepancies between the idealized new home and one's desires to experience motherhood in ways that resemble native traditions and norms. For others, there may be, for the first time, a sense of belonging, a sense of settling in an adopted home.

Language is deeply linked to historical and cultural meaning and as such, the teaching of the native or heritage language becomes an important means in retaining the cultural identity (Akhtar, 2011; Suarez Orozco et al., 2002). For many immigrant mothers, the sharing of a language with their children symbolizes a special bond that resembles the connection to the native culture. The mother tongue becomes crucial in framing thinking, emotions, and shaping a cultural identity. Often, the first language remains the language of emotions and thus, for mothers, there may be great anxiety around the loss of the native language; as it may represent the loss of the cultural identity (Akhtar, 2011). Moreover, the ways that children and parents vary in the degree of native language fluency may also symbolize the different generational perspectives on culturally pertinent issues. For children, the loss of native language in the second and third generations may add to a sense of cultural identity crisis. While the native language may be one of the most powerful tools to preserve cultural ties, immigrant women also wish for their children to learn the language of the new country. This desire is often connected to a strong hope for children to successfully negotiate a bicultural identity. It also channels mothers' hopes for children's upward mobility in U.S. society and economic attainment. As such, immigrant parents tend to place high importance on education. Research suggests that immigrant-origin parents have higher academic motivation, aspirations, and expectations for their children, regardless of their own educational background (APA, 2012). For example, in Germany, a qualitative study demonstrated that Turkish-origin mothers were most invested in having their daughters receive an excellent education and emphasized a wish for their daughters to have autonomy in making life decisions (Edthofer & Oberman, 2007). Thus, while there is often a desire to maintain cultural values, there may be hope that the next generation of women, specifically, may have more opportunity and freedom.

The formation of maternal identity in the immigrant context also encompasses conflicts between dominant parenting styles in the culture of origin and those in the new cultural environment. Over the past several decades, there has been an increasing emphasis in the U.S. on an intensive style of mothering in which a central task of motherhood is to develop the ability to emotionally attune to the needs of the child and to fulfil his/her physical and psychological needs. The "independent" mother is thought to be someone who chose to have children either biologically or through adoption and pursues a career without the support of community support (Eckardt, 1998; Tummala-Narra, 2009). D.W. Winnicott's (1971) concepts of good-enough mothering and primary maternal preoccupation support the primacy of the mother-infant/mother-child emotional relationship. The quality of affective experience is at the heart of psychoanalytic models of optimal mothering. Yet, these conceptions have often excluded the effects of external realities, especially stress associated with loss of and separation from loved ones, trauma, and cultural upheaval.

The value of intensive mothering in mainstream U.S. society contrasts with a value of interdependence and multiple caretakers prevalent in many other countries and in many subcultures within the U.S. (Tummala-Narra, 2009). Maintaining an interdependent system of interactions within the family and ethnic and/or religious community is of great importance to many immigrant families and, yet, is difficult to sustain in the face of broader cultural message in the U.S. that emphasize the importance of individual autonomy and separation of children from parents. These contradictory experiences can contribute to ongoing anxiety and confusion about negotiating varying conceptions of attachment and parenting styles (Tummala-Narra, 2004). Sometimes, these conflicts can be overwhelming, resulting in the questioning of the earlier decision to migrate to the U.S., and fantasies of returning to the country of origin. One client, a mother of a 16-year-old daughter, stated, "Nothing I do feels right. I can't be a good Brazilian mother and I can't be a good American mother. I'm trying to show my daughter that you can be both Brazilian and American, but how can I do that, when I feel like I can't be both?" This mother, who had been victimized by sexual violence as a child, struggled with messages from her non-Brazilian friends that her attempts to protect her daughter by restricting her from dating were too "traditional". On the other hand, her fellow Brazilian immigrant friends often warned her about not allowing her daughter to socialize too much with boys since this would result in harm to her daughter and to the family's reputation.

These types of conflicts call for a broader construction of good enough mothering (Winnicott, 1971), as for immigrant mothers, they raise important concerns about not only separation from their heritage cultures but also the potential loss of their children to a new cultural context. Carola Suárez-Orozco (2000) described the concept of "social mirroring", an expansion of Winnicott's notion of mirroring (1971), to describe messages that immigrant children and adolescents receive from others outside of their families and ethnic communities. Positive social mirroring in which immigrant youth experience mainstream society as accepting fosters a positive bicultural identity, whereas negative social mirroring in which youth receive negative messages about their ethnicity, race, or religion can pose challenges to a positive sense of self (Suárez-Orozco, 2000). Stress related to negative messages from mainstream society can be detrimental to immigrant parents' relationships with their children. Immigrant parents and their children often contend with conflicting cultural values rooted in mainstream U.S. context and in their ethnic and religious communities, and as such may experience acculturation gaps and problems in communicating effectively with each other (Akhtar, 2011; Birman & Simon, 2014). Such challenges intensify parents' fears of losing their children and/or disconnecting from them. A 56-year-old Mexican American mother of a son in his 30s stated, "I don't know what he will remember from our culture. I think he wants to, but he never grew up with people who know much about Mexico. Maybe when I'm not here anymore, he won't know much at all". For this mother, a critical function of her mothering entails maintaining a sense of continuity between her life in Mexico and her son's life in the U.S. She spoke at length in a number of psychotherapy sessions about how her son passes as White and that no one seems to see his Mexican heritage, until they meet her, as her phenotype appears "more Mexican" than that of her son. Further, she and her son, throughout their years in the U.S., had heard negative, derogatory comments about Mexicans at school, their neighbourhood, and in the media. As she discussed her concerns about her son's acculturation, she expressed feeling as though she is "losing him".

Immigrants' pre-migration fantasies of creating a new and better life with their partners or spouses for their children are challenged by feelings of

disillusionment and loss of hope when they and their children face a negative reception in the new country. Sometimes, the need to ensure the physical and economic survival of children in a new country results in intensified
efforts to prepare children to cope in a hostile environment. For example,
there has been increasing attention on parenting styles thought to characterize parenting styles of Asian American parents, especially the mother.
The notion of the **"tiger mom"**, most commonly popularized Amy Chua's
book, *Battle Hymn of the Tiger Mother* (Chua, 2011), depicts a strict, rigid
form of Chinese mothering, in contrast to permissive Western parenting, as
essential to the academic and professional success of Chinese Americans
(Cheah et al., 2013; Guo, 2013). This description of the "tiger mother" has
garnered considerable attention from the media and has served to reify
stereotypes (e.g., model minority) and misconceptions of Asian immigrant
parenting. It is important to recognize that there is great variation in how
Chinese American women and men approach parenting their children and
that these approaches in part rely on finding ways to combat discrimination
(Cheah et al., 2013). Interestingly, there are very few media accounts and
public discourse that acknowledge the role of a "negative social mirror"
(Suárez-Orozco, 2000) on parenting practices, including pressures that exist
within school systems for immigrant children and parents. Such distor-
tions are problematic in that parents' and children's attempts to negotiate
and work through divergent cultural values are masked by stereotypes and
marginalization.

Although psychoanalytic theories emphasize the role of the maternal
figure in the outcome of children's development, scholars have noted that
children have significant relationships with other people, such as extended
family, nannies and babysitters, parents' friends, neighbours, teachers, and
peers (Akhtar, 2011; Tummala-Narra, 2004). Immigrant mothers' identities are influenced by their interactions across multiple contexts. Mothers'
interactions and engagement within their children's schools, for example,
form an important dimension of their experiences as parents, contributing
to sense of belonging or isolation in a new cultural environment. In some
cases, children translate both linguistically and culturally for their parents, which can be both a source of burden and a source of self-esteem for
children and for parents (APA, 2012). The reciprocal, mutual nature of
caregiving in immigrant families may be interpreted as non-adaptive by
important figures (e.g., teachers, co-workers, neighbours, doctors, therapists) in the child's and the mother's daily life. However, it is important to
recognize that the developmental trajectories of immigrant children and
adolescents and those of their parents influence each other (Mann, 2004).
For many immigrant mothers, connecting with an ethnic and/or religious
community is an important source of support and "refuelling", in the face
of negotiating parallel acculturation with their children. Engagement in
these communities is especially important when there is limited access

to extended family who may have been involved with child-rearing in the country of origin (Akhtar, 1999; 2011).

Over the past two decades, psychoanalytic scholars have emphasized the bidirectional influence of mothers and children (Beebe & Lachman, 1988; Malberg & Mayes, 2013; Mitchell, 1997; Stern, 2005). The mother is no longer seen as the only being that drives the relationship with her child, but rather the mother-infant/mother-child relationship is a site of mutual recognition and influence (Beebe, 2014; Benjamin, 2005; Harris, 2005). Jessica Benjamin (2005, p. 38) described the presence of a "third" in the mother-infant relationship, which "allows for accommodation and exchange of recognizing responses". She described this thirdness as related to Winnicott's (1971) conception of transitional experience, which links subjective experience with objective reality. Mutual recognition encompasses the mother's efforts to recognize her infant's or her child's distress and engage in soothing him/her in a way that is not overridden with her own anxiety (Benjamin, 2005). In this perspective, the mother's subjectivity is critical to the subjectivity of the child. As such, it is especially important to consider the impact of contextual realities that help to shape the mother's subjectivity. The impact of trauma, migration, and cultural adjustment must be recognized as organizing factors in the experience of immigrant mothers and their relationships with their children. Immigrant mothers' love and willingness to bear personal losses and separation from the heritage culture for the sake of their children's well-being in a new land should also be viewed as a mark of their resilience. It is important that clinicians recognize that the complexities faced by immigrant mothers in the formation of identity in a new cultural context co-exist with resilience, as many immigrant mothers, despite challenges, strive to protect the integrity of their relationships with their children, families, and communities.

Case vignette

Suda is a 37-year-old woman who immigrated to the U.S. from Thailand when she was in her early 20s. Suda sought treatment to cope with increasing anxious mood over a course of several months. She reported feeling overwhelmed with grief after learning that her mother was terminally ill a few months prior to beginning psychotherapy. Suda met and married her husband approximately one year after moving to the U.S. Her husband, Chet, is a Thai American man who was born and raised in the U.S. She and her husband have a 12-year-old son and an 8-year-old daughter. While Suda grew up in a middle-class home in Thailand and migrated to the U.S. for educational opportunities, Chet's parents had endured political persecution in Thailand prior to their escape to the U.S.

Throughout the first few months of psychotherapy, Suda expressed feeling overwhelmed by sadness related to her mother's illness. She stated, "I can't really imagine how I'm going to move on. I'm not ready to for her to leave". She travelled to Thailand as often as possible to spend time with her mother whom she adored. Her mother's illness triggered the loss of her father who had died several years earlier from a heart attack. Suda had only one aunt who remained in Thailand and had no living siblings. Her older sister had died in an automobile crash as a child. Suda's mother was her "pillar" and someone who encouraged her to pursue her professional dreams in the U.S. For several months in psychotherapy, Suda told her therapist (first author) that she found herself withdrawing from her husband and children and wished that she had never made the decision to leave Thailand. At other moments, however, she could acknowledge that she feared more loss (especially her children) and living away from Thailand intensified this fear. In one session, she stated, "I can't go through anymore loss. It hurts to think about it". Her mother passed away during our seventh month of working together, and Suda took leave from her workplace to cope with the painful loss of her mother.

As she mourned her loss, she began to question her own ability to mother her children without the guidance and physical presence of her mother. Suda expressed that she feels lost in helping her children to grow up in a different culture. She worried that her children did not know their heritage culture to the extent that she would have liked. Her fears were compounded by her husband's second-generation status. Suda stated, "Chet is more American. He is Thai but he is more American. He doesn't always get what it feels like to have grown up in Thailand. I guess that is what my kids will be like". When I asked her to tell me what it felt like for her to know that her children will have a very different experience of their Thai heritage than her, she responded, "I don't like thinking about it. It's hard to feel different from your kids". She proceeded to talk about how she felt "left out" at times when she noticed that she was the only member of her family to speak in English with a Thai accent. Her accent made her more visible to others in some ways, and yet her internal life, including images and memories of growing up in Thailand, remained invisible even at times to her husband and to her children.

This experience was enacted in psychotherapy with me. In one session, she stated, "Well, you were born here too. So, it's probably hard to imagine what it is like to grow up in another country". In fact, I was born in India and arrived at the U.S. in childhood and, therefore, do not have a visibly foreign accent. For Suda, I too was a second-generation immigrant, one without a trace of memories of India. However, my internal experience is quite different than what Suda imagined. The images and memories that I have of my early childhood in India are an important part of my identity, often unseen by others. We proceeded in psychotherapy to talk about the differences in our experiences as immigrant-origin women, and over time, Suda gradually came to wonder if I had actually been born in India. After I told her that I was born in India, she told me that she felt as though I may be able to relate to her grief. At the same time, she wondered whether I could fully relate to her experience of raising children in the U.S. Suda struggled with a longing to return to Thailand and with a longing to stay in the U.S. where she had placed enormous hope in her own future and that of her children. She would vacillate between feeling "grateful" for having more freedom in the U.S. as a woman and having a sense of home in Thailand.

In the course of our work, she came to bear her ambivalence and her grief and began to work through her fears of losing her children to a cultural environment that she sometimes experienced as unfamiliar and hostile. Suda worried that, similar to Chet, her children would not escape the problem of discrimination. Suda's preoccupation with her children's future often interfered with her ability to feel present with her children. At times, she expressed, "I still need to work on enjoying my time with them. I'm too worried most of the time". Gradually, Suda spoke more about missing her mother. She shared with me that the most peaceful times in her life were the days when she and her mother spent calm afternoons talking with each other. She recognized that these days were few in number, as she and her mother had suffered numerous losses and crises which had overridden any sense of calm. Nevertheless, she was able to access her mother's calm demeanour, which helped her to feel more present over time with her children.

Psychotherapy was a space in which Suda could express both her anxiety and her desire to "just be" with her children and her husband without the intrusions of loss and separation from Thailand and the hostility she experienced in the U.S. She continued to mourn the loss of her mother and of the reality that she would likely not return to Thailand as often as she had previously. The mourning process was essential to her emerging ability to imagine the possibility of her children having happy and fulfilling lives in the U.S.

Conclusion

We have attempted to present the experience of immigrant mothers as one that is complex and one that is driven by an interaction of intrapsychic, interpersonal, and sociocultural factors. Psychoanalytic perspectives offer an important lens into the internal life of immigrant mothers, and how the subjectivity of the mother interacts with that of the child. The mutual influence of the mother-child relationship is reflected and enacted in the therapist-patient relationship (Benjamin, 2005). In the immigrant context, these subjectivities are shaped by layers of hope, connection, marginalization, isolation, and anxiety. It is important that therapists recognize the importance of the migration process (pre, transit, and post), the losses and separations incurred in this process, and the interwoven nature of intrapsychic, interpersonal, and cultural conflicts. Therapists should also attend to the deep sense of love and connection experienced alongside anxiety in the mothering process. Psychotherapy offers a space to attend to and potentially bridge divergent cultural value systems and their accompanying affective experiences. It also holds the potential to explore the possibility of bearing seemingly contradictory identifications with the heritage and adoptive cultures. As immigrant mothers and their children have become more visible in public discourse in contemporary U.S., it is our hope that clinicians, researchers, and educators will continue to expand understandings of the internal and external realities inherent to immigrant mothers' experiences.

Note

1 Tummala-Narra, P., & Claudius, M. Immigrant mothers. In S. Akhtar (Ed.), *New Motherhoods.* Lanham, MD: Rowman & Littlefield) Reproduced from NEW MOTHERHOODS PATTERNS OF EARLY CHILD Edited by Salman Akhtar, published by Rowman & Littlefield Publishers. © 2016 by Rowman & Littlefield, reproduced by arrangement with Rowman & Littlefield Publishers.

References

Ackman, P. (2012). Helping the helpers: Consultation to childcare staff using psychoanalytically informed developmental concepts. *Psychoanalytic Inquiry, 32,* 186–204.

Ahmed, A., Stewart, D.E., Teng, L., Wahoush, O., & Gagnon, A. J. (2008). Experiences of immigrant new mothers with symptoms of depression. *Archives of Women's Mental Health, 11*(4), 295–303.

Ahmad, F., Riaz, S., Barata, P., & Stewart, D. E. (2004). Patriarchal beliefs and perceptions of abuse among South Asian immigrant women. *Violence Against Women,* 10(3), 262–282.

Akhtar, S. (1999). *Immigration and identity: Turmoil, treatment, and transformation.* Jason Aronson.

Akhtar, S. (2011). *Immigration and acculturation: Mourning, adaptation, and the next generation.* Jason Aronson.

American Immigration Council. (2014). *Immigrant women in the United States: A portrait of demographic diversity.* Washington, DC. Retrieved from http://www.immigrationpolicy. org/just-facts/immigrant-women-united-states-portrait-demographic-diversity

American Psychological Association, Presidential Task Force on Immigration. (2012). *Crossroads: The psychology of immigration in the new century.* Retrieved from http://www.apa.org/topics/immigration/report.aspx

Beebe, B., & Lachmann, F.M. (1988). The contribution of mother-infant influence to the origins of self-and object representations. *Psychoanalytic Psychology, 5*(4), 305–337. http://dx.doi.org/10.1037/0736-9735.5.4.305

Beebe, B. (2014). My journey in infant research and psychoanalysis: Microanalysis, a social microscope. *Psychoanalytic Psychology, 31(1),* 4–25.

Benjamin, J. (2005). What mothers and babies need: The maternal third and its presence in clinical work. In S.F. Brown (ed.), *What do women want? developmental perspectives, clinical challenges* (pp. 37–54). Routledge.

Berger, R. (2004). *Immigrant women tell their stories*. NY: Routledge.

Berry, J. W., Phinney, J. S., Sam, D. L., & Vedder, P. (2006). *Immigrant youth in cultural transition*. Mahwah, NJ: Lawrence Erlbaum Associates.

Birman, D., & Simon, C. D. (2014). *Acculturation research: Challenges, complexities, and possibilities*. Washington, DC: American Psychological Association.

Bowlby, J. (1983). *Attachment and loss*. Basic Books.

Bronfenbrenner, U., & Morris, P. A. (2006). The bioecologicalmodel of human development. In W. Damon & R. M. Lerner (Eds.), *Handbook of child psychology: Vol.1. Theoretical models of human development* (6th ed., pp. 793–828). Hoboken, NJ: Wiley.

Brown, S.F. (ed.) (2005). *What do women want? Developmental perspectives, clinical challenges*. Routledge.

Cheah, C. S. L., Leung, C. Y. Y., & Zhou, N. (2013). Understanding "Tiger Parenting" through the perceptions of Chinese immigrant mothers: Can Chinese and U.S. parenting coexist? *Asian American Journal of Psychology, 4*(1), 30–40.

Chodorow, N. (2000). The psychodynamics of the family. In S. Saguaro (Ed.), *Psychoanalysis and woman* (pp. 108–127). New York University Press.

Chua, A. (2011). *Battle hymn of the tiger mother*. Penguin.

Comas-Diaz, L. (2010, Summer). *Sin nombre*: Female immigrants and the anti-immigration laws. *The Feminist Psychology, 37* (3), 7–14.

Eckardt, M. H. (1998). The changing challenges in the lives of three generations of professional women. *American Journal of Psychoanalysis, 58*, 351–359.

Edthofer, J., & Obermann, J. (2007). Familienstrukturen und Geschlechterrollen in der Migration Eine qualitative Analyse von Müttern und Töchtern türkischer Herkunft. *SWS-Rundschau, 47*(4), 453–476.

Eng, D. L., & Han, S. (2000). A dialogue on racial melancholia. *Psychoanalytic Dialogues, 10*(4), 667–700. doi:10.1080/10481881009348576

Feliciano, C. (2001). The benefits of biculturalism: Exposure to immigrant culture and dropping out of school among Asian and Latino youths. *Social Science Quarterly, 82*(4), 865–879.

Ferenczi, S. (1909). Introjection and transference. In M. Balint (Ed.), *First contributions to psychoanalysis* (pp. 35–93). Karnac Books.

Freud, S. (1905). Three essays on the theory of sexuality. In J. Strachey (Ed. & Trans.), *The standard edition of the complete psychological works of Sigmund Freud* (Vol. 7, pp. 123–246. Hogarth Press.

Guo, K. (2013). Ideals and realities in Chinese immigrant parenting: Tiger mother versus others. *Journal of Family Studies, 19*(1), 44–52.

Harris, A. (2005). *Gender as soft assembly*. The Analytic Press.

International Organization for Migration (IOM). (2006). *Female migrants: Bridging the gaps throughout the life cycle*. New York, NY: IOM.

Jung, C.G. (1959). *The archetypes and the collective unconscious*. New York, NY: Random House.

Kim, S., Conway-Turner, K., Sherif-Trask, B., & Woolfok, T. (2006). Reconstructing mothering among Korean immigrant working class women in the United States. *Journal of Comparative Family Studies, 37(1)*, 43–58.

Lazarre, J. (2005). Listen to my words: Maternal life in colors and cycles of time. In S.F. Brown (ed.), *What do women want? Developmental perspectives, clinical challenges* (pp. 213–222). Routledge

Levi, M. (2014). Mothering in transition: The experiences of Sudanese refugee women raising teenagers in Australia. *Transcultural Psychiatry, 51(4),* 479–498.

Livingston, G., & Cohn, D. (2006). *The new demography of american motherhood.* Pew Research Center.

Main, M., & Solomon, J. (1990). Procedures for identifying disorganized/disoriented infants during the Ainsworth Strange Situation. In M. Greenberg, D. Cicchetti, & M. Cummings (Eds), *Attachment in the preschool years* (pp. 121–160). Chicago: University of Chicago Press

Malberg, N. T., & Mayes, L. C. (2013). The contemporary psychodynamic developmental perspective. *Child and Adolescent Psychiatric Clinics of North America, 22*(1), 33–49. doi:10.1016/j.chc.2012.08.002

Mann, M.A. (2004). Immigrant parents and their emigrant adolescents: The tension of inner and outer worlds. *The American Journal of Psychoanalysis, 64*(2), 143–153.

Marks, A. K., Ejesi, K., & García Coll, C. (2014). Understanding the US immigrant paradox in childhood and adolescence. *Child Development Perspectives, 8*(2), 59–64.

Migration Policy Institute (2015). Retrieved from http://www.migrationpolicy.org/research

Miranda, J., Siddique, J., Der-Martirosian, C., & Belin, T. R. (2005). Depression among Latina immigrant mothers separated from their children. *Psychiatric Services, 56*(6), 717–720.

McCarroll, J. (2009). Analysis of an undocumented Latina immigrant. *Psychoanalysis, Culture, & Society, 14*(3), 225–236.

Mitchell, S. A. (1997). *Influence and autonomy in psychoanalysis.* Hillsdale, NJ: Analytic Press.

Moon, S. (2003). Immigration and mothering: Case studies from two generations of Korean immigrant women. *Gender & Society, 17*(6), 840–860.

Morash, M., Bui, H., Zhang, Y., & Holtfreter, K. (2007). Risk factors for abusive relationships: A study of Vietnamese American immigrant women. *Violence Against Women, 13*(7), 653–675.

Paris, R. (2008). "For the dream of being here, one sacrifices…": Voices of immigrant mothers in a home visiting program. *American Journal of Orthopsychiatry, 78*(2), 141–151.

Parrado, E. A., & Flippen, C. A. (2005). Migration and gender among Mexican women. *American Sociological Review, 70*(4), 606–632.

Passel, J. S., & Cohn, D. (2008). *U.S. Population Projections: 2005-2050.* Pew Research Center. Retrieved from http://www.pewhispanic.org/2008/02/11/us-population-projections-2005-2050/

Perez Foster, R. (2001). When immigration is trauma: Guidelines for the individual and family clinician. *American Journal of Orthopsychiatry, 71*(2), 153–170.

Phoenix, A., & Seu, B. (2013). Negotiating daughterhood and strangerhood: Retrospective accounts of serial migration. *Feminism and Psychology, 23*(3), 299–316.

Ruddick, S. (2005). What do mothers and grandmothers know and want? In S. F. Brown (ed.), *What do women want? developmental perspectives, clinical challenges* (pp. 69–85). New York, NY: Routledge.

Rytovaara, M. (2014). The great mother and the terrible mother: Mimesis, alterity and attachment in adolescence. *The Journal of Analytical Psychology, 59,* 211–228.

Sam, D.L. (2006). Acculturation of women and children. In D. L. Sam and J. W. Berry (Eds.), *Acculturation Psychology* (pp. 403–428). Cambridge University Press.

Sam, D. L., & Berry, J. W. (2006). *Acculturation psychology*. Cambridge University Press.

Smith, J. M. (2003). *A potent spell*. Boston, MA: Houghton Mifflin Company.

Stern, D. N. (1985). *The interpersonal world of the infant: A view from psychoanalysis and developmental psychology*. New York, NY: Basic Books.

Stern, D.N. (2005). The psychic landscape of mothers. In S. F. Brown (ed.), *What do women want? Developmental perspectives, clinical challenges* (pp. 3–18). Routledge.

Suárez-Orozco, C. (2000). Identities under siege: Immigration stress and social mirroring among the children of immigrants. In A. C. G. M. Robben & M. M. Suárez-Orozco (Eds.), *Cultures under Siege: Collective violence and trauma* (pp. 194–226). Cambridge University Press.

Suárez-Orozco, C., Suárez-Orozco, M., & Todorova, I. (2008). *Learning a new land: Immigrant students in American Society*. Cambridge, MA: Harvard University Press.

Suârez-Orozco, C., Todorova, I. L., & Louie, J. (2002). Making up for lost time: the experience of separation and reunification among immigrant families. *Family Process*, 41(4), 625–643. https://doi.org/10.1111/j.1545-5300.2002.00625.x

Takeuchi, D. T., Zane, N., Hong, S., Chae, D. H., Gong, F., Gee, G. C., Walton, E., Sue, S., & Alegria, M. (2007). Immigration-related factors and mental disorders among Asian Americans. *American Journal of Public Health*, 97(1), 84–90.

Tsai, T., Chen, I., & Huang, S. (2011). Motherhood journey through the eyes of immigrant women. *Women's Studies International Forum*, 34(2), 91–100.

Tummala-Narra, P. (2004). Mothering in a foreign land. *The American Journal of Psychoanalyis*, 64(2), 167–181.

Tummala-Narra, P. (2009). Contemporary impingements on mothering. *The American Journal of Psychoanalysis*, 69, 4–21.

Tummala-Narra, P. (2013). Women immigrants: Developmental shifts in the new culture. In L. Comas-Diaz & B. Greene (Eds.), *Psychological health of women of color: Intersections, challenges, and opportunities* (pp. 257–274). Westport, CT: Praeger.

Tummala-Narra, P. (2011). A psychodynamic approach to recovery from sexual assault. In T. Bryant-Davis (Ed.), *Surviving sexual violence: A guide to recovery and empowerment* (pp. 236–255). Lanham, MD: Rowman & Littlefield Publishers, Inc.

Winnicott, D.W. (1971). *Playing and reality*. New York, NY: Routledge.

Zelkowitz, P., Saucier, J. F., Wang, T., Katofsky, L., Valenzuela, M., & Westreich, R. (2008). Stability and change in depressive symptoms from pregnancy to two months postpartum in childbearing immigrant women. *Archives of Women's Mental Health, 11* (1), 1–11. doi: 10.1007/s00737-008-0219-y.

Chapter 6

Spirit possession and motherhood

Geneviève Welsh

In a changing world, millions of people move to escape from conflict, perse-cution, or poverty. Transculturality is often problematic because of racism and xenophobia, but it has benefits including cultural enrichment and crea-tivity. In transcultural clinical contexts, anthropology can help clinicians to see how "cultural systems attain their social force by tapping into people's unconscious beliefs and desires" (Gammeltoft & Buch Segal, 2016, p 402).

How ethnographic concepts and data can be put to work in a psycho-analytic treatment is the main question this chapter will tackle about the case of an African mother, Djenaba. With Djenaba, I have learned not only that possession can affect the mothering process, but also that vulnerability related to perceived discrimination, acculturative stress can co-exist with creativity. I am grateful to Djenaba for what she made me discover.

Outline of the clinical picture

Djenaba, a 30-year-old woman born in Africa, was referred to me for a depres-sion following the birth of her first child, Amanda. She is married to Paul, a Caucasian man, with whom she shares a creative way of life. I was told she had not been able to handle or hold the baby since she was born, 5 months ago.

On the first session, a tall and elegant woman comes into my consult-ing room and immediately asks a quite unexpected question: "Why can't I get along with women?". It is as if this question had been thought of as the core of her difficulties and the aim of our encounter. She is composed, speaks easily of her history, and seems unconcerned by the relation to her baby. She goes on telling me her history. Djenaba is of a Muslim family; she was born in Africa, the third child of 10 and was sent to France when she was only 7 to relatives who had settled there long ago, and where it was for-bidden to speak her native language. She had to speak only French. Later, when her parents and her siblings moved to France, she joined them, but she could not feel safe in her own family because her brothers were brutal. So much so that she sometimes fled and ran away back to her relatives. She went to school, where she did poorly, enjoying only art class where she proved to be

DOI: 10.4324/9781003174684-7

talented; she feels she is "completely ignorant" especially in science and has acquired what she qualified a "basic and lacunar" knowledge. After she had finished school, she tried to start a business, but it failed. When she met Paul, she was pleased to see that he appreciated her artwork. Although Amanda is their first child, she did not speak much of her at first. She did not look concerned by her relation to motherhood, rather annoyed by the fact that her husband and her stepmother seemed reproachful to her. Rather puzzled by this unusual post-birth depression and by the fact that Djenaba did not seem to be concerned by her relation to her baby, I proposed weekly sessions.

Out of the blue, after a few sessions, she told me that she had been possessed by a spirit, since early childhood and was, thus, regarded by her family as someone both potent and dangerous: she was viewed alternatively as lunatic or possessed. During her pregnancy, she told me, "I was not present". Right after delivery, she could neither hold nor handle her baby. She had to get to grips with all the changes occurring after childbirth: her relationship with the spirit, but also with her husband and his family. As she was excluded from her own family, no blessing, no welcome, no rituals were performed, so she was on her own to face all this turmoil.

First steps to explore possession

I was taken aback by this situation. I had previously met other patients with a history of possession in my practice with Cambodian refugees. After a trustful relationship had been established, they had revealed that some spirits were living within them. In the context of genocide and its aftermath, I had thought of these spirits as wandering souls of relatives who had disappeared, had been slaughtered, and were not properly buried. (Welsh, 2018). I had learned from a Cambodian patient that for years he had not mentioned the spirits that possessed him for fear I would not "believe" him.

In the case of Djenaba, I had to check my counter-transferential reactions: this kind of possession evoked images of the film "the Exorcist" that had frightened me when I was an adolescent. In addition, other ghastly pictures emerged: the Convulsionaries of Saint Medard graveyard, voodoo cults, connecting possession to death and zombies. I also realized that possession has of course sexual meanings, related to childhood sexual fantasies. I was able to identify these reactions as typical cultural countertransference reactions calling for a need to decenter urgently!

Once I had come to realize that my reactions might prevent me from listening quietly to Djenaba, I could resort to psychoanalytically checking my countertransference and see what this uncanny feeling was conveying in a set of images combining sex, death, and evil. I was aware to be at risk of being either fascinated or frightened.

Exploring the psychoanalytic field of possession, I realized that possession was seen in the earliest steps of psychoanalysis as "nothing more than hysteria" (Wikstrom 1980). It was related to demonic possession, for instance, in the famous case of Johann Christoph Haizmann (1651–1700) described by Freud (1923). Haizmann was a painter who had pledged in a pact he had made with the Devil that he would belong to him 9 years later. He had sold his soul to the Devil to be cured of his melancholia, and subsequently, he displayed symptoms of possession such as convulsions and visions. When Freud read his manuscript, he "assumed that the Devil was a substitute for his father and that the state of possession was a struggle against his own feminine passive wishes including a desire to bear a child for his father" (Wikstrom, 1980). Thus, in Freud's analysis, possession was understood as connected to a conflict over the unconscious fantasy of homosexuality leading to a persecutory-paranoid state of anxiety. Haizmann's case was later viewed differently, as related to procreation fantasies accompanied by sex confusion.

Overall, contemporary psychoanalysis tends to see demonic possession along the lines of object relations theory, namely the internalization of bad objects as Taylor (1978) explains: "psychoanalytic treatment of a case of demoniacal possession is described to indicate the multiple dynamic meanings which possession may have and to demonstrate the necessity for integrating and applying aspects of libido and object relations theories. Current trends in psychoanalysis are towards recognising the psychotic core which is frequently masked by an apparently psychoneurotic illness so that analysis must reach beyond Oedipal conflicts to the primitive internalised object relations". As most of psychoanalytic literature is on demoniacal possession, it did not apply to Djenaba: she was not persecuted by the spirit, it had lived in her. I did not think she was psychotic, and was it through internalization of bad objects that possession occurred. I was left with many questions: if the dominant concept of man in non-Western cultures is more relational than individualistic, then how can Western traditional psychoanalysis be used in a case of possession acknowledged by a group as non-pathological? How could I work psychoanalytically with Djenaba, based on drive theory or object relations? I decided to suspend my theoretical framework for a while and try to build a narrative.

Whatever unconscious personal resonances the material had on me, I needed to explore what possession meant for Djenaba and to understand who she is as a person, and what makes her suffer. In another situation, I would have met her relatives and try to understand the dynamic of her family. The choice of a psychotherapeutic setting was guided by her situation and her initial question.

Dialogue with ethnography

I am grateful to Michèle Fiéloux, an anthropologist and a friend of mine, whose interest and fieldwork on spirit-possession has helped me to reflect on this case. Together, we have conducted a seminar on "Psychoanalysis and Anthropology" (2010–2013) at the Maison de Solenn and learned to deepen the dialogue between our disciplines, bearing uncertainties and enjoying discoveries this dialogue entails. In addition, we both participated in another seminar held as part of the courses of the Paris Psychoanalytic Society on "cultural aspects of countertransference" (2008–2014). Fiéloux's works in Burkina Faso, Senegal, and Malagasy (2014) have enabled me to understand both the complexity of ethnographic fieldwork and the different levels needed to understand the construction of subjectivity focusing on family and lineage, in contrast to the psychoanalytic focus on individual psychic reality.

Of course, at first, I thought I could apply complementarism to my clinical work, based on Devereux (1983) and his epistemology of complementarity. But how was I to construct the anthropological side of possession? No analyst can be familiar with all cultures, albeit analysts can be trained to develop a familiarity with Culture in general. I also thought I was not to work in the manner of an ethnologist and ask questions that would put Djenaba in the position of an informer. I needed to recourse to information on the patient's culture, whilst maintaining, in the context of Djenaba's recent motherhood, the setting of a standard psychoanalytic treatment, based on free association, handling, and holding the transference, analyzing resistances, and a particular attention to counter transferential phenomena. Thus, the cultural and uncanny aspects of the clinical material were to be integrated into the psychoanalytic process.

Therefore, we decided that I would present Djenaba's case in our seminar. In another setting such as Moro's transcultural consultation, the group of therapists would have provided a large variety of associations stemming from the therapists' varied cultural backgrounds and could have been used as therapeutic levers. In my consulting room, I was alone with Djemba and decided to use our seminar as a setting to elaborate some of the questions that arose during the sessions. I exposed the clinical material to Michèle Fiéloux, who shed an ethnographic light on possession, based on what I presented. Later, I invited Fiéloux to participate in sessions with Ego, an African patient in the consultation for exiled patients I had set up in the Psychoanalytic Centre Evelyne et Jean Kestemberg. Thus, we felt our way to work in transcultural situations (Fiéloux, 2021).

The first thing I discovered is that possession is a worldwide phenomenon, viewed as an ordinary mode of communication in many social groups. Later, I discovered according to Fiéloux and Lombard's studies (in press) of "tromba" in Malagasy that possession involves women in most cases and can be "conceived as the process of a spirit choosing a person, generally on the model of an amorous relationship". In childhood, the future possessed girl often displays some oddities or symptoms of illness that are interpreted as predicting the subsequent possible occurrence of possession. When possession is established – after an itinerary that can last for several years – "the spirit will always occupy the place of primary husband". Of course, possession in Madagascar is connected to rituals and cults that ethnographic work can document, whereas I could know nothing of possession status, rituals, and cults which might have been set up in Djenaba's birthplace. Nevertheless, it can be assumed that there are common traits shared worldwide regarding possession, whether possession is transitory or permanent, private, or public.

In particular, one of the common traits is that it is not seen as a personal fantasy or a delirium: it is a mode of communication inside a group and across generations. Often a person may be possessed by several spirits and spirits can possess more than one person in the lineage group: "spirits are frequently passed on from generation to generation and thus associated, though not exclusively, with particular families" (Lambek 1980). Possession cannot be understood as an individual phenomenon, it speaks of all the relations in a given group and it enables what cannot be told in a direct way to be expressed through the voice of the spirit. What has to be repressed according to the accepted rules of communication can be attributed to the spirit's speech (Fiéloux, 2021).

In the field of sociology, it is noteworthy that Graham (1976), based on a series of interviews of pregnant women in England, made the hypothesis that "pregnancy equated to possession by the unborn child" and that possession is "a phenomenon principally described in non-western societies", whereas in western societies "spirit possession is seen as an outcome of a mental disturbance rather than placing it within the social and political context in which it occurs". Indeed, perhaps Djenaba had no room to place the unborn child in her psychic life since she was already possessed.

At first, I could not have insights on the context of her family as she had been excluded at an early age and had subsequently broken up. She was actually in a transcultural situation with her Caucasian husband who was raised in a very traditional nuclear Christian family. There was no co-mother to help her welcome her daughter. Step by step, she spoke more and more of her relatives and I could better picture her family.

All this input led me to a first hypothesis: Djenaba could not take care of her daughter because she was caught by the bond she had had for so long with the spirit. I explored this hypothesis during the sessions. It was confirmed that she was constrained to keep a bond with him, to wish he would stay with her, but also to "spare" her child. She feared he could turn to her daughter and possess her. During pregnancy and in the months following childbirth, she told me, becoming a mother, being a spouse, and a woman was not easy in part because of these "negotiations" (her words) with the spirit and because she had to elaborate a new relation with her human husband. Step by step, I was able to construct a narrative intertwining the clinical material and the ethnographic approach, co-constructed for 3 years. I met her on the basis of one weekly session, then less frequently when she found a job she could enjoy. On some occasions, she came with her husband, mainly when there were conflicts between them regarding child-rearing.

Artificially, I shall divide this narrative in three threads: Djenaba's construction of femininity, motherhood and mothering, conflicts in a mixed couple.

Constructing narratives

Djenaba's construction of femininity

When she was a baby, her excision took place, as a purification ritual to enter paradise after death. She received the name of a grandmother. During her childhood, she once pointed at an animal and was thereafter thought to be possessed by the spirit of a grandfather. This oddity can be seen as a sign predicting subsequent possession as was mentioned above. When she had her first periods, her mother locked her up and warned her not to be touched by a man least she become pregnant. She had thereafter always felt disgusted by blood, another "oddity". When she began to dress pretty, her mother often treated her as a "whore".

After a kind of "odd" illness, she was thought to be "strange". Her father told her she would never give birth, her mother said she wished she would have a child as mean as Djenaba had been with her and predicted she could "never be a good mother anyway". Never did her mother accept her as a woman. Djenaba recalls she was a melancholic child, she did not like her life, and would write imploring poems to figures of death. No doubt when she moved to France at the age of 7, she had to face a huge number of losses.

During adolescence, a spirit visited her and became her lover. At this stage, it can be assumed she had followed the itinerary of possession described by Fiéloux and Lombard (2014). Sometimes she wonders whether the spirit is a transformation of another spirit who appeared previously as a man with a horrible face, related to her grandfather.

Her mother and she had frequent fights. She once explained: her mother's spirit could not get along with hers. She assumed her mother's spirit was a female one, weaker than hers. This shed a new light on her opening question: "why can't I get along with women?". She could not identify with a good enough mother since her mother vilified her as a woman and since her male spirit was attacking and defeating the female spirit inhabiting her mother. Of course, I thought that, in part, Oedipal and castration issues were, thus, staged and that this fight with the maternal image was jeopardizing her access to motherhood.

The only woman who had loved her was her grandmother: she carried her on her back, let her play with her breast, comforted her when she had nightmares, protected her when she ran away from her family. Even after her death, she sent her dreams and even stung her when she was near her grave under the disguise of a mosquito. Her brothers were often mean with her, even brutal, but she got along rather well with a younger sister. She resented her father when he left the family and later came back with a young second spouse. Thereafter, there was a time when she felt "funny", went into a kind of trance and, thanks to the spirit, her anger towards her father could be expressed. The rivalry with the second spouse was violent. Daring to express her hatred was possible and probably put on behalf of the spirit as possession is offering "an unusual chance to directly and subjectively express acts, intentions, and emotions" (Fiéloux, personal communication) that otherwise could not be uttered. Djenaba could never date any African man. When she met Paul, she was passionately in love. She let him know that she was possessed, and it did not prevent him from loving her, at least in the beginning of their relationship.

Motherhood and mothering

When she got pregnant, she had mixed feelings: after all, she realized, she was not cursed, she was going to give birth, despite fibroids, against all the odds! She thought the fibroids had mysteriously disappeared to "let the baby out" despite the curses. There was also a kind of implicit permission the spirit had given her to become pregnant. During her pregnancy, she was very creative, but she did not think much of the baby. While pregnant, she told me that she would look at a photo of herself and realize she had to part with the child she was, albeit she felt the little girl was still present. Sadly, she told me she had not "<u>felt</u>" her pregnancy; it was as though she was staring at an "abstract painting", meaningful for others, but meaningless for her. Later, she wished she could be pregnant again and be "present".

When her daughter was born, she could not take her in her arms after delivery: "she was kind of blue, covered with blood..." Her husband said she looked absent and depressed, even suicidal. She was sleeping all the time and could hardly wake up to breastfeed the baby. It was as though she was not able to <u>see</u> her daughter. At first, Djenaba's mother was not around because they had quarrelled: no cultural blessing or welcoming was done. She decided not to give her daughter an African name. Later, she went to family gatherings with her daughter.

But right after childbirth, her stepmother called upon by Paul, took over, rather brutally according to Djenaba. She recalled she had the feeling her husband and her stepmother were trying to "possess" her. When at this point of her account, I said that sometimes after delivery, mothers can be overwhelmed, or can even be in a state of nightmare, she nodded and told me that she was afraid the spirit would either abandon her or go after her daughter or both. She had to have a "discussion" with him. She does not know whether she had to do this because she wished so, or because of all the "African stuff" her parents had put in her mind. Once again, I verified that the relation an individual has with his own culture can be ambivalent and changing.

Anyway, she begged the spirit to protect her daughter, to give her what she wants. Yet, she kept watch: sometimes, at night, she had a strange feeling. It means the spirit was arriving, so she tried to avoid his visit by making specific gestures. Thus, he is out and will not bother her nor her daughter. Should she fail to do this, it is as if she would let him in, a door would open, and the spirit would make love to her. Her ambivalence was striking as she wished she would not lose him in part because she liked to feel the powers he gave her. Thanks to him, she can have premonitions, say soothing words to people who suffer, speak bluntly to her father...The outcome of the "discussion" was not clear, or perhaps she did not want to make it clear and kept it secret. I could see how difficult it was for Djenaba to become a mother: to some extent, a mourning work had not occurred, she was caught in curses and possession conflicting with procreation fantasies; no good-enough mother had been interiorized and she could not speak with anyone but her analyst of her inner struggles. I had the feeling that I needed to be a container, trying to transform for her as well as for myself "protomental" (Bion, 1961) phenomena into words, reveries, and thoughts.

Conflicts in a mixed couple

Right after Amanda's birth, different levels of misunderstanding occurred between Djenaba and Paul. When he realized that she was unable to take care of the child, he became anxious and at first chose to call help from his own mother who immediately tried to control the household.

Then, as Amanda was growing, he resented the way Djenaba was raising her. According to him, she was not gentle or tender; she seemed to care only for the child's body needs. Djenaba thought Paul was overprotective, too much a kind of "hen-father", arguing that in Africa, children are bathed, combed, massaged, fed, carried on different backs, free to play with other children. Whereas Paul, she said, was still having to "solve his Œdipus complex!"

In fact, beyond the differences in child-rearing, this "lack of tenderness" was connected to his fear of Djenaba's supposed madness and/or possession. He recalls how he was scared when she once looked entranced and had covered her face with jam. Upon hearing his account, she laughed and explains that she had smeared her face with jam and fruit juice because she was jealous of her daughter getting more attention from Paul than she.

He did not know what to think when Djenaba expressed unexpected fantasies about their daughter: for instance, she feared that she could be kidnapped. When she looked at her daughter's pretty body, she thought it did not resemble hers. Paul does not know what to do with her fantasies, he knows how jealous she can be and could face her jealousy, but her fantasies leave him voiceless. All the love Paul was giving to Amanda made Djenaba feel neglected and abandoned. She even cried during a session with her husband when she realized, she "never felt loved by anyone"; she felt she was always treated as "special" or "lunatic".

What is at stake is also the question of the ominous presence of the spirit in the house. Amanda became interested in cartoons featuring witches and monsters. One night, she had a nightmare and woke up shouting: "Ha! a monster!". Djenaba immediately thought it could be related to a Japanese cartoon she saw albeit she had forbidden her to watch TV. For Djenaba, it could also be the spirit who visited their daughter in a dream thereafter. Paul disagreed, it was not "**her** spirit": all children are afraid of monsters, and it is likely it is another monster. They began to worry because Amanda was afraid to go to bed. I then proposed a session with both parents, based on exploring the child's needs at bedtime. Soon after that session, they were relieved to see that Amanda could sleep. They both had found new ways to comfort her. Paul had decided to sing lullabies and Djenaba to read a story to Amanda.

Right after a conference I gave on possession, an African woman introduced herself to me as a physiotherapist and said she was glad of the way I had presented possession. She herself had been possessed by a spirit since childhood and, when she married a Caucasian man, she told him that she would need to keep contact with her spirit and they both agreed that he and their children would let her spend an evening every week with him. This harmonious compromise did not occur in Djenaba's couple. I can only assume that Djenaba's relationship to her spirit was too ambivalent and that she could not let it go since the power it gave her prevented her from a depression she had experienced when she was a child imploring Death to take her into her arms.

Uncertainties, questions, and hypotheses

The plurality of levels of listening and the complexity of the clinical picture were puzzling.

Yet, the clinical elements I have described show the vitality of the transference-countertransference process: she was getting along with her analyst, a woman who had overcome the anxiety possession had stirred up and was looking at her in a benevolent and interested way. I had suspended my theoretical framework to listen to different levels of the material, as I would listen to a polyphony. I shall now artificially describe three themes, three levels of listening.

Intrapsychic level and splittings

"Why can't I get along with women?" was Djenabas's opening sentence during our first meeting; yet, she had a grandmother who was always protective and loving and a sister whom she dearly loved. In her family, she had always been seen as "strange", "special", "soothsayer", "whore", worthless, yet she is aware she has achieved great pieces of art. Her shame is of being nearly illiterate, but she finds pleasure exposing her knowledge with a good sense of humour when she shows how well read she is in art, philosophy, and literature. She is pleased to surprise me when she comments on paintings displayed in my consulting room

She had sticked to her African background and beliefs in spirits, premonitions, but at times, she is skeptical about all this African "stuff", akin to brainwashing according to her. She would like to get rid of her possessing spirit but does not wish to lose the power he gives her (dreams, premonitions, use of hard talk); she tries sometimes to resort to alternative powers, but praying Jesus for instance proved rather deceptive.

When she speaks of her violence, she says she is feeling like a volcano, a warrior, a tiger, a jealous, and potential murderer, all this violence inside her is scary: where does it come from, she wonders? From jealousy towards women for sure, not only from the strength of her warrior spirit. Yet, during the course of the therapy, she realized that she could behave as a good enough mother, friend, colleague in a group of women.

My main hypotheses are that she had never been seen for herself, as she was caught in a network of projective identifications. She had never been seen for someone who is trying to achieve her own identity and to come to terms with powerful drives, ambivalence, and splittings. Of course, achieving one's identity is a lifetime process: we are all made of heterogeneous elements we integrate provided we do not avoid elaborating ambivalence and conflicts. But in the transcultural situations Djenaba had been experiencing, the heterogeneity of the cultural repertories she could resort to is so substantial that there were times she could not integrate all the ingredients or metabolize them and then she literally was "absent". There were times when she put the unintegrated (violent, shameful) parts in the spirit or enacted them in violent fits. She had to resort to different logics both conscious and unconscious.

Interpersonal level

Of course, right after Amanda's birth, many conflicts between Djenaba, Paul, and Paul's mother arose. They seemed staged as conflicts on cultural affiliations in child-rearing: one does like this in Europe versus one does like that in Africa. But both Paul and Djenaba deepened their understanding and managed to somehow elaborate their conflicts. Djenaba rightly pointed out that the difference she could see in Paul was not only that of a Caucasian man, but also that of a son who had not "solved his Oedipus complex" and needed to behave like a good mother. He then argued that he had to be like a mother since she was not as motherly as he had expected.

Paul was frightened by Djenaba's potential violence and her lack of tenderness and found more sensible to take her daughter away when Djenaba became too jealous and violent; she felt some relief to be sure that he would protect Amanda from her violence. Paul could not do without her mother's help to look after Amanda, and he acknowledged that Djenaba could not stand her stepmother. So, they agreed Amanda would spend some time at her paternal grandparents' place without Djenaba. Djenaba and Paul could not understand why Amanda could not go to sleep easily: each of them found a way to put Amanda to sleep. However, some aspects could not be integrated because Paul quite often resented Djenaba for being "ill" and reluctant to be treated. As Paul was assigning certain aspects of Djenaba's behaviour as pathological and unbearable, they reached the limit of what could be achieved in the interfamilial transculturality of the mixed couple.

Transgenerational level

Djenaba was very ill when she was a baby, and it is said that a healer saved her. The family sent her to France when she was 7 for unknown reasons. As she had already been labelled "strange", I can only wonder whether she was sent abroad for that matter. When she was an adult, the intrafamilial violence was in part due to her status of a possessed and every time she went back to Africa, she would be sent to healers. She named one of them "grandfather" and was pleased to meet him because he had foreseen that she would be cured on the day she would have a dream in which she would see a woman and then a man. He also predicted she would become a clairvoyant. Unfortunately, I have not gathered enough insights to understand what kind of transgenerational mandate was transmitted to Djenaba by her lineage group and what meaning was attributed to her possessed state.

Conclusion: Motherhood and transference

Thus, Djenaba was navigating on turbulent waters, slowly integrating heterogeneous aspects, and feeling stronger as she made her own synthesis during her psychotherapy. During the last session, she said: "I do not see my mother or my aunt in every woman anymore. Whenever it occurred, I wanted to hit them, destroy them. You gave me confidence when I was afraid one could realise I was inefficient. I can see now that there is a part of me who can be rather paranoid and pretends to be omniscient; it is not like the other part, the one that is connected to dreams, and wonders what messages they are sending. I want to leave you, I am no more a baby, I want to see if I can walk on my own".

In sum, Djenaba felt in the transference that she could be seen as a person, a talented artist, a woman, and a mother, and not as a lunatic or evil being. I assume it helped her reduce the splitting between two parts: the evil archaic omnipotent phallic mother-figure and a good enough sensible nurturing mother/woman who can get along with other women.

References

Bion, W. R. (1961). *Experiences in groups and other papers*. London, UK: Tavistock

Devereux, G. (1983). *Essais d'ethnopsychiatrie générale*. Gallimard.

Fiéloux, M., & Lombard, J. (2014). Chronique familiale quotidienne avec Personnages, le sujet et l'imaginaire social à Madagascar. *Etudes Océan Indien*, 51–52. https://doi.org/10.4000/oceanindien.1641

Fiéloux, M., & Lombard, J. (in press). A day-to-day family chronicles with "personages" in Madagascar. In E. Pocs & A. Zempléni (editors), *Spirit Possession: Multidisciplinary approach to a worldwide phenomenon* (pp. 207–223). CEU Press.

Fiéloux, M. (2021). Une expérience ethnologique de thérapie transculturelle. In Y. Mouchenik & M. R. Moro (eds.), *Pratiques transculturelles* (pp. 39–61). In Press.

Freud, S. (1923/1971). *Une névrose démoniaque au XVIIème siècle*. Gallimard.

Gammeltoft, T. M., & Buch Segal, L. (2016). Anthropology and psychoanalysis: Explorations at the edges of culture and consciousness. *ETHOS, 44*(4), pp. 399–410. doi: 10.1111/etho.12138

Graham, H. (1976). The social image of pregnancy: Pregnancy as spirit possession. *The Sociological Review, 24*(2), 291–308. https://doi.org/10.1111/j.1467-954X.1976.tb00114.x

Lambek, M. (1980). Spirits and Spouses: possession as a system of communication among the Malagasy speakers of Mayotte. *American Ethnologist, 7*(2), 318–331.

Taylor, G. (1978). Demoniacal possession and psychoanalytic theory. *British Journal of Medical Psychology, 51*(1), 53–60. doi: 10.1111/j.2044-8341.1978.tb02445.x. PMID: 623714.

Welsh, G. (2018). Que nous disent les fantômes à propos du Mal? Approche transculturelle. In E. Darchis & H. Bartoli (eds.), *Le Mal, traumas, hantise et mélancolie* (pp 65–77). L'Harmattan.

Wikström, O. (1980). A case of "possession". *Archive for the Psychology of Religion*, 14(1), 212–227. doi: https://doi.org/10.1163/157361280X00197

Chapter 7

Special challenges faced by children of immigrants

Salman Akhtar

Children of immigrants face many specific challenges. To be sure, such dilemmas exist side by side with the ubiquitous intrapsychic and interpersonal problems of childhood and adolescence. The hardships caused by being a child of immigrants and the ordinary phase-specific developmental difficulties rarely stand apart. More often than not, the two symbolize each other, defend against each other, or get condensed and accentuate the emotional intensity of whatever is going on at a given moment. It then becomes hard to tease them apart.

Nonetheless, the specific burdens upon children of immigrants do warrant individual consideration. These include (i) straddling between cultures, (ii) experiencing shame at having parents who are "different" from the parents of friends and peers, (iii) feeling taxed by the high expectations of their parents, (iv) having tight restrictions on their autonomy, (v) being forced into the role of their parents' teachers and "'translators'", (vi) managing the guilt induced into them by immigrant parents, (vii) parental prohibition on socialization, especially dating, drinking, and mingling with the opposite sex, (viii) facing discrimination and prejudice and, (ix) having to defend their being "American". A discussion of these burdens follows.

Straddling between cultures

Children of foreign-born parents are faced with biculturalism from the very beginning of their lives. Most are given names that reflect the parental language and culture and this can have a Janus-faced impact. On the one hand, it endears them to the parents and keeps them closer to the latter's inner world of memory and aspiration. On the other hand, having a name that is "different" (and sometimes, difficult to pronounce) can be a source of shame and a sense of alienation from peers. A similar early split is evident in the child's being bathed in the sonorous lullabies of the mother's mother tongue and being wrapped in the children's shows on television which not only use a different language but also might convey a discordant sense of autonomy and selfhood. What all this reveals is that the biculturalism faced

DOI: 10.4324/9781003174684-8

by children of immigrants begins at home and lies at the core of their beings. It is not something that crops up in adolescence or even with the start of formal schooling, though these epochs certainly underscore and intensify the bifurcated experience of such children.

Entry into school pushes the child into a wider segment of society. Differences between home culture and culture-at-large force themselves upon the child's awareness. The sense of being "different" from peers in terms of skin-colour, name, accent, and even the contents of one's lunch box can burden the child; discernment of such anxieties and empathic support from parents is crucial at this stage.

Often, however, the immigrant parents are too over-worked, tired, and struggling with their psychosocial turmoil to the extent that they cannot pay attention to their child's distress. Under such circumstances, the early experiences of biculturalism become traumatic and intensify ordinary developmental conflicts, setting up a vicious circle whereby problems at school and problems at home begin to compound each other.

Navigating between diverse cultures becomes even more of a challenge as the child enters adolescence. He or she is now faced with the task of bringing together the cultural idiom of his home, the standards of his peers, and the values upheld by his school; the three, not infrequently, are considerably divergent. "Immigrant children today may have their breakfast conversation in Farsi, listen to African-American rap with their peers on the way to school, and learn about the New Deal from their social studies teacher in mainstream English" (Suarez-Orozco & Suarez-Orozco, 2001, p. 92).

The impact of such discontinuities on identity consolidation during adolescence is a matter of great importance and will be taken up in a later section (see below). Here it would suffice to underscore that biculturalism suffuses the psychosocial existence of children of immigrants throughout their life span. Aptly titled *"Masks"*, the following poem by Neera Tewari, the teenage daughter of immigrant parents from India[1], captures the bitter-sweet dimensions of belonging to two worlds.

> The clock strikes six.
> We take off our masks of formality.
> Now we're in our own world.
> We bustle around, tend to
> different businesses.
> The familiar aromas of
> *dal, roti*, and *chaval*
> fill the air.
> We talk in our language
> And then the doorbell rings.
> Time freezes in its tracks.

We put our masks back on
And answer the door
in English.

Experiencing shame at having parents who are "different"

Children of immigrants often feel ashamed that their parents are different from those of their friends and peers. Their parents speak English with an accent, and, at times, do not know the language at all. They dress differently from others, especially at home, cook and eat foods that the child's peers are not familiar with. They seem ignorant of all sorts of cultural facts and practices ranging from baseball to senior prom, from "texting" to rolling admissions, and from the Civil War to Kurt Cobain. Children of Indian parents often complain that their parents talk too loudly in department stores and shopping malls. Children of immigrants from Muslim countries are embarrassed by their elders (mostly men) offering religious prayers in public. Other children feel a sense of shame at their parents' way of dressing and even at the jewelry they wear. Zeeshan Javid, a Philadelphia-based psychiatrist, whose parents came to the United States from Pakistan, captures such anxieties in poignant detail:

> "One of my least favorite memories from grade school was the parent-teacher conference, held quarterly throughout the academic year. Four times a year, teachers would meet each student's parents to hand them a report card and update them on their child's progress. These sessions would last fifteen minutes and were fairly rudimentary. Like many South Asian families, my parents emphasized education, and my report card reflected the hard work ethic they instilled in me. My teachers would hand my mother a card with all A's, and comment that I was both cooperative and disciplined. Given that I was a model student, it was never the content of the report that made me feel uncomfortable. It was the possibility that my classmates would identify my mother and her cultural identity that made me anxious.

> Being the only Asian-American in my class, I wanted to fit in with my peers. I knew that when my mother would appear in the school with her colorful *shalwar qameez*, the traditional Pakistani dress, it would attract attention. I would be embarrassed by her thick accent, which one of my teachers once called 'cute and exotic', after my mother had invited her to our house for some *chai*. (To my relief, the teacher politely declined.) All other students would take instant notice of the foreign woman visiting the school and would link her to me. They would ask me questions like, 'why does your mom have an earring in her nose?' I had no answer to offer them, other than to explain a *coca* was a common piece of jewelry

in my culture. They would also comment on my mother's long, braided hair, and tease me for days afterwards. While the taunts were easy to deflect, it was difficult not to feel out of place. I felt a great sense of unease as I defended my culture while trying to distance myself from it at the same time" (personal communication, June 3, 2010).

Shame over the culture of one's parents can contribute to the child's reluctance to accompany them on their visits "back home". In one study (Kibria, 2009), children of Bangladeshi immigrant parents were noted to be "far less cheerful" (p. 108) about their trips to Bangladesh than their parents. Humaira Siddiqi, a Northern Virginia-based Pakistani American psychiatrist also recalls such feelings from her childhood:

"I visited Pakistan once when I was twelve years old for the summer. The shock of meeting so many relatives and having the handicap of language and mottled cultural upbringing, was difficult for a child who had been raised in a nuclear family in America. I felt the relatives to be 'intrusive', something I now view differently. In fact, I now realize that they were simply being interested and loving. But, as an 'American' youngster, I found it annoying" (personal communication, May 8, 2009).

While acknowledging positive aspects of such visits (e.g., meeting cousins), bicultural youngsters often feel deep unease about returning to their parents' culture. Such resistance is compounded if the portrayal of the original country in history books and popular media is largely negative. D'Alisera (2009) talks of this in the context of children of immigrants from Sierra Leone.

"For the children, their parents' attempts to construct a homeland that challenges the popularly-constructed Western capital images of a continent often fall on deaf ears. As parents evoke positive images, children are bombarded outside the home and community with more powerful negative images that construct their lives in terms of disease, war, and corruption, endemic and spreading. If yesterday's images of Africa came from Sierra Leone and Rwanda, today's come primarily from Darfur and Congo. The conflict between the positive images of their parents' nostalgic longing and the negative image plays itself out in children's lives in profound ways. The children often experience a profound sense of displacement that is conveyed in the way in which they present themselves to the world. Often their presentation is a mixture of pride and shame" (p. 122).

Regardless of its source, (e.g., popular media, teasing by peers, displaced intrapsychic conflicts) shame over one's parents being different is common among children of immigrants. This makes the developmentally necessary identifications with them difficult and might result in premature disidentification with them; a gaping hole in the psychic structure is, thus, created. Adolescent identity formation becomes difficult. Even in full adulthood, children of immigrants – especially if they have been upwardly mobile – tend to experience shame over their less affluent and old-fashioned parents.

Feeling taxed by high parental expectations

Children of immigrants are often subject to exceedingly high expectations of achievement from their parents. Value of education is inculcated in them from early on and the pressure, subtle though it may be, never lets up. Some of this pressure comes from the idea that higher education is the key to success in America and some from the parents' own cultural backgrounds. Writing of Chinese families, for instance, Zhou (2009) states that parents who were raised in the Confucian tradition tend to be especially demanding of their children as far as educational achievement is concerned. And there are some unique features to such emphasis:

> "First and foremost, the children's success in school is tied to face-saving for the family. Parents constantly remind their children that achievement is a duty and an obligation to the family goal, and that if they fail, they will bring shame to the family. Not surprisingly, children are under tremendous pressure to succeed... The parents are keenly aware of their own limitations as immigrants and the structural constraints blocking their own mobility – for example, limited family wealth even among middle-income immigrants, lack of access to social networks connecting them to the mainstream economy and various social and political institutions, and entry barriers to certain occupations because of racial stereotyping and discrimination. Their own experience tells them that a good education in certain fields will allow their children to get good jobs in the future. These fields include science, math, engineering, medicine, and, to a lesser extent, business and law. Parents are more concerned with their children's academic course work, grades, and majors in these preferred fields than with a well-rounded learning experience and extra-curricular activities. They actively discourage their children from pursuing interests in history, literature, music, dance, sports, or any subject that they consider unlikely to lead to well-paid, stable jobs" (p. 30).

The tendency to pressure children into entering fields that assure a high income is hardly restricted to Chinese immigrant parents, though. Indians living in the United States are especially keen on "making" their children physicians and take great pride if the child can accomplish this in a lesser time by the way of a six-seven-year combined college-medical school program. The fact is that such accelerated progress often deprives the youth of socialization experiences essential for normal growth. The kid then fails to get into medicine and, even if he or she succeeds in entering into a medical school, feels overwhelmed, socially inexperienced, and below par with his or her peers. The 1996 cluster of suicides by six older adolescents and young adult offspring of Indian American parents in the affluent suburbs of Detroit (Mehta, 1998) speaks to this very point since all these tragedies were precipitated by academic failures[2].

Fortunately, such occurrences are rare. And the high expectations of parents are internalized to form not a punitive superego but an exalted ego-ideal. Knowledge that parents have undergone actual suffering in the course of migration can then add an object-related poignancy and concern to do well in life. Lorriann Tran, the physician daughter of Vietnamese refugee parents, gives voice to such sentiment.

"My parents left Vietnam in a small fishing boat in 1979, sailing towards the Philippines. It was a dangerous and unpredictable journey that resulted in either freedom and opportunity or torture and death, depending on who they ran into first. But now living comfortably in Harrisburg, PA, their biggest uncertainty is no longer their own lives, but rather the futures of their children. They fear that everything they survived would be in vain if no one carried on their courage, diligence, and faith. This has become my strongest motivating factor in almost everything I do. It is a blessing, but also a curse at the same time. I am extremely proud of my parents and the culture they have shared with me, but I also have a tremendous desire for that pride to be reciprocated, which has proved to be a lifelong task.

I feel like I owe them something for everything they've undergone to give me the opportunities I have now. But few things could amount to the physical torture my father endured in the re-education camps or the mental anguish my mother suffered as a 6-year-old girl after her father was killed in battle. I am left with this burden to find my own way in carrying on my parents' noble legacy. As a first generation American, I feel a tremendous amount of pressure to succeed, to take full advantage of my parents' sacrifices on their arduous journey here, and to make something of myself. The biggest question that remains is how to define that success. Do I measure it against my parents' expectations? Or by America's stereotypical standards of popularity and luxury? Or maybe even my own elusive happiness" (personal communication, January 22, 2009).

Being forced into the role of their parents' teachers

Children of immigrants often learn the ways of local culture in more rapid and deeper ways than do their parents. They speak the local language better and with less pronounced accents than their parents or with no accent at all. They know the local games, sports, movies, and movie stars. They read the local history as "their" history and regard the national heroes as theirs. They sing the national anthem without conflict and they are almost invariably more familiar with electronic gadgets and modern information technology[3].

Such "acculturation gap" (Prathikanti, 1997) between immigrant parents and their children has the potential of causing role-reversal between them. As a result, children can be placed in a position where they have to "translate" (literally or metaphorically) the ways of the culture-at-large for their parents. This may range from innocuous advice on how to operate a VCR or a computer to the more serious advocacy in medical and legal settings that are beyond the full comprehension of immigrant parents; clearly, this is more likely to occur if the older generation is less educated, less optimally acculturated, and not proficient in English. Lan Cao (1997), a Vietnamese-American writer, describes such role reversal in poignant terms:

"The dreadful truth was simply this: we were going through life in reverse, and I was the one who would help my mother through the hard scrutiny of ordinary suburban life. I would have to forgo the luxury of adolescent experiment and temper tantrums, so that I could scoop my mother out of harm's way and give her sanctuary. Now, when we stepped into the exterior world, I was the one who told my mother what was acceptable and unacceptable behavior. And even though I hesitated to take on the responsibility, I had no choice" (p. 35).

A matching, though less painful, account is provided by Christine Lin, the 20-year-old daughter of immigrants from Canton, China.

"My parents, who immigrated to the States in 1985, stay largely in the society of Chinese-speakers and have not really assimilated. My mother has learned enough English to have a meaningful conversation, but not to read the paper. She votes when it suits her fancy and is active in the community. My father never bothered to apply for citizenship.

I moved across the country after high school and built myself a life on the East Coast. But it is a difficult decision, being the only child and knowing that my parents will likely depend on others more, not less, as they age. Even now, they depend on me to read their letters, write their emails, call customer service on their behalf and serve as interpreter. Though my mother is clever enough to feel her way around a computer, her lack of English vocabulary means I have to Google things for her, and phone her with the results" (personal communication, July 9, 2009).

The consequences of such role-reversal are that the child comes to know the family's financial, medical, and legal secrets somewhat prematurely. This can burden his ego[4]. More importantly, seeing one's parents in a socially compromised position is deleterious to the development of healthy self-esteem in the child (Kohut, 1971; 1977). And, finally, the parental dependence makes the child's developmentally appropriate movement towards separation and autonomy conflict-ridden (hence, the reciprocal difficulty on the immigrant parents' part in letting go of the child).

Managing the guilt induced by the parents

Children of immigrants often carry an undue amount of unconscious guilt. Such guilt is usually of three types: (i) *separation guilt*: children of immigrants tend to feel guilt at their developmentally appropriate and culturally encouraged move towards independence and autonomy. This "separation guilt" (Modell, 1984) is compounded by their parents' dependence upon them as the youthful ambassadors of the new culture that the family is forced to deal with; (ii) *parentally-induced guilt*: children of immigrants often feel the burden of the guilt induced into them by their parents. Often, they grow up hearing their parents say, "We came to this country so that you can have a better life". Espiritu (2009) notes that "we did it for the children" is a common refrain among Phillipino immigrants. However, this might apply to many other groups including those from Indian, Pakistani, Mexican, African, and Central American countries. The refrain has a more nefarious twin: "we stay in this country because of you guys". This conveys to the child that the parents are suffering on a daily basis and are tolerating it only for the sake of their children. Working in unison, such declarations on the parents' part can saddle the immigrants' offspring with much guilt. In a different context, the genesis of such guilt is described by Asch (1976) to certain revelations by the mother to the child. Statements such as "your birth nearly killed me", or "I was so torn up inside" come across as accusations and can lead the child to life-long guilt, (iii) *deposited parental guilt*: children of immigrants can also become the "containers" (Bion, 1967) of the parental guilt which is deposited into them. Though idiosyncratic and highly personal variables can lie at their roots, such parental guilt is usually the result of their having left family members and friends behind in the country of origin, becoming more affluent than them, and, living in the new country with less than complete loyalty to it. Such guilt is greater if the move has been from less affluent and politically unstable countries (Akhtar, 1999). And, if the grief over leaving one's country and the associated guilt are not adequately "mentalized" (Fonagy & Target, 1998) and mitigated by the means of reparative measures, it can be passed on to the next generation, neatly gift-wrapped in cultural rationalizations. Kahn's (1997) observation is pertinent in this context.

> "The need of parents to insulate themselves and maintain their native culture or, alternatively, their desire to become part of the dominant society, significantly affects the children. Sometimes the children bear the brunt of their parents' fear of losing their bearing" (p. 278).

Having tight restrictions on their autonomy

Unlike American culture which encourages (and even pushes) children to become self-reliant, most "Third World" cultures hold their children tightly close to the family's orbit. Individuals who come to the United States from such backgrounds tend to allow less autonomy to their offspring. Children are expected to show parents and family elders (and, not infrequently, those outside the family as well) a degree of reverence that is far greater than expected in modal North American families. In the Chinese cultural context, this manifests as the "filial piety complex" (Gu, 2006) by which the customary oedipal themes are reconfigured by Confucian morality and the material takes the disguised form of parental demands for devotion and children's commitment to the resulting duties. According to Zhou (2009), the child's filial responsibility, in its ideal form, is

> "the debt of life owed to parents; a child is expected to suppress his or her own self-interests to satisfy parental needs, whether or not those needs are appropriate or rational. Related to filial piety is the notion of unconditional obedience, or submission to authority – to the parent, the elder, and the superior. The parent is the authority in the home, as is the teacher in the school. The parent, often the father, is not supposed to show too much affection to his children, to play with them, or treat them as equals. This stone-faced, authoritative image often inhibits children from questioning, much less challenging, their parents" (p. 29).

Scenarios of this sort are found to some extent in most Asian-immigrant families. Children are encouraged to achieve but not to individuate (e.g., "we will pay all your tuition if you go into medicine"). Not only are the future career paths chosen by the parents, where the child can go to study is also often dictated by them. This degree of restriction is more common among the less-educated, more ethnocentric, and needy parents. Many others are able to put the love of their child above their instinctive wish to hold on to him or her. Kabir Hamdani, a Los Angeles-based journalist, recalls the following interaction with his Pakistani father around the time he was choosing a college for himself.

> "When I was selecting colleges to apply to, my father decided to have a talk with me. He said that I could go anywhere within the geographical triangle that stretched between Boston, Chicago, and North Carolina (we lived in Philadelphia). I was taken aback and said, 'That sounds awfully like immigrant talk.' My father, who deeply loved me and had a sense of humor, responded with, 'You want immigrant talk? Okay, then, you stay in Philadelphia or, at best, you can go to New Jersey.' The twinkle in his eye, however, told me that he understood my point and would

not preclude my autonomous choice in this matter. The funniest thing is that I ended up staying in Philadelphia, but hey, it was at Penn, an Ivy League institution" (personal communication, January 11, 2009).

Not all immigrant parents are so flexible. And many are permissive with their sons but not with their daughters (Dasgupta and Warrier, 1996). Such gender differences in parental attitudes become more evident when it comes to mingling with members of the opposite sex, dating, and premarital sexuality.

Parental prohibition of socialization, especially dating, drinking, and mingling with the opposite sex

Though exceptions exist, most children of Asian immigrants feel their freedom to be curtailed in the realm of dating (Akhtar, 1999; Espiritu, 2009; Foner, 2009; Zhou, 2009). Their parents tell them that it is a distraction from studies, that it is not safe (hinting at rape and unwanted pregnancy), and that it is not done in "our culture". While overtly strict towards both their sons and daughters, many immigrant parents are covertly permissive towards the former; a "boys-will-be-boys" sort of logic prevails. A certain amount of vicarious gratification might also be extracted by both fathers and mothers from the son's dalliances with girls. The attitude is often sharply different when it comes to the daughter.

An adolescent girl or young woman is made to feel "non-ethnic", "non-traditional", and not caring about family and its ancestral traditions, if she is "found" dating. Such accusatory labeling causes immense pain to the growing child and/or adolescent. The stricter the parental prohibition, the greater the likelihood of it leading to problematic outcomes. Two scenarios are common: (i) *psychosocial infantilism,* whereby sexuality becomes too conflict-laden, body is not fully known and "owned" (Laufer, 1968), masturbation is suppressed or highly guilt-laden, and the tyranny of repression can extend to include intellectual functions, and (ii) *situational dishonesty,* whereby the child begins to date behind the parents' backs, lies about her whereabouts, loses respect for the parents while simultaneously feeling guilty about such internal attack against them. Often the secret life comes unhinged in an out of control and traumatic manner. The parents then exclaim, "Who are you? You are not our daughter! We had raised a good girl and you have turned out to be a whore! We don't even know who you are!" To such melodramatic declarations, the girl responds, "Dad, Mom, this is the first time you are really seeing me! I have not become somebody else today. You had driven me to lie, to have a secret life, and to split myself into two parts. Today, I have become one!" If matters do not get out of hand, such crises possess the potential of spurring psychic growth on the part of all concerned – with or without formal psychotherapeutic interventions.

Another source of difficulty involves the growing children's exposure to drugs and alcohol. Communication between parents and children is relatively easy and clear-cut in reference to drugs. Parents have little difficulty telling their children – usually around the time they are entering high school – to avoid using drugs and children, in turn, readily assure their parents that they would do what they are told. Leaving an occasional experimentation with "softer" drugs (e.g., marijuana) aside, most children abide by the parental guidance, societal condemnation of drug use, and their own common sense.

Alcohol is a different ballgame, though. It is everywhere, readily available, and an integral part of Western culture. For immigrant parents who come from religious backgrounds (e.g., Islam) that strictly prohibit drinking alcohol, what to say to their teenagers is obvious; indeed, their children have most likely heard the ban on alcohol a hundred times before reaching their teenage years. The fact that most Muslim parents do not drink alcohol and do not keep any at home renders the parents' command justified and, once internalized, relatively ego-syntonic. This, however, does not rule out that peer pressure at school can tax the teenagers' resolve and, at times, lead to some guilt-ridden or counterphobic imbibing of alcoholic drinks (Mann, 2008). Such transient rebellion subsides with time, especially if the parent-child relationship has essentially been loving. If that has not been the case, indulgence in alcohol might become an intoxicating (pun intended) token of freedom and independence from parental strictures.

For non-Muslim immigrant parents, especially those who drink themselves (and for those Muslim parents who drink), the message to be conveyed to children depends less upon the words used and more upon the parental conduct itself. If the parents drink responsibly and occasionally, then the child follows the example. If the parents drink excessively, their guidance and prohibition reek of hypocrisy. All in all, raising the bar too high (pun unintended) when it comes to advising children to drink responsibly and wait until legal age is almost never helpful. It creates unrealistic expectations and has the potential of mobilizing much anxiety and guilt in the child.

Facing discrimination and prejudice

While those from affluent and professional families might manage to remain unscathed, most children of immigrants sense that their American counterparts and Americans, in general, have somewhat negative perceptions of them. When Suarez-Orozco and Suarez-Orozco (2001) asked a group of Chinese, Dominican, Central America, Haitian, and Mexican children to complete the sentence, "Most Americans think that we (people from my country) are —", they got the following results:

"Most Americans think that we are stupid" (ten-year old Haitian girl).

Most Americans think that we can't do the same things as them in school or at work (ten-year old Mexican girl).

> Most Americans think that we are garbage (fourteen-year-old Dominican boy).
>
> Most Americans think that we are members of gangs (nine-year-old Central American girl).
>
> Most Americans think that we are thieves (thirteen-year-old Haitian girl).
>
> Most Americans think that we are lazy, gangsters, drug-addicts that only come to take their jobs away (fourteen-year-old Mexican boy).
>
> Most Americans think that we are bad like all Latinos (twelve-year old Central American boy).
>
> Most Americans think that we don't exist (twelve-year old Mexican boy)" (pp. 96–97).

All in all, 65 percent of the study participants gave a negative response to this sentence completion item. This goes to show that the feeling of being looked down upon – regardless of it being factually true or untrue – is rampant among the children of immigrants. A caveat needs to be added here, though. The sample in this study did not include children of European immigrants whose fair skin and Anglo-Saxon names might render them more "acceptable" to Americans. The same might be true of immigrant children from highly affluent families. The schools they attend tend to have children and teachers from demographically better-informed strata of society; a greater tendency towards "political correctness" might also prevail in such circumstances. The presence of physical beauty and an extraordinary talent (e.g., playing a musical instrument, painting, gymnastics) can also protect the child from being prejudicially treated.

Conversely, there exist variables that increase the chances that a child of immigrant parents would be treated with prejudice by his or her peers. Overt neurotic habits (e.g., tics, excessive shyness), anatomical and physiognomic divergences from the modal group (e.g., short stature, dark skin, prominent epicanthic folds), and a socioeconomic status that is visibly different from peers can all become "justifications" for prejudicial attitudes on others' part. Since the September 11, 2001, attack on the Twin Towers in New York, being Arab and/or Muslim (often conflated with each other, ignoring the fact that not all Arabs are Muslims and not all Muslims are Arabs) can also expose one to others' mistrust, avoidance, and dislike. Given this, it can become very difficult for high school-aged children of Arab and/or Muslim immigrants to voice their true feelings about world affairs including the Israeli-Palestinian conflict. Sarah Badin, a freshman at an Ivy League university, however, stands out as a shining exception to this. She recalls her experience of having written a paper on this topic that brought out the Middle Eastern perspective that is less known to the American public.

"The assignment was to research and write a paper on a controversial issue. My classmates wrote from perspectives that were largely accepted in our school, like arguing for the importance of environmental awareness, or in favor of animal rights, but I wrote about a topic I knew would not be well-received. In my years of following current events, I had always noticed a bias against Middle-Easterners in the media, and as the daughter of Syrian immigrants who had been exposed to the Palestinian point of view, I was able to see just how big the communication gap was and I wanted to make my peers aware of it too.

The plan was to point out common prejudices in Americans and challenge them with facts that contradicted accepted beliefs. My research progressed smoothly until people in the student body, which is mostly racially homogeneous and extremely unsympathetic to the Palestinian point of view, began to show their disapproval for the types of questions I was raising by coming up to me and starting one-on-one debates. These approaches and their resulting discussions happened more frequently and involved increasingly more people until I found myself in a heated debate against an entire class. I knew I probably would not change anyone's mind, but I persisted in communicating what I believed was true about the portrayal of Middle-Easterners in the American media because I was passionate about the topic, and about getting others to open their minds and acknowledge the presence of another side to the issue.

Everyone is raised with fundamental beliefs that become their core. When people attack that core, it becomes extremely difficult to stay composed and defend yourself and your beliefs while staying collected and poised. In this moment, in this classroom, my core was being attacked. As I sat there thinking how to respond to the arguments of others, which on more than one occasion contained personal criticisms and direct accusations, I could feel my face getting hot and vulnerability setting in. For an instant I wished I could somehow just end the discussion and get out of the room as quickly as possible. I was almost surprised when my words broke through my tightening throat, but as I rebutted I was scared of how my argument would be received and nervously anticipated the next barrage of comments. It is true my parents gave me the right genes so I could maintain a calm appearance, but more importantly, they instilled in me a strong sense of self that gave me the confidence to collect myself and form my next argument and the drive to continue stating what I believed despite the great amount of opposition" (personal communication, December 18, 2009).

Not all encounters with prejudice are as confrontational and emotionally charged, however. Many times, subtle and "unmentalized xenophobia" (Akhtar, 2007) seeps into seemingly ordinary workplace conversations. To be sure, this too is hurtful although given some resilience and a sense of humor, the situation can be defused. Deeana Nobleza, a Filipino-American physician, recounts one such experience.

> "After making my morning rounds on the inpatient unit of a college health center, I was sitting at the nursing station writing up my notes. A physician colleague (and close friend) of mine came into the room gesturing with her arms in a frustrated manner. She began to tell the head nurse about a student she had just seen who was complaining of vague abdominal discomfort and whom she suspected was seeking a medical excuse in order to get out of an exam. She suddenly stopped herself in mid-sentence, looked at me and said, 'I was just about to say something'. Her face had a smile with a hint of embarrassment, and as she looked at me, she continued uncensored – 'I was about to say…Asians are so wimpy'. In my shock, I responded 'OH! So, that's what you really think of me?!' The three of us shared a hearty laugh, although I can't be sure we were all laughing for the same reason" (personal communication, July 10, 2010).

Having to defend their being "American"

The question "where are you from?" (or its variant, "where were you born?" is frequently asked of the children of immigrants. While children of European immigrants, especially those with education, money, and English proficiency tend to escape such interrogation, most others have to struggle with the feelings such a question stirs up. Factually, it is easy to answer. It is the implication that somehow one is not "really" American, or one can't be American or one is not American enough which hurts. Regrettably, the vulnerability to such narcissistic injury often persists over the entire life span. As adults, American-born children of immigrants are often asked (e.g., during a job interview) where are they from. Gloria Wise (2005) a Filipino-American journalist, has provided a touching account of her tackling this question and of her conviction that where she is from is far less important than who she is and what she wants to be in the future.

Stereotypes and caricatured images popularized by media also come into play and put the individual's status as an "American" into question. To complicate matters, the assumption that someone with an unfamiliar name, dark skin, and/or "oriental" facial features cannot be *really* American gets coalesced with ignorance of differences among various immigrant groups themselves.

> "Thus, a fourth-generation Japanese American who proudly serves in the U.S. military is outraged when asked by people in the street – while in uniform – whether he is in the 'Chinese Army.' The message he hears

is that he 'can't be a real American'. The Latina student in the Advanced Placement Calculus class is routinely told by her classmates that she 'must be' Asian – the stereotype of the successful minority student. The dark-skinned Dominican is told that he cannot be Latino – he 'must be' black" (Suarez-Orozco & Suarez-Orozco, 2001, p. 65).

Some caveats

This survey of the challenges faced by children of immigrants needs to be "softened" by a reminder that such children also enjoy some benefits that are often not available to their native-born peers. Divorce rates are lower in immigrants than the mainstream population of the United States (Brooks, 2006; Das Gupta and Warrier, 1996) and far fewer children of immigrants are brought up in single-parent households. Most grow up in an intact family with much closeness among siblings and extended family members. The glow of such warmth comes through in the following account by Leah Doghramji, the 17-year-old daughter of an Armenian-American colleague of mine.

"My Bebaba and Memama (my grandparents) are family-oriented and use every excuse they can to gather the family to their house: Thanksgiving, Christmas, anniversaries, Easter, and any other holiday. Regardless of the holiday, all family get-togethers seem to be similar. My family usually arrives second or last of the three families. My uncles are watching the most current sports team of Pennsylvania and drinking beer. My cousin Kristen sits cross-legged on the couch talking with her mom. My cousin Nicky follows around my brother and my three other boy cousins. My Memama shuffles around the kitchen preparing the abundance of rice pilaf, cheese berug, and other Armenian/Turkish foods. My cousin Paul mimics my Bebaba's accent and mannerisms. My uncles yell angrily or cry out joyfully at whatever is happening in the game. My uncle Jimmy usually ends up on the piano playing 1940's show tunes. This is the true of almost all our family get-togethers.

Like many kids from foreign cultures, I have about five hundred relatives I have no idea about. My mom will tell me about someone and say how she or he is my cousin or second cousin or great uncle or aunt. I'm constantly told that I've met them before, and they always ask me if I remember them, even though I was three when I met them. Looming in the distance is a family reunion of all the Armenian clan members, which I am sure will be filled with many Armenian men and women who will claim they've met me before, yet I will not remember any of them.

At home, my family is no different than any other family. We do things that normal families do, such as eating dinner, watching movies talking, etc. Perhaps the only difference is my dad's love for Armenian music and the occasional outburst of Armenian yelled at my mom in jest, but other than that our household is the same as the one next door.

Any family that is Greek or Russian or Italian will have similar aspects to their families. Of course, there are differences like the frequency of family get-togethers and the overload of far away family members. My friends who aren't of foreign origins have minimal cousins and almost never see their relatives. Family is the most important thing in foreign cultures, and it really shows in my family" (personal communication, June 27, 2010).

Familial cohesion and warmth of this sort enrich the formative years of children of immigrants. It enlarges the child's object-relational world, anchors his or her identity in the historical legacy of the family as revealed by different relatives, and strengthens the child's ego. Moreover, immigrant parents are often very hard-working and serve as good models for their children. They also readily offer financial support and are more than willing to bail their children out in times of financial need. They strongly wish to see their children succeed and accommodate many sacrifices to this end. While actuarial data is not available, anecdotal evidence suggests that children of immigrant parents end up with less student loans to pay at the end of their academic road. All this has beneficial effects on their psychosocial lives.

The bicultural idiom that pervades the developmental years of children of immigrants can also have a salutary impact upon their personality functioning.[5] A capacity to see issues from multiple perspectives, greater empathy with other immigrant and minority peers, and a broader, international viewpoint are among the positive results of being raised in a bicultural environment. Even the parental strictures and expectations that appeared annoying during children and adolescence can lead to greater discipline and self-care once adulthood begins. There is, for instance, some evidence that children of Asian-Americans perceive themselves as more prepared and likely to have greater success than their White counterparts (Wong et al., 1998). Compared with other ethnic groups, they are also less likely to have unprotected sex (So et al, 2005). All in all, therefore, it seems that both extra psychosocial burdens *and* extra protective factors characterize the developmental background of children of immigrants. Matters are not one way or the other.

Notes

1   Neera is a now an adult and practices anesthesiology in Stony Brook, NY.
2   In my 31 years of service at Jefferson Medical College in Philadelphia, PA, only four students have committed suicide. To the best of my recollection, three (if not all four) of them were enrolled in accelerated studies programs.
3   They are not only better in the actual handling of electronic gadgets, but also more proficient in the language that has recently emerged in this context. For a comprehensive review of the cell phone-internet lexicon and its impact upon the communicative functions of language, see Akhtar and Nayar (2010).

4 A "non-cultural" parallel to this is found in Sylvan Keiser's (1969) delineation of neurogenesis in a bright child. According to Keiser, such a child can see parental limitations before he's able to emotionally handle them. The result is traumatic and often accompanied by the development of neurotic symptoms.

5 Most impressive are the results of a recent study involving 12,580 kindergarten-aged children (11,060 White and 1,520 local-born children of Asian immigrants) who were followed up till they entered the fifth grade. Of the first group, 210 were bilingual and of the second group, 910 were bilingual. At the five-year follow-up, it became clear that the bilingual children were doing emotionally and behaviorally better than those who spoke one language. Moreover, the bilingual children of Asian immigrants performed at a higher level than the bilingual White children.

References

Akhtar, S. (1999). *Immigration and identity: Turmoil, treatment, and transformation.* Jason Aronson.

Akhtar, S. (2007). From unmentalized xenophobia to messianic sadism: Some reflections on the phenomenology of prejudice. In H. Parens, A. Mahfouz, S. W. Twemlow, & D. E. Scharff (eds.), *The future of prejudice: Psychoanalysis and the prevention of prejudice* (p. 7–19). Jason Aronson.

Akhtar, S., & Nayar, K. I. (2010). The cell phone-internet lexicon: Overview and implications. In S. Akhtar & M. D. Lanham (eds), *The electrified mind: Development, psychopathology, and treatment in the era of cell phones and internet* (p.1–21). Jason Aronson.

Asch, S. (1976). Varieties of negative therapeutic reaction and problems of technique. *Journal of the American Psychoanalytic Association* 24, 383–407.

Bion, W. R. (1967). *Second thoughts.* Heinemann.

Brooks, D. (2006). Immigrants to be proud of. *The New York Times*, 03/30/2006.

Cao, L. (1997). *Monkey bridge.* Penguin Books.

D'Alisera, J. (2009). Images of a wounded homeland: Sierra Leonian children and the new heart of darkness. In N. Foner (ed.), *Across generations: Immigrant families in america* (pp. 114–134). New York University Press.

Dasgupta, S. D., & Warrier, S. (1996). In the footsteps of "Arundhati": Asian Indian women's experience of domestic violence in the United States. *Violence Against Women*, *2*, 23–259.

Espiritu, Y. L. (2009). Emotions, sex, and money: the lives of Filipino children of immigrants. In N. Foner (ed.), *Across generations: Immigrant families in America* (pp. 47–71). New York University Press.

Fonagy, P., & Target, M. (1998). Mentalization and the changing aims of child psychoanalysis Psychoanalytic dialogues. *The international Journal of Relational Perspectives*, *8*(1), pp. 87–114.

Foner, N. (2009). ed. *Across generations: Immigrant families in America.* New York, NY: New York University Press.

Gu, M. D. (2006). The filial piety complex: Variations on the Oedipus theme in Chinese literature and culture. *Psychoanalytic Quarterly*, *75*, 163–195.

Kahn, C. (1997). Four women: Immigrants in cross-cultural marriages. In P.H. Elovitz & C. Kahn (eds), *Immigrant experiences: Personal narrative and psychological analysis* (pp. 199–220). Associated University Presses.

Keiser, S. (1969). Superior intelligence: Its contribution to neurosogenesis. *Journal of the American Psychoanalytic Association, 17*, 452–473.

Kibria, N. (2009). "Marry into a good family": Transnational reproduction and intergenerational relations in Bangladeshi American families. In N. Foner (ed.), *Across generations: Immigrant families in America* (pp. 98–113). New York University Press.

Kohut, H. (1971). *Analysis of the self*. International Universities Press.

Laufer, M. (1968). The body image, the function of masturbation and adolescence: Problem of the ownership of the body. *Psychoanalytic Study of the Child, 23*, 114–137.

Mann, M. (2008). Religious identity formation in the children of immigrant Muslim parents. In S. Akhtar (ed.), *The Crescent and the couch: Crosscurrents between Islam and psychoanalysis* (pp. 181–195). Jason Aronson.

Mehta, P. (1998). The emergence, conflicts, and integration of the bicultural self: psychoanalysis of an adolescent daughter of South-Asian immigrant parents. In S. Akhtar & S. Kramer (eds.), *The colors of childhood: Separation-individuation across cultural, racial, and ethnic differences* (pp. 129–168). Jason Aronson.

Modell, A. (1984). *Psychoanalysis in a new context*. International Universities Press.

Prathikanti, S. (1997). East Indian American families. In E. Lee (ed.), *Working with Asian Americans: A guide for clinicians* (pp.79–100). Guilford.

So, D.W., Wong, F.Y., and DeLeon, J.N. (2005). Sex, HIV risk, and substance abuse among Asian Americans. *Aids Education and Research 17*, 457–468.

Suarez-Orozco, C., & Suarez-Orozco, M. (2001). *Children of immigration*. Harvard University Press.

Wise, G. (2005, February 11). *Where are you from? Is not the right question*. Philadelphia Inquirer, pp. B–2C.

Wong, P., Lai, C. F., Nagasawa, R., & Lin, T. (1998). Asian Americans as a model minority: self-perceptions and perceptions by other racial groups. *Sociological Perspectives, 41*, 95–118.

Zhou, M. (2009). Conflict, coping, and reconciliation: intergenerational relations in Chinese immigrant families. In N. Foner (ed.), *Across generations: Immigrant families in America* (pp. 21–46). New York University Press.

Chapter 8

Holding and handling a child from a different cultural cradle

Parenting in a context of international adoption

Mayssa' El Husseini, Aurélie Harf,
Sara Skandrani, and Marie Rose Moro

Being parents in a transcultural context, with new and different under-standings to being a parent, is what is referred to as Parenthood in migra-tion. There are not many references tackling the subject of being a parent to a child with different "cultural origins" in international adoption cases. Worth mentioning at this point that the notion of "cultural origins" needs to be questioned in early adoption cases.

Parental representation of the adopted child's cultural identity and the child's cultural identity itself was the center of observation through clinical work and research with families in the International Adoption consulta-tion at the Adolescent's department at Cochin Hospital[1]. The international adoption consultation team constituted of different professionals (pae-dopsychiatrists, psychologists, nurses) conducts a research and a clinical activity. It deals with early and late adoption cases. The consultation pro-vides different settings according to various needs: parents in the procedure of adoption, wondering how to welcome the adopted child; families in the first steps of the adopting process who need guidance; and families experi-encing difficulties.

The setting is based on a theoretical combination of psychoanalysis, sys-temic therapy, and transcultural theories. Different questions arise in late adoption cases when little is known about the familial and cultural origins of a child such as in the adoption of Daniel: for his adopting parents, the question of cultural identity was fraught with conscious and unconscious burdens.

Clinical vignette

Daniel is adopted by a French Caucasian couple, Mr and Mrs Y, who went to a sub-Saharan country in a war zone, to fetch Daniel, with a registered association which has prepared them for adoption. They are both in their fifties, Daniel is 6 when they meet him in an orphanage. Daniel was found in the streets; his history is unknown. The parents have decided not to change his first name. Three months after Daniel's arrival in France, his father calls

DOI: 10.4324/9781003174684-9

the consultation: he is upset because of Daniel having fits of violence, and embarrassing gestures on the parents' genitals. Daniel is unable to sleep on his own so much so that the parents have taken turns to sleep with him. They have noticed scars on Daniel's body and have been puzzled by his eating paper and pencils. Daniel is doing rather well at school, especially in gym, learning French, forgetting his native tongue.

An appointment is scheduled with a group of therapists. The group is made up of three therapists of different backgrounds: nurse, psychologist, psychopaediatrician. The same group will have time for the parents and the child together, for the parents on their own, and later, Daniel will have individual sessions.

At first, Daniel is silent and watchful while his parents express their love and their concerns. Overall, everything is fine, but Daniel has crises of violence: he hits them and bites them. They think that Daniel might have been ill-treated because of the scars they have noticed on his body. Daniel only complains of pain in the knees, elbows, ears, and back.

The group takes time to let them unload their pains, but the therapists feel that time is frozen in a fixed violent present tense, they feel unable to think.

Slowly, the violence is contained by the group of therapists who can deal with ambivalent feelings as they debrief and go on elaborating in supervision sessions. As the therapists acknowledge their ambivalence, the parents' ambivalence comes to light. For some of the therapists, the parents picture the colonialist stance, and they frown at statements made by the parents such as: "this is how it is in Africa". But they have in mind that to co-construct a narrative of filiation and a narrative of adoption takes time. Gradually, Daniel can put words on his violence: right after a crisis, he has a revival of his leg being stabbed by a man with a knife as he was sleeping. He also expresses concerns about the children left in the orphanage and why can't he have the same skin colour as his parents'?

The time parents and child were living a state of fusion is followed by a time when Daniel can sleep on his own. It occurs in a parallel to what is happening within the setting: parents sometimes come on their own without Daniel: they have their own space with the therapists. Thus, they can unfold their own family histories: Mrs Y is depressed, sometimes delusional, her relationship with her own mother is distant. Mr Y's brother killed himself 3 months after the couple Y married. The couple is infertile. Mr Y became impotent after his brother's violent death. Thus, violent death and sexuality are connected and reverberate with the supposedly traumatic aspects of Daniel's early childhood. Through providing a maternal attuning the therapists opened a space where many elements could be disentangled: the father's impotence, the family trauma, Daniel's unknown history and the war in his country, the transition to France, the otherness, and the explosive encounter with a troubled family and their expectations. Based on this intensive work, later the parents will be able to have a representation of the child's cultural identity. Currently, and after 4 years of therapy, Daniel is journeying into adolescence relatively peacefully, with episodic turbulences specific to the adolescence process. The parents have an adjusted reflective function and feel more confident about their parenting and more secure with their child.

There is something special about the internationally adopted children who come from a different country and culture, this is due to the fact that they have migrated alone. When looking at this category, one should consider the place of birth, place of early interactions, receiving country, and where they live. The "transracial adoption paradox", the term coined by Lee, to describe the status of adopted children who differ, in their appearance, from their parents; how they grow up in a certain race and be treated like an honorary member of this race, but be looked at, by the rest of the society, as belonging to another race (Lee, 2003). Also, over the past decade, the number of children adopted at an older age has drastically increased. Their pre-adoptive past can reveal traumatic experiences following abandonment, violence, or deprivation of the biological family or orphanage. The account of this previous life experience, disrupted by the traumatic effect, had an impact on the encounter between the child and their adoptive parents and the parental representations of their child.

Research field: First encounters in international adoption

This chapter discusses, through the results of the research carried out by the authors, the experience of adoptive parents at the moment of the first parent-child encounters in international adoptions. It collaborates in the establishment of early prevention methods by working with adoptive families on family dynamics. The subject of the adopted children's cultural belongings can become a point of hardship during the creation of their identity and within the parent-child connection (Hjern et al., 2002; Juffer & Van Ijzendoorn, 2005; Soulé & Lévy-Soussan, 2002).

Eventually, as situations arise, adoptive families will question the multiple cultures to which their children belong. The situations can range from an experience of racism, discrimination, questions resulting from a voyage to the child's country of birth, a claim of belonging to the country of birth in adolescence. Parental questions about the choice of a first name and whether it should be French for instance or whether they should keep the name given at birth also play a role in questioning the multiplicity of cultures.

The influence of parental attitudes on identity development in adopted children, particularly in multicultural families, was the subject of numerous studies. Many argue that the children's level of bicultural competence depends on how much importance do parents place on bicultural socialization: to what extent do they want their child to participate in cultural events of his or her birth country, to learn its history and language? Is the parents' social network inclusive of people coming from the same country, or belonging to the same ethnic group as the child, potentially serving as role models? Do parents take active steps to link the child with the community from the birth country, to nurture identification with the ethnic group, and to claim the child's cultural heritage? (Andujo, 1988; Basow et al., 2008; Carstens & Juliá, 2000; DeBerry et al., 1996; Hollingsworth, 1998; Lee et al., 2006; Lee & Quintana, 2005; Rushton & Minnis, 1997; Thomas & Tessler, 2007; Vonk, 2001; Yoon, 2004).

There is abundant English-language literature tackling the subject of adoption and the question of the cultural identity of adopted children, mostly advocating for parents maintaining links with the child's birth culture. Qualitative methods were applied to observe the adoptive parents' views regarding their child's cultural belonging. While some paid particular attention to parents' feelings (Scherman & Harre, 2010) and showcased inconsistencies these families faced in their identity-work (Friedlander et al., 2000; Harrigan, 2009; Tessler et al., 1999), others have zoomed on communication within adoptive families, as side of family interactions (Docan-Morgan, 2010; Suter, 2008; Wrobel et al., 2003). Qualitative studies are acclaimed when the aim is to unravel the common and unique experiences of individuals who have first-hand knowledge of the phenomenon of interest (Malterud, 2001; Whitley & Crawford, 2005).

There is not much information about parental representation of the cultural belonging of adopted children in the French scene, and there is a big gap in the literature between Europe and the United States, therefore we decided to conduct this research based on a qualitative approach. Authors take the discourse of adoptive parents and their positionality in relation to the appropriation of the children's cultural identity as origination of the analysis. Our objective is, therefore, to explore qualitatively adoptive parents' representations of their child's cultural belonging in a French context. This study explores how parents tell of their child's cultural identity. Our qualitative methodology gives us access to arguments parents use to explain their beliefs: the reasons why they consider it important to foster links with the child's country of birth and its culture, or conversely, why they see that it is not in the child's advantage. It also allows us to observe the impact of the traumatic experience of pre-adoption on the parents' dynamics and the representations of their child.

Method

Participants

People chosen to participate should have at least one adopted child from another country, other than France. 51 French adoptive parents volunteered to take part of the study among which 13 fathers and 38 mothers. If the children were adopted by couples, both parents were asked to join the research.

Interviews were conducted separately for each parent. These parents were 12 couples in which both parents (father and mother) participated, so 24 parents. The remaining parents were 26 mothers among which 16 adopted as single mothers, while 10 adopted with their husbands (who did not participate in the study). The last parent was 1 father who is married but whose wife did not participate.

We interviewed 11 parents who had 2 internationally adopted children twice (one interview for each child), and we interviewed 2 parents who had 3 internationally adopted children 3 times, therefore a total of 66 interviews, which took place between May 2011 and January 2013.

Parents' ages at the time of their children's adoptions fluctuated from 28 to 49 years (average = 41) and their ages at the time of the interview ranged from 31 to 60 years (average = 47). They lived in urban areas of France and 86% were college-educated professionals.

Of the 48 internationally adopted children, 27 were girls and 21 were boys. At the time of adoption, their ages fluctuated from 2 weeks to 7 years (average = 2.1). Children who were younger than 1 year old summed to 18 at the time of their adoption, 13 were 1 or 2 years old, and 17 were 3 years or older.

At the time of the interview, the children's ages ranged from 15 months to 17 years (average age = 8.6). The time between the adoption and the interview ranged from 1 year to 16 years (average = 6.6). Of the 66 interviews, 15 children were adopted within 2 years of the interview, 11 children were adopted 2 to 5 years before the interview, and 40 children adopted more than 5 years earlier. We had 14 parents who had both adopted and biological children. The number of children per family ranged from 1 to 4, and the number of adopted children from 1 to 3.

The sample was varied in terms of age, life stage (families with young children as well as those with adolescents), and family structure (single parents and married couples). Sampling in qualitative research involves purposive sampling of individuals likely to provide the most informative description of the studied phenomenon (Mays, 2000). Our sampling technique was indeed purposive, as we selected subjects typical of the population of interest (Patton, 2002). Participants were recruited from the general population through adoption associations and connections with adoptive parents.

Data collection procedure

The data were collected via semi-structured interviews. The authors reviewed the literature on international adoption to develop a guide for these interviews with parents. The main topics covered included the stages in the adoption process, the choice of country, the trip to the child's country of origin, what is known of the child's history before the adoption, links to the child's country of birth and its culture, and any racism or discrimination of which the child may have been the victim.

Questions were designed to elicit specific information while remaining flexible so that the interviewees can tell their stories. The open-ended questions allowed participants to interpret the meaning of the question and respond based on their personal feelings. Interviewers used prompts and probes as needed to enrich the discussion. We chose to gather data through semi-structured interviews because this method combines an approximate standardization of questions with the possibility for subjects and interviewers to broaden their answers when appropriate. The interview process produced data that was both deep, broad, and focused on the research question: the connections adoptive parents have with their child's country of birth and culture and parents' representations of the cultural identity of their child.

The parents chose the site for the interview: the researcher's office or their own home. The participants and what they had to say determined the length of the interviews, which lasted on average one hour. Each interview was recorded for later transcription, with the permission of the participants, and transcribed verbatim in French. Two different researchers conducted these interviews separately. Each has been trained in adoption and qualitative research methods (AH, SS).

Data analysis

A phenomenological research plan was used to understand parents' representations of their children's cultural identity. Phenomenology is a nonprescriptive approach to research which allows the essence of experience to emerge, while anchoring the analysis of the data in the unique representations of participants (*ibid.*). The aim is to explore personal experience and the subjective perception of an object or event. Our research approach is phenomenological in that it involves a detailed examination of the personal perceptions and lived experiences of the participants.

To analyze the data from our interviews, we employed the Interpretative Phenomenological Analysis (IPA) method (Eatough & Smith, 2008; Smith & Osborn, 2008) a prominent qualitative methodology used to research profoundly how individuals perceive the particular situations they face and how they give meaning to their personal and social world. Following the IPA, we conducted a thorough qualitative analysis. It began with a detailed case-by-case study of each interview transcript, using an iterative inductive process. We started with several careful and detailed reads of each interview to provide a holistic perspective, noting points of interest and significance. Through a step-by-step analysis, we proceeded to describe the analytic themes and their interconnections, while making sure to keep a link with the original account. IPA, therefore, involves navigating between different levels of interpretation (Eatough & Smith, *op. cit.*). The last step is to produce a coherent ordered table of themes (Smith & Osborn, *op. cit.*). The data analysis was an inductive procedure as it was performed secondarily. The sample size was determined by data saturation, that is, the point at which in-depth interviews analysis no longer leads to the emergence of new themes.

Due to the chosen qualitative methods (theoretical sampling and no statistics), we had no predetermined ideas of the number of parents to incorporate. The data collection and analysis took place concurrently, and inclusions continued as long as the analysis of the material continued to come up with new information beneficial for the investigation of the phenomenon. In this type of study, sampling, continued data collection and the development of themes and sub-themes are interrelated. When data analysis becomes repetitive and no longer brings new insights, it is time to conclude that we reached data saturation and we can stop including new topics. As with the inductive procedure, data collection and analysis of the results continued simultaneously until the sample was saturated. Analysis influences data collection by driving us to redefine the research question, to find counterexamples and seek new avenues (Mays & Pope, 1995).

Throughout, we used computer software to aid our analysis: QSR NVivo9 for data management, extracting topics transcripts, and recording them thematically.

Validity

We compared the coding of the researchers to ensure the validity of our qualitative research. Two trained researchers independently coded and interpreted all data from the parent interviews. The two coders discussed the emerging codes in repeated meetings with other members of the research team who had read the transcripts. These conversations helped identify potential themes in the data that might not yet have been captured by the codes and allowed us to clarify or modify the coding to increase the consistency and coherence of the analysis by ensuring that the themes we identified accurately reflected the data and that the analysis was not limited to one perspective. Multiple discussions allowed us to eliminate systematic differences due to variations in interpretation. Validity has also enhanced our care to clearly distinguish between what respondents said and how we interpreted it or took account of it (Smith & Osborn, *op. cit.*).

Member-checking (also known as informant feedback or respondent validation) has been practiced because it is a vital way for interpretive researchers to verify the reliability of their research (Baxter & Babbie, 2004). After the qualitative analysis of the parents' data was completed, a summary of the thematic findings was sent to the parents, who were invited to provide feedback, reactions, and comments. Participants were also asked to share these preliminary results with spouses who were unable to participate in the interview. Ten of 51 parents provided written or verbal feedbacks, which were incorporated into the final results. This methodological aspect of the study provided a source of testimonial validity for the qualitative results; it also allowed us to take participants' feedbacks into account in their interpretation (Plummer, 2001) and to assess the degree to which the themes resonate with the parents' experience.

Ethics statement

Parents were fully informed of the voluntary nature and the objectives of the study. Written informed consent was obtained from all parents included in the study prior to the interview. Participants were told that all responses would be confidential, that the transcripts contain no identifying information, and that they would be free to withdraw at any time. All indicating information was removed from the transcripts, and participant anonymity was further ensured through disguise or withholding of descriptive data. The Ethical Review Committee[2] officially agreed on this research protocol.

Results

The phenomenological analysis of the 51 interviews with the parents showed three groups of parents, corresponding to three types of parental representations of their adopted child and their cultural belonging: the first group of parents who kept no association with the country of birth of children. They refused all multiplicity of cultural identities; a second group of parents who actively maintained regular associations with the country of birth and the culture of the children and said they are a multicultural family; and a third group of parents adjusted their ties with the country of birth and culture based on the questions and interests of the child. They accepted the multiplicity of their child's feelings of cultural belonging.

In half of the interviews, parents reported traumatic pre-adoptive experiences lived by their child: sudden loss of their biological mother, repeated experiences of neglect or abandonment in the biological family, emotional deprivation at the orphanage, major health problems or accidents or serious injuries. Five themes emerged from the analysis pertaining to the impact of these traumatic experiences on the parents: lack of affect in the narrative; denial of the meaning of the traumatic experiences of the child; perceptions of strangeness concerning the child; parental worry about the child reliving a repetition of the trauma, therefore worrying about the new narrative structure.

Discussion

Qualitative phenomenological analysis of interviews with adoptive parents in our research population shows three major groups of parental representations of the cultural identity of their internationally adopted child and five indicators of the traumatic pre-adoptive experiences' impact of parents.

In group 1, which included 12 of the 51 parents (24%), the parents considered, above all, that their child had the same culture as them, and that the maintenance of associations, which they considered artificial, with the country of birth, would prevent the child from feeling the belonging to their new family. Parents in group 1 declared that they had to "pretend" their children were French children, born in France, in order to be able to integrate them into their family and so that they were not considered foreigners. They insist that there is no difference between an adopted child and a biological child. The parental position consisting in acting as if the child had been born to them corresponds to certain parental positions described in the literature (Bowie, 2007). Parents in group 1 need to cancel the differences that exist between them and the child they have gone to look for on the other side of the world.

This position, taken by the parents in group 1, also resembles that of some authors, notably European, who consider that making children members of the culture of the host country allows them to be assimilated and fully integrated both in their family and the country of adoption (Howell, 2003; Levy-Soussan, 2010). It is also akin to the first parenting strategy described by Lee in his review of the literature on transracial adoptions: cultural assimilation, which includes parental behaviors that reject differences or downplay the child's unique racial and ethnic experiences (Andujo, *op. cit.*; DeBerry et al., *op. cit.*). This results in the acculturation of the child in the majority culture (Lee, 2003). A variant of cultural assimilation is a humanistic strategy emphasizing a "colorblind" orientation or a view of humanity without reference to ethnicity and race (*ibid.*). Several authors have described the colorblind approach to parenthood (Hubinette, 2012; Neville et al., 2000). Friedlander speaks of a "universalist strategy" to describe the parental attitude which denies or minimizes the issue of discrimination (Friedlander et al., 2000). This attitude seems to be detrimental to the child (Huh & Reid, 2000).

In group 2 (18 parents of 51: 35%), as opposed to group 1, the parents actively defended the bicultural identity of their children. Through active links with the culture of the country of birth of children, they enable them to develop skills in that culture. Studies show that the level of cultural competence of children (for their culture of birth) depends on the beliefs of their parents (Thomas & Tessler, 2007; Vonk, 2001; Lee et al., 2006). Parental cultural competence (Vonk, *op. cit.*) is defined by active measures aimed at promoting the development of a positive cultural and ethnic identity in children as well as by an awareness of the importance and role that ideas of ethnicity and culture occupy in the life of each person. The consequence of this second point is the strong involvement of parents in helping their adopted children develop the capacity to protect themselves from racism and discrimination, even if the parents themselves do not experience it. Parents in group 2, therefore, have a high level of parental cultural competence. The analysis of the interviews in group 2 shows the conviction of these parents that is important to transmit cultural elements of their country of birth to their children, to facilitate their identity work. The pride of their cultural heritage allows for better self-esteem.

In group 3, which includes 21 of the 51 parents (41%), adoptive parents have a fluid position that changes over time, determined by the child's questions. These parents believe that the feeling of belonging of children to their country of birth and its culture changes with their age, their experience of discrimination, their questions about their identity, etc.

This position resembles what Tessler, Gamache, and Liu describe as the child's choice, that is to say adapting the links with the country of birth and its culture according to the interest or choices of the child (Friedlander et al., *op. cit.*). These views follow transnational and postcolonial approaches which reject a static, categorical, and reductive concept of cultural identity (Bhatia & Ram, 2001; Hermans & Kempen, 1998). This criticism was initially formulated in the context of research on the identity building of immigrants and their children. Above mentioned authors describe identity negotiations and feelings of cultural belonging as subjective, complex, and dynamic (Bhatia & Ram, *op. cit.*). Parents in group 3 also express their conviction that their children's feelings of cultural belonging are not resolved and affirm that their role as parents is to adapt to the process of their child's identity building, regardless of its direction.

In all 3 groups, the interviews, therefore, show the parents' desire to protect the child. Parents in group 1 say they protect their children by assimilating them completely to the biological child they might have had; parents in group 2 say that they protect their children by actively developing their bicultural identity; and parents in group 3, by supporting and accompanying their children in the direction of their choices, whether it is a refusal or, on the contrary, a demand for connections with aspects of the culture of their country of birth.

It is worth reflecting on the parental representations of their child's cultural origins considering the personal experiences of parents of their children's pre-adoptive past. They question the traumatogenic impact of these traumatic experiences on them and their repercussions on parental representations of the child. They could be interpreted as the transmission of trauma from children to their parents (Lachal, 2015).

The denial by some parents of a painful and traumatic past may reflect an attempt to reverse, in hindsight, its existence, and the impact on their child. Several studies have shown that the mechanisms of denial and minimization of hostile experiences are criteria found in the accounts of traumatized subjects (Lachal, 2006; Waintrater, 2003).

This lack of affect in parents' accounts and denial of the importance of their child's traumatic personal experience shows a poor reflective function on the part of parents. The reflective function as defined by Fonagy (Fonagy et al., 1991) is the ability of parents to represent their child's emotional and internal experience, to allow themselves to be influenced and to adapt to it, in order to mentalize it. Parents' mental capacity helps the child to identify meaningfully with their own disrupting experiences and, thus, integrate it in their storyline and their experience of the world. This process mitigates the traumatic impact on the child in his/her emotional development. This internal/psychological dimension, silenced or canceled, shows the specific difficulties parents have in identifying themselves with their children when their pre-adoptive past is brought up. This inability to identify – limited to a period of time – can be interpreted as a way to distance oneself from the unbearable, the unthinkable in their child's traumatic personal experience. On the other hand, when other difficult moments in their child's life were brought up, events after their child's adoption, parents were quite able to talk about their child and their own personal emotional experience, thus demonstrating a good reflective function. This observation supports the understanding that the absence of reference to internal personal and emotional experiences is a form of defensive reaction to the traumatic personal experience of the child. Temporarily, they find themselves unable to identify with their children or to put themselves in their place. This sudden and temporary interruption of their reflective function is a sign of trauma. The findings regarding reflective function seem all the more important, as other research works have shown its significance as a predictor of the child outcomes, especially for abused adoptees (Steele et al., 2003; Steele et al., 2007). A high reflection function allows parents to identify with their children, preserving them from an intense feeling of otherness and strangeness.

This position of otherness of the adoptee is reflected precisely in our results. We postulate that the parental experience of the child's strangeness and otherness portrays their reaction to the pre-adoption trauma. The terms used by parents to describe their child, express a certain dehumanization of their child. Parents' stories provide insight into what cannot be thought or worked out by parents. The inability to represent what children have experienced could exclude these children from the human community, thus hampering any process of identifying parents. The child takes on an unsurpassable otherness. This otherness has already been described in studies on children's skin color (Golse, 2012) or on their foreign genetic heritage (Lévy-Soussan, 2002; Soulé, 1995). The present results add another dimension to the child's otherness, linked to the impossible representation of his/her pre-adoptive experiences. The adoptees carrying this trauma through scars on their bodies or through the stories of their parents could be stuck between two filiations and condemned to wander between affiliations: they have been uprooted from their past world and the process of rooting in their present is hampered by the trauma's radioactivity (Gampel, 2003) on parental representations of the child. They find it difficult to be identified as the same by their biological family and their birth culture as well as by their adoptive family and their new host culture.

The uncanny (Freud, 1919) generates fear in the psyche of the parents and triggers defense mechanisms. Negotiating fear can lead to distancing oneself and rejecting the source of the fear, that is, the traumatic residue lodged in the child. This process is echoed in the poor reflective function. Some parents attribute their children's traumatic experiences to fantasized characteristics of the country of birth, which could be interpreted as an attempt to make sense of their children's personal experience, to give it a place. The difficulty in dealing with trauma leads to ignoring cultural interpretations and resorting to generalizations to make sense of an extremely painful situation. It also provides a protective distance with the person's culture of origin (El Husseini et al., 2016). Parents' accounts show how they deal with traumas that cannot be remembered/worked out. The culture of origin allows them to fill the void of representation. It is the original culture, foreign and strange, which explains the violence suffered by children. The trauma is attributed to the culture of origin. Thus, parents are confronted with a double otherness: the otherness of the trauma and that of the culture of birth. This undermines their ability to identify and empathize with their child, who is kept at a bay due to this overwhelming otherness.

The current results, showing the traumatogenic impact of the pre-adoption traumatic experience of children on their parents and on the representations of parents of their children, can be interpreted from concepts developed by Wilson et al. (1994). These authors have suggested two types of countertransference reactions to a traumatic narrative. While this model was developed from a therapist's reaction to his patient's accounts, it seems interesting in exploring parents' reactions to what is transferred to them – by the children themselves or by others – the pre-adoptive experience of their child. The first type of countertransference is characterized by avoidance and the second by over-identification. Our results indicate an over-representation of the first type in the interviews. The empathic tension experienced triggers empathic repression (*ibid.*). These types of reactions to a traumatic account include forms of denial, trivialization, distortion, avoidance, detachment, and withdrawal toward the subject; these are reactions that were highlighted in our interviews with parents.

The themes that emerged from the analysis of the interviews showed some evidence of trauma transmission among adoptive parents facing the pre-adoptive traumatic experiences of their child. This is confirmed by other studies conducted on the subject, highlighting the traumatic effects in parents after their confrontation with the trauma of their children (Cairns, 2008) and symptoms of depression, stress, or anxiety they may develop (Wilburg, 2014).

Conclusion

Working with adoptive parents about their representations of their children's cultural affiliation is an important issue. These representations, present from the very early stages of adoption, determine the ways in which parents respond to their children when they ask inevitable questions about their difference in physical appearance, their experiences of discrimination, their country of birth, and sometimes their desire to return there. Exploring these parental representations is also essential if we are to understand family interactions and provide more effective support to these adoptive families. Systematic training for professionals around this issue of parental representations of their child's cultural affiliation must be put in place in all countries receiving children in international adoptions, to allow early prevention, beginning with the child's arrival.

The current results highlight the need for specific therapeutic support for adoptive parents, and even more so the need for a support program for these parents in their adoption process. This support would allow better parental preparation for the reception of a child who has experienced pre-adoptive traumatic events. This is even more true as children are adopted at increasingly later ages, thus increasing their risk of prior confrontation with hostile environments or traumatic life events. In a previous study, we showed an increased risk of traumatic experiences for parents when they first encounter their child. A pre-adoption program for parents could sensitize them to the reactions and needs of traumatized children, but also to the challenges faced by those who care for them, especially families. Some authors have emphasized the need for parental preparation, in order to prepare them to be parents and also therapists for their child. Numerous studies in recent years have underlined the usefulness of specific trauma training for parents – both to welcome the child and to deal with the risk of trauma transmission.

Notes

1 Maison de Solenn – Hôpital Cochin in Paris, France. Department of Professor Marie Rose Moro.
2 Institutional Review Board of Paris North Hospitals, Paris 7 University, AP-HP, N° IRB00006477.

References

Andujo, E. (1988). Ethnic identity of transethnically adopted Hispanic adolescents. *Social Work*, *33*(6), 531–535.
Baden, A. L. (2002). The psychological adjustment of transracial adoptees: An application of the Cultural-Racial Identity Model. *Journal of Social Distress and the Homeless*, *11*(2), 167–191.

Basow, S. A., Lilley, E., Bookwala, J., & McGillicuddy-Delisi, A. (2008). Identity development and psychological well-being in Korean-born adoptees in the U.S. *American Journal of Orthopsychiatry*, *78*(4), 473–480. doi: 10.1037/a0014450 PMID: 19123769

Baxter, L. A., & Babbie, E. (2004). *The basics of communication research*. Wadsworth.

Bhatia, S., & Ram, A. (2001). Locating the dialogical self in the age of transnational migrations, border crossings and diasporas. *Culture and Psychology*, *7*, 297–309.

Bowie, F. (2007). Cultures of transnational adoption. *Anthropological Quarterly*, *80*(2), 623–627.

Cairns, K. (2008). Enabling effective support: secondary traumatic stress and adoptive families. In D. Hindle & G. Shulman (Eds), *The emotional experience of adoption: A psychoanalytic perspective* (pp. 90–98). Routledge/Taylor & Francis Group.

Carstens, C., & Juliá, M. (2000). Ethnoracial awareness in intercountry adoption: US experiences. *International Social Work*, *43*(1), 61–73.

Castle, H., Knight, E., & Watters, C. (2011). Ethnic identity as a protective factor for looked after and adopted children from ethnic minority groups: A critical review of the literature. *Adoption Quarterly*, *14*, 305–325.

Cederblad, M., Höök, B., Irhammar, M., & Mercke, A. M. (1999). Mental health in international adoptees as teenagers and young adults. An epidemiological study. *Journal of Child Psychology and Psychiatry*, *40*(8), 1239–1248. PMID: 10604402

DeBerry, K. M., Scarr, S., & Weinberg, R. (1996). Family racial socialization and ecological competence: Longitudinal assessments of African-American transracial adoptees. *Child Development*, *67*(5), 2375–2399.

Docan-Morgan, S. (2010). "They don't know what it's like to be in my shoes": Topic avoidance about race in transracially adoptive families. *Journal of Social and Personal Relationships*, *28*(3), 336–355.

Eatough, V., & Smith, J.A. (2008). Interpretative phenomenological analysis. In C. Willing & W. Staiton-Rogers (Eds.), *Qualitative research in psychology*. Sage Publications. https://dx.doi.org/10.4135/9781848607927.n11

El Husseini, M., Skandrani, S., Sahab, L. T., Dozio, E, & Moro, M. R. (2016). Countertransference in trauma clinic: A transitional breach in the therapists' identity. In G. El Baalbaki & C. Fortin (Eds.), *A multidimensional approach to post-traumatic stress disorder*. BoD – Books on Demand.doi: 10.5772/64842

Fonagy, P., Steele, M., Steele, H., & Moran, G. S. (1991). The capacity for understanding mental states: the reflective self in parent and child and its significance for security of attachment. *Infant Mental Health Journal*, *12*(3), 201–18. doi: 10.1002/1097-0355(199123)12:3<201:AID-IMHJ2280120307>3.0.CO;2-7

Freud, S. (1919). The "uncanny". In *The standard edition of the complete psychological works of Sigmund Freud vol. XVII (1917–1919): An infantile neurosis and other works* (pp. 217–256).

Friedlander, M. L., Larney, L. C., Skau, M., Hotaling, M., Cutting, M. L., & Schwam, M. (2000). Bicultural identification: Experiences of internationally adopted children and their parents. *Journal of Counseling Psychology*, *47*(2), 187–198.

Gampel, Y. (2003). Violence sociale, lien tyrannique et transmission radioactive. In A. Ciccone (Ed.), *Psychanalyse du lien tyrannique* (pp. 102–125). Dunod.

Golse, B. (2012). La double étrangeté de l'enfant venu d'ailleurs, accueilli en adoption internationale. *L'autre, Cliniques, Cultures et Sociétés*, *13*(2), 144–150. www.revuelautre.com

Harf, A., Skandrani, S., Radjack, R., Sibeoni, J., Moro, M. R., & Revah-Levy, A. (2013). First parent-child meetings in international adoptions: A qualitative study. *PLoS ONE, 8*(9): e75300. doi: 10.1371/journal.pone.0075300 PMID: 24086500

Harf, A., Skandrani, S., Mazeaud, E., Revah-Levy, A., & Moro, M. R. (2015). Le concept d'identité culturelle chez les enfants adoptés, quelle pertinence? *Psychiatrie de l'enfant, 58*(1), 299–320.

Harrigan, M. M. (2009). The contradictions of identity-work for parents of visibly adopted children. *Journal of Social and Personal Relationships*, 26, 634–658.

Hermans, H. J. M., & Kempen, H. J. G. (1998). Moving cultures: The perilous problems of cultural dichotomies in a globalizing society. *American Psychologist, 53*, 1111–1120.

Hjern, A., Lindblad, F., & Vinnerljung, B. (2002). Suicide, psychiatric illness and social maladjustment in intercountry adoptees in Sweden: A Cohort Study. *The Lancet, 360*, 443–448. PMID: 12241716

Hollingsworth, L. D. (1998). Adoptee dissimilarity from the adoptive family: Clinical practice and research implications. *Child and Adolescent Social Work Journal, 15*(4), 303–319.

Howell, S. L. (2003). Kinning: Creating life-trajectories in adoptive families, *Journal of the Royal Anthropological Institute (N.S.)*, 9(3), 465–484.

Hubinette, T. (2012). Post-racial utopianism, white color-blindness and "the elephant in the room": Racial issues for transnational adoptees of color. In J. L. Gibbons & K. S. Rotabi (Eds.), *Intercountry adoption: Policies, practices, and outcomes* (pp. 221–231). Ashgate Publishing Limited.

Huh, N.S., & Reid, W. (2000). Intercountry, transracial adoption and ethnic identity: A Korean example. *International Social Work, 43*, 75–87.

Johnston, K. E., Swim, J. K., Saltsman, B. M., Deater-Deckard, K., & Petrill, S. A. (2007). Mothers' racial, ethnic, and cultural socialization of transracially adopted Asian children. *Family Relations, 56*, 390–402.

Juffer, F., & Van Ijzendoorn, M. H. (2005). Behavior problems and mental health referrals of international adoptees: a meta-analysis. *JAMA, 293*(20), 2501–2515.

Lachal, C. (2006). *Le partage du traumatisme: Contre-transferts avec les patients traumatisés*. La Pensée sauvage. doi: 10.3917/jdp.253.0050

Lachal, C. (2015). *Comment se transmettent les traumas? Traumas, contre-transferts, empathie et scénarios émergeants*. La Pensée sauvage.

Lee, D. C., & Quintana, S. M. (2005). Benefits of cultural exposure and development of korean perspective taking ability for transracially adopted Korean children. *Cultural Diversity and Ethnic Minority Psychology, 11*(2), 130–143.

Lee, R. M. (2003). The transracial adoption paradox: history, research, and counseling implications of cultural socialization. *Counseling Psychology, 31*(6), 711–744. PMID: 18458794

Lee, R. M., Grotevant, H. D., Hellerstedt, W. L., Gunnar, M. R., & the Minnesota International Adoption Project Team. (2006). Cultural Socialization in families with internationally adopted children. *Journal of Family Psychology, 20*(4), 571–580. PMID: 17176191

Lévy-Soussan, P. (2002). Travail de filiation et adoption. *Revue Française de Psychanalyse, 1*, 41–69. doi: 10.3917/rfp.661.0041

Levy-Soussan, P. (2005). Adoption internationale: spécificités et risques psychiques. *Journal de Pédiatrie et de Puériculture, 18*, 13–19.

Levy-Soussan, P. (2010). *Destins de l'adoption*. Fayard.

Malterud, K. (2001). Qualitative research: Standards, challenges, and guidelines. *The Lancet, 358* (9280), 48–488.

Mays, N. (2000). Qualitative research in health care. Assessing quality in qualitative research. *BMJ, 320*(7226), 50–52.

Mays, N., & Pope, C. (1995). Rigour and qualitative research. *BMJ (Clinical Research ed.), 311*(6997), 109–112. PMID: 7613363

Neville, H. A., Lilly, R. L., Duran, G., Lee, R. M., & Browne, L. (2000). Construction and initial validation of the color-blind racial attitudes scale (CoBRAS). *Journal of Counseling Psychology, 47*(1), 59–70.

Patton, M. Q. (2002). *Qualitative research and evaluation methods* (3rd ed.). Sage Publications.

Phinney, J. S., & Kohatsu, E. L. (1997). Ethnic and racial identity development and mental health. In J. Schulenberg, J. Maggs & K. Hurrelman (Eds.), *Health risks and developmental transitions during adolescence* (pp. 420–443) University Press.

Phinney, J. S., & Ong, A. D. (2007). Ethnic identity development in immigrant families. In J. E. Lansford, K. Deater-Deckard & M. H. Bornstein (Eds.), *Immigrant families in contemporary society* (pp. 51–68). Guilford Press.

Plummer, K. (2001). *Documents of Life 2*. Sage.

Rotherham, M. J., & Phinney, J. S. (1987). Introduction: Definitions and perspectives in the study of children's ethnic socialization. In J. S. Phinney & M. J. Rotherham (Eds.), *Children's ethnic socialization: Pluralism and development* (pp. 10–28). Sage.

Rushton, A., & Minnis, H. (1997). Annotation: Transracial family placements. *Journal of Child Psychology and Psychiatry, 38*(2), 147–159. PMID: 9232462

Scherman, R., & Harre, N. (2010). Interest in and identification with the birth culture: An examination of ethnic socialization in New Zealand intercountry adoptions. *International Social Work, 53*(4), 528–541.

Skandrani, S., Harf, A., Mestre, C., & Moro, M. R, (2012). La question culturelle dans l'adoption internationale. *L'Autre, Cliniques, Cultures et Sociétés, 13*(2), 151–159.

Smith, J. A., & Osborn, M. (2008). Interpretative phenomenological analysis. In J. A. Smith (Ed.), *Qualitative psychology: A practical guide to research methods* (2nd ed.). Sage Publications. doi: 10.1111/jocn.12421. PMID: 24313229

Soulé, M. (1995). Le fantasme de la recherche de ses géniteurs par l'enfant adopté ou le roman familial. *Neuropsychiatrie de l'Enfance, 43*(10–11), 465–469.

Soulé, M., & Lévy-Soussan, P. (2002). Les fonctions parentales et leurs problèmes actuels dans les différentes filiations. *Psychiatrie de l'enfant, 45*(1), 77–102.

Steele, M., Hodges, J., Kaniuk, J., Hillman, S., & Henderson, K. (2003). Attachment representations in newly adopted maltreated children and their adoptive parents: implications for placement and support. *Journal of Child Psychotherapy, 29*, 187–205. doi: 10.1080/0075417031000138442

Steele, M., Henderson, K., Hodges, J., Kaniuk, J., Hillman, S., & Steele, H. (2007). In the best interests of the late-placed child: A report from the attachment representations and adoption outcome study. In L. Mayes, P. Fonagy & M. Target (Eds), *Developmental science and psychoanalysis: Integration and innovation* (pp. 159–191). Karnac Books. doi: 10.4324/9780429473654-12

Suter, E. A. (2008). Discursive negotiation of family identity: A study of U.S. families with adopted children from China. *Journal of Family Communication, 8*(2), 126–147.

Tessler, R. C., Gamache, G., & Liu, L. (1999). *West meets east: Americans adopt Chinese children*. Bergin & Garvey.

Thomas, K. A., & Tessler, R. C. (2007). Bicultural socialization among adoptive families. Where there is a will, there is a way. *Journal of Family Issues, 28*(9), 1189–1219.

Vonk, M. E. (2001). Cultural competence for transracial adoptive parents. *Social Work, 46*(3), 246–255.

Waintrater, R. (2003). *Sortir du génocide*. Payot

Westhues, A., & Cohen, J. S. (1998). Ethnic and racial identity of internationally adopted adolescents and young adults: Some issues in relation to children's rights. *Adoption Quarterly, 1*, 33–55.

Whitley, R., & Crawford, M. (2005). Qualitative research in psychiatry. *Canadian Journal of Psychiatry, 50*(2), 108–114.

Wilburg, B. (2014). Adopting a traumatized child: A phenomenological investigation of eight families' postadoptive experience of the psychological and neurobiological impact of early childhood trauma. *Dissertation Abstracts International: Section B. Sci Engineering, 74*(10-B).

Wilson, J. P., Lindy, J. D., & Raphael, B. (1994). Empathic strain and therapist defense: Type I and II CTRs. In J. P. Wilson & J. D. Lindy (Eds.), *Countertransference in the treatment of PTSD* (pp. 31–61). The Guilford Press.

Wrobel, G. M., Kohler, J. K., Grotevant, H. D., & McRoy, R. G. (2003). The Family Adoption Communication (FAC) Model: Identifying pathways of adoption-related communication. *Adoption Quarterly, 7*(2), 53–84.

Yoon, D.P. (2004). Intercountry adoption: The importance of ethnic socialization and subjective well-being for Korean-born adopted children. *Journal of Ethnic and Cultural Diversity in Social Work, 13*, 71–89.

Chapter 9

Going through adolescence with immigrant parents in Chile

*Gabriela Guzman (1977–2017)**

Gabriela Guzman came to France to work with us in the transcultural clinic at the Maison de Solenn in Paris; it was a great honor to have her as a resident, then as an assistant, later as a child and adolescent psychiatrist, and psychotherapist in the transcultural clinic. Together we went to Chile, her childhood country, to Santiago, Valparaiso, Punta Arenas, where we talked about clinics, encounters, cooking, arts, cocktails. We went to China, which she discovered with joy and a sharp eye and to the United States for symposiums and conferences. She had an amazing contact and empathy with adolescents and their families. In transcultural consultations with migrant families, she radiated. With migrant mothers and babies, she was extremely creative. Her research topics were eating disorders in migrant children and the evaluation of transcultural psychotherapies. She was a great ambassador of the transcultural clinic in the Spanish and English-speaking world and a great friend.

Gabriela, we miss you so much.
Marie Rose Moro
May 1, 2021

Gabriela was more than a colleague; she was a close friend. We discovered the Maison de Solenn together, both young residents 13 years ago, and we matured together. We shared a taste for work, a passion for the transcultural clinic, and a desire to transmit. Gabriela marked us by her numerous qualities, in particular, by her humanism, her enthusiasm, her rigor, and her federative qualities. She will always have an important place in our hearts and memories. Gabriela, you left far too soon, but what an honor to transmit one of your writings, because writings are endowed with immortality.

Rahmeth Radjack
May 4, 2021

The migratory phenomenon has been rapidly increasing over the last decades, occurring all over the world, in different countries and different societies.

DOI: 10.4324/9781003174684-10

As different cultures encounter, acculturative processes occur, and mixed cultures emerge. Acculturation finds expression at both group and individual levels. At an individual level, these changes challenge parents in the ways they become parents, and they challenge their children in their identity construction.

Parenthood in migration is more complex. Parents frequently lack support from significant others, the enculturation of the child is complicated, harmonic early parent-child interactions can be harder to develop and difficulties in transgenerational transmission can be found (Moro, 2010).

In addition to this, migrants' children have a specific vulnerability that emerges from a phenomenological split between the inside world (family, native language, the intimate sphere) and the outside world (the host country, school, among others): they are exposed to a transcultural risk (Moro, 1994; 2010). Upon reaching adolescence, the child can no longer continue to accommodate this split. Thus, the quest for identity that is inherent to adolescence is stressed by the need to achieve a bicultural identity. Furthermore, the transcultural risk may express itself via an organic and/or mental pathology at some point of the child's development (Moro, 1994), but it can also be transformed into creative potential.

In Chile, the migratory flow from neighbour countries (Peru, Argentina, Bolivia, Ecuador, Colombia) has augmented considerably in the past ten years. This immigration is mostly economic, related to the search of better employment opportunities, aiming to achieve higher living standards and eventually improve social position. Chile has a more stable economic and politic situation, when compared to the other countries in South America.

In clinical settings, we are now encountering adolescents born in Chile from immigrant parents. According to the acknowledged migration objectives, their parents frequently have high expectations regarding their education and their future occupations. How do these adolescents cope with this pressure? How do they grow up and construct their identity in a country other than that of their parents? How can we, clinicians, help these teenagers when they face acute psychological distress?

To better apprehend situations involving migrant patients (first, second, or third generation), a transcultural approach seems necessary. Georges Devereux initiated ethno-psychoanalysis in the 1960s (Devereux, 1967; 1972). His method is a "complementarist" approach, defined as involving systematic but not simultaneous analysis of cultural representations and any psychopathological elements that emerge during consultations, calling on the disciplines of anthropology, linguistics, or history, alongside psychoanalysis, to assess each situation. The ethno-psychoanalytical paradigm has been developed in Avicenne Hospital, Bobigny, Paris starting in 1979, first by Tobie Nathan, and then by Marie Rose Moro, who took particular interest in second-generation migrants. This approach has been used in Cochin Hospital, in Paris, since 2008, where I trained for several years, living in Paris as an immigrant myself.

To illustrate the aspects mentioned above, I will discuss the case of a young adolescent with Peruvian parents who attempted suicide after being sexually abused by another adolescent.

Suicide is considered by Freud to be a form of aggression that is directed toward others; the suicidal individual feels great hostility and aggression toward a frustrating person with whom he or she identifies and with whom there is a libidinal connection. The frustrating person is then internalized and the individual is not able to separate himself from that person, becoming overwhelmed with the aggressive impulses (see quotation by Freud in Huprich, 2004). From a transcultural point of view, many studies have found that acculturation stress and intergenerational conflicts are related to suicide attempts in adolescents of migrant parents (Skandrani & Bouche-Florin, 2013).

I met Caroline[1], a 14-year-old, at a public hospital in the suburbs of Santiago. She lived with her parents, Peruvian immigrants who had arrived in Chile a few years before her birth, and her younger sister.

She entered ambulatory treatment at the adolescent unit of the hospital after a suicide attempt, by prescription drug overdose. She explained that her act was an impulsive reaction to a sexual abuse by a friend, and more particularly to the fear of her parents acknowledging it, and the dread of defrauding them.

At the adolescent unit, Caroline and her parents received therapy with the pluri-professional team, composed by paediatricians, a nurse, a social worker, a psychologist, and a child and adolescent psychiatrist. Individual and parent-child interviews were performed for six months. At the beginning of treatment, Caroline was reluctant to talk about herself when alone in interviews, especially when it came to search for meanings surrounding her suicide attempt. During the treatment, the family began to prepare another migration, this time to Germany, her father being of German ascendance. This subject was used as a therapeutic lever, and enabled Caroline to further elaborate on her relations with her parents, her family history, her own history, and her bicultural identity.

This case seemed of particular interest to discuss the passage through adolescence in transcultural situation, as it allows showing how a suicide attempt can be a manifestation of separation-individuation conflicts – inherent to the process of identity construction – stressed by acculturation.

Notes

* In memoriam.
1 In order to protect the patient anonymity I have used the name Caroline as a pseudonym.

References

Devereux G. (1967). *From anxiety to method in the behavioral sciences*. Mouton & Co.
Devereux G. (1972). *Ethnopsychanalyse complémentariste*. Flammarion.

Huprich, S. K. (2004). Psychodynamic conceptualization and treatment of suicidal patients. *Journal of Contemporary Psychotherapy*, *34*(1), 23–39.

Moro M.R. (1994). *Parents en exil. Psychopathologie et migrations*. PUF.

Moro M.R. (2010). *Grandir en situation transculturelle*. Editions Fabert.

Skandrani S. & Bouche-Florin L. (2013). Adolescence: la construction identitaire et ses aléas. In Baubet T. & Moro M. R. (Eds.), *Psychopathologie transculturelle* (pp. 203–220). Elsevier Masson.

Index

For Product Safety Concerns and Information please contact our EU
representative GPSR@taylorandfrancis.com
Taylor & Francis Verlag GmbH, Kaufingerstraße 24, 80331 München, Germany

www.ingramcontent.com/pod-product-compliance
Lightning Source LLC
Chambersburg PA
CBHW070343270326
41926CB00017B/3969

9 7 8 1 0 3 2 0 0 5 5 0 8